Interactive Reports in SAS® Visual Analytics
Advanced Features and Customization

Nicole Ball

sas.com/books

Contents

About This Book xi

About The Author xix

Chapter 1: Introduction 1
    Introduction 1
    SAS Visual Analytics 2
    SAS Viya 2

Chapter 2: Creating Advanced Data Items and Filters 5
    Introduction 5
    Example: Creating a Calculated Item and a Basic Filter 6
    Example: Grouping an Aggregated Measure 10
    Example: Using a Common Filter 15
    Example: Creating a Periodic Aggregated Measure and Adding Time Filters 19
    Example: Creating a Moving Average 27
    Example: Creating a Tabular Aggregated Measure 33

Chapter 3: Linking to External Websites 41
    Introduction 41
        Step 1: Research 41
        Step 2: Hardcode 42
        Step 3: Parameterize 42
        Step 4: Test 42
    Example: Creating a Static URL Link 42
    Example: Creating a Web Link 44
        Step 1: Research 44
        Step 2: Hardcode 45
        Step 3: Parameterize 46
        Step 4: Test 47
    Example: Searching a Web Page 48
        Step 1: Research 48
        Step 2: Hardcode 49
        Step 3: Parameterize 49
        Step 4: Test 51
    Example: Linking to a File 51
        Step 1: Research 52
        Step 2: Hardcode 54

Step 3: Parameterize 55
Step 4: Test 55
Example: Viewing a Map Location (Additional) 56
Step 1: Research 57
Step 2: Hardcode 57
Step 3: Parameterize 57
Step 4: Test 59
Example: Linking to a Parameterized Report (Additional) 60
Step 1: Research 60
Step 2: Hardcode 64
Step 3: Parameterize 64
Step 4: Test 65

Chapter 4: Applying Numeric Parameters **67**
Introduction 67
Step 1: Create 68
Step 2: Populate 68
Step 3: Apply 68
Step 4: Test 68
Example: Highlighting Values below a Threshold 68
Step 1: Create 70
Step 2: Populate 71
Step 3: Apply 71
Step 4: Test 72
Example: Displaying Countries with Orders above a Minimum 72
Step 1: Create 74
Step 2: Populate 74
Step 3: Apply 74
Step 4: Test 74
Example: Showing Top Customers 76
Step 1: Create 78
Step 2: Populate 78
Step 3: Apply 78
Step 4: Test 78
Example: Grouping Values Based on a Threshold 78
Step 1: Create 81
Step 2: Populate 81
Step 3: Apply 82
Step 4: Test 82
Example: Viewing Data for the Next N Years 82
Step 1: Create 85
Step 2: Populate 85
Step 3: Apply 86
Step 4: Test 87

Chapter 5: Using Character Parameters.. **89**
  Introduction.. 89
    Step 1: Create 89
    Step 2: Populate.. 89
    Step 3: Apply 90
    Step 4: Test... 90
  Example: Searching for a String 90
    Step 1: Create 91
    Step 2: Populate.. 91
    Steps 3 and 4: Apply and Test 92
  Example: Selecting Characteristics for Indirect Filtering... 95
    Step 1: Create 96
    Step 2: Populate.. 96
    Step 3: Apply 97
    Step 4: Test... 99
  Example: Ranking Top or Bottom Values 100
    Step 1: Create 100
    Step 2: Populate.. 101
    Step 3: Apply 102
    Step 4: Test... 103
    Alternate Solution.. 104
  Example: Choosing Multiple Measures 106
    Step 1: Create 107
    Step 2: Populate.. 107
    Step 3: Apply 108
    Step 4: Test... 109
  Example: Selecting a Region (Additional) 109
    Step 1: Create 110
    Step 2: Populate.. 110
    Step 3: Apply 110
    Step 4: Test... 114

Chapter 6: Working with Date Parameters **117**
  Introduction.. 117
    Step 1: Create 117
    Step 2: Populate.. 117
    Step 3: Apply 118
    Step 4: Test... 118
  Example: Highlighting a Selected Month 118
    Step 1: Create 119
    Step 2: Populate.. 120
    Step 3: Apply 121
    Step 4: Test... 121

Example: Choosing a Month to Compare Values..122
   Step 1: Create 124
   Step 2: Populate...124
   Step 3: Apply..124
   Step 4: Test..125
Example: Viewing the Last Five Years of Available Data 128
   Step 1: Create 128
   Step 2: Populate...130
   Step 3: Apply..131
   Step 4: Test..131
Example: Viewing 10 Years after a Selected Year..132
   Step 1: Create 133
   Step 2: Populate...133
   Step 3: Apply..134
   Step 4: Test..135
Example: Displaying Data within a Selected Range 135
   Step 1: Create 136
   Step 2: Populate...136
   Step 3: Apply..137
   Step 4: Test..137

Chapter 7: Using SAS Graph Builder to Create Custom Graphs 139
Introduction..139
   Step 1: Choose Graph Elements...139
   Step 2: Lay Out Elements...140
   Step 3: Configure Roles..140
   Step 4: Adjust Appearance...140
   Step 5: Save and Use..140
Example: Using a Data-Driven Lattice...141
   Step 1: Choose Graph Elements...141
   Step 2: Lay Out Elements...142
   Step 3: Configure Roles..142
   Step 4: Adjust Appearance...143
   Step 5: Save and Use..144
Example: Syncing Hierarchies..145
   Step 1: Choose Graph Elements...146
   Step 2: Lay Out Elements...146
   Step 3: Configure Roles..147
   Step 4: Adjust Appearance...148
   Step 5: Save and Use..148
Example: Creating a Chart with Overlays...148
   Step 1: Choose Graph Elements...148
   Step 2: Lay Out Elements...149
   Step 3: Configure Roles..150
   Step 4: Adjust Appearance...150
   Step 5: Save and Use..151

Example: Using Overlays with a User-Defined Lattice 151
    Step 1: Choose Graph Elements 152
    Step 2: Lay Out Elements 152
    Step 3: Configure Roles 152
    Step 4: Adjust Appearance 153
    Step 5: Save and Use 154
Example: Building a Custom Map 154
    Step 1: Choose Graph Elements 155
    Step 2: Lay Out Elements 156
    Step 3: Configure Roles 156
    Step 4: Adjust Appearance 157
    Step 5: Save and Use 157
Example: Building a Custom Map with Polygon Layers 157
    Step 1: Choose Graph Elements 157
    Step 2: Lay Out Elements 158
    Step 3: Configure Roles 158
    Step 4: Adjust Appearance 160
    Step 5: Save and Use 160

Chapter 8: Using Data-Driven Content to Create Custom Graphs **163**
Introduction 163
    Requirements 163
    Benefits 164
Example: Using a Circle Packing Plot 164
Example: Using and Modifying a Sunburst Plot 168
Example: Creating a Visualization 172
    Displaying Sample Data 174
    Displaying JSON-Formatted Data 177
Example: Incorporating a Visualization into SAS Visual Analytics 179
    Using Utilities 180
    Creating Dynamic Variables 181
    Setting Up Callback Functions 181
    Initializing and Validating Data 182
    Drawing/Updating the Visualization 183
    Viewing in SAS Visual Analytics 183
Example: Using a Visualization as the Target of an Action 185
    Using Sample Data when No Data Is Available 185
    Updating the Visualization 185
    Viewing in SAS Visual Analytics 186
Example: Highlighting Selected Values in the Visualization 189
    Updating CSS Styles 189
    Applying CSS Styles 189
    Viewing in SAS Visual Analytics 191

Example: Using a Visualization as the Source of an Action...192
Updating CSS Styles 192
Deselecting All Elements...192
Applying CSS Styles to Selected Elements 193
Viewing in SAS Visual Analytics..195
Additional Considerations 196
Handling Axes 196
Managing Resize Events..196
Saving URL Mappings..197

Chapter 9: Working with Jobs in SAS Visual Analytics...199
Introduction...199
Step 1: Create the SAS Program...200
Step 2: Create the Job Definition 200
Step 3: Create the Job Form...200
Step 4: Execute and Test 201
Example: Returning SAS Results 203
Step 1: Create the SAS Program...203
Step 2: Create the Job Definition 204
Step 3: Create the Job Form...205
Step 4: Execute and Test 206
Example: Returning SAS Results Using an HTML Form..207
Step 1: Create the SAS Program...207
Step 2: Create the Job Definition 207
Step 3: Create the Job Form...208
Step 4: Execute and Test 210
Example: Adding Data to a Table 211
Step 1: Create the SAS Program...211
Step 2: Create the Job Definition 214
Step 3: Create the Job Form...216
Step 4: Execute and Test 219
Example: Updating Data in a Table 221
Step 1: Create the SAS Program...221
Step 2: Create the Job Definition 224
Step 3: Create the Job Form...226
Step 4: Execute and Test 230
Example: Deleting Data from a Table 231
Step 1: Create the SAS Program...232
Step 2: Create the Job Definition 233
Step 3: Create the Job Form...234
Step 4: Execute and Test 237
Additional Considerations 239

Chapter 10: Sharing Reports **241**
   Introduction...241
   Viewing Reports in SAS Visual Analytics 241
   SAS Visual Analytics Apps 244
   SAS Visual Analytics SDK..244

Appendix A: Loading Geographic Polygon Data to CAS...**247**

Appendix B: Working with Data-Driven Content **255**

Appendix C: Additional Resources **273**

About This Book

What Does This Book Cover?

This book contains a variety of examples that enable you to create interactive reports in SAS Visual Analytics using advanced features and customization. You can create interactive links to external websites, use parameters to give the viewer more control over the report, create and add custom graphs and third-party visualizations, execute SAS code using SAS Viya jobs, and even embed report content in your own web pages and apps.

This book does not discuss basic functionality in SAS Visual Analytics, like how to create reports, use report objects, apply filters, or add basic actions or links. It is intended for users that are already familiar with both basic and advanced functionalities in SAS Visual Analytics and want to create more advanced interactive reports that enable viewers to exert more control over their report-viewing experience.

Is This Book for You?

This book is intended for users who are familiar with both basic and advanced features in SAS Visual Analytics. If you do not have any experience with SAS Visual Analytics, see "An Introduction to SAS Visual Analytics: How to Explore Numbers, Design Reports, and Gain Insight into Your Data" by Tricia Aanderud, Rob Collum, and Ryan Kumpfmiller. You can also take the SAS Visual Analytics 1 for SAS Viya: Basics course and the SAS Visual Analytics 2 for SAS Viya: Advanced course.

What Are the Prerequisites for This Book?

Before reading this book and working with the examples, you should know how to do the following:

- Access SAS Visual Analytics
- Build a basic report
- Create calculated items and aggregated measures and understand the difference between the two
- Use objects in SAS Visual Analytics to build reports
- Modify roles and options for report objects
- Create basic filters, actions, links, display rules, and ranks

How to Use This Book

This book can be used as a resource for you to incorporate more advanced functionality and interactivity into your SAS Visual Analytics reports. You don't have to read the book in order! There are many ways you can approach learning and applying the information in this book:

- *Just-in-time learning*: Use the chapters and examples as you need them. For example, if you need to learn different ways that you can create advanced links, see **Chapter 3: Linking to External Websites**.
- *Learn more about using the Data pane*: Focus on creating more advanced data items using the Data pane and apply them to your reports. For this approach, see **Chapter 2: Creating Advanced Data Items and Filters**, **Chapter 4: Applying Numeric Parameters**, **Chapter 5: Using Character Parameters**, and **Chapter 6: Working with Date Parameters**.
- *Learn more about customizations*: Focus on creating your own custom graphs and experiences. For this approach, see **Chapter 7: Using SAS Graph Builder to Create Custom Graphs**, **Chapter 8: Using Data-Driven Content to Create Custom Graphs**, **Chapter 9: Working with Jobs in SAS Visual Analytics**, **Chapter 10: Sharing Reports**, and **Appendix B: Working with Data-Driven Content**.
- *Learn about using date data items*: Focus on creating and using date data items for your reports. For this approach, see the following examples:
  - **Chapter 2**- Example: Creating a Calculated Item and a Basic Filter
  - **Chapter 4**- Example: Viewing Data for the Next N Years
  - All examples in **Chapter 6: Working with Date Parameters**
- *Learn about Geo maps*: Learn about creating different types of geographic data items (using predefined roles, using latitude and longitude, and using custom polygonal shapes). For this approach, see the following examples:
  - **Chapter 3**- Example: Linking to a File (coordinate geo map using latitude and longitude)
  - **Chapter 3**- Example: Viewing a Map Location (coordinate geo map using latitude and longitude)
  - **Chapter 3**- Example: Linking to a Parameterized Report (region geo map using predefined geographic roles)
  - **Chapter 4**- Example: Grouping Values Based on a Threshold (region geo map using predefined geographic roles)
  - **Chapter 4**- Example: Viewing Data for the Next N Years (coordinate geo map using latitude and longitude)
  - **Chapter 5**- Example: Selecting a Region (region geo map using custom predefined geographic roles and custom polygonal shapes)
  - **Chapter 6**- Example: Highlighting a Selected Month (coordinate geo map using latitude and longitude)
  - **Chapter 6**- Example: Viewing 10 Years after a Selected Year (coordinate geo map using latitude and longitude)
  - **Chapter 7**- Example: Building a Custom Map (coordinate geo map using latitude and longitude)

- o **Chapter 7**- Example: Building a Custom Map with Polygon Layers (region geo map overlaid with coordinate geo map using custom polygonal shapes and latitude and longitude)
- o **Chapter 9**- Example: Adding Data to a Table (coordinate geo map using latitude and longitude)
- o **Chapter 9**- Example: Updating Data in a Table (coordinate geo map using latitude and longitude)
- o **Chapter 9**- Example: Deleting Data from a Table (coordinate geo map using latitude and longitude)

Note: For more information about creating and using custom polygonal shapes in SAS Visual Analytics, see **Appendix A: Loading Geographic Polygon Data to CAS**.

What Should You Know about the Examples?

This book includes tutorials for you to follow to gain hands-on experience with SAS. Before trying the examples, you need to load the data sets to SAS Visual Analytics and import the reports. Most chapters contain starter reports in which you can start working on the example and ending reports that have the final solution.

Note: An administrator might need to import the data and reports for the examples in your environment.

To access the starter reports and ending reports in SAS Viya, do the following:

1. Download the data and the JSON file.
   Note: There is a JSON file that contains all examples in the book and separate JSON files for each chapter. If you are using SAS Visual Analytics 8.5, download the files with the suffix _85. If you are using SAS Visual Analytics 2020.1 (November 2020) or later, download the files with the suffix _2020.1.
2. Using SAS Data Explorer, load data to CAS. You can choose any caslib that you have access to; just make a note of the name of the caslib. For this book, the **Public** caslib was used for most examples and a **Jobs** caslib was created for **Chapter 9: Working with Jobs in SAS Visual Analytics**. Make note of the caslib that you import to in your environment. You'll need this information in the next step.
3. In SAS Environment Manager, on the Content page, do the following:
   a. Click the **Import** icon.
   b. For the **Import file** field, navigate to the location where the JSON file is stored.
   c. On the left side of the Import tab, click **Mapping**.
   d. Click **Tables**.
   e. If your CAS server has a different name than the one used to create the JSON file (cas-shared-default), modify the **Target Server** field to match your server.
   f. If your caslib is different than the ones used to create the JSON file (**Public** and/or **Jobs**), modify the **Target Caslib** field to match your caslib.

      g. Click **Import**.

         The reports should be stored in the SAS Content/InteractiveReports folder and are organized by chapter.

To access the starter reports and ending reports in SAS®9, do the following:

1. Download the data and the SPK file.

   Note: There is an SPK file that contains all examples in the book and separate SPK files for each chapter. If you are using SAS Visual Analytics 7.5 on SAS®9, download the files with the suffix _75.

2. Using self-service import in SAS Visual Analytics, load data to the SAS LASR Analytic Server. You can choose any LASR server and library that you have access to; just make a note of the name of the server and library. For this book, the **LASR Analytic Server** and the **Visual Analytics LASR** library were used for all examples. Make note of the library that you import to in your environment. You'll need this information in the next step.

3. In SAS Management Console, on the Folders tab, do the following:

   a. Right-click the folder where you want the book content to be stored and select **Import SAS Package**.

   b. For **Enter the location of the input SAS package file**, navigate to the location where the SPK file is stored.

   c. Click **Next**.

   d. Verify that all objects are selected and click **Next**.

   e. Click **Next** for the About Metadata Connections step.

   f. If your SAS Application Server has a different name than the one used to create the SPK file (SASApp), modify the **Target** field to match your server name and click **Next**.

   g. If you loaded the data to a different LASR library than the one used to create the SPK file (Visual Analytics LASR), modify the **Target** field to match your library name and click **Next**.

   h. Verify that all tables are available in the library you selected and click **Next**.

   i. View the Summary page and click **Next**.

   j. Click **Finish** when the objects are imported.

   The reports should be stored in the InteractiveReports folder and are organized by chapter.

Software Used to Develop the Book's Content

All the examples in this book were developed using SAS Viya 2020.1 (November 2020). All examples should work in later versions of SAS Viya and in SAS Visual Analytics 8.5, and some examples should work in SAS Visual Analytics 7.5. Any examples that will not work in earlier versions are noted in the text, and, in some cases, an alternative approach is suggested.

Example Data

The following data sets are used in the examples in this book:

- **Accidental_Drug_Deaths**: This data set contains details about accidental drug-related deaths in Connecticut between 2012 and 2018. It has information about the geographic location and the person. This data set is used in the following examples:
  - **Chapter 6**- Example: Highlighting a Selected Month
  - **Chapter 7**- Example: Building a Custom Map with Polygon Layers

- **Austin_Intakes_By_Type**: This data set contains details about animals that were surrendered at an Austin animal shelter. It has information about the number of each type of animal surrendered by date. This data set is used in the following examples:
  - **Chapter 2**- Example: Creating a Moving Average
  - **Chapter 5**- Example: Choosing Multiple Measures

- **Books**: This data set contains details about book ratings from Goodreads (www.goodreads.com). It has information about the books (including the title, ISBN, publication year, authors, and a link to the cover image) and ratings. This data set is used in the following examples:
  - **Chapter 3**- Example: Creating a Web Link
  - **Chapter 8**- Example: Creating a Visualization
  - **Chapter 8**- Example: Incorporating a Visualization into SAS Visual Analytics
  - **Chapter 8**- Example: Using a Visualization as the Target of an Action
  - **Chapter 8**- Example: Highlighting Selected Values in the Visualization
  - **Chapter 8**- Example: Using a Visualization as the Source of an Action

- **Counties_States_US**: This data set contains polygon information for United States counties, states, and the country. The county polygon information was created using shapefiles from the Census. This data set is used in the following examples:
  - **Chapter 5**- Example: Selecting a Region
  - **Chapter 7**- Example: Building a Custom Map with Polygon Layers

- **Customers_Clean**: This data set contains details about customers who purchased products from a fictitious sports and outdoors store, Orion Star. It has information about the customers (including their geographic location) and their orders (including the order type, the amount purchased, and the order date). This data set is used in the following examples:
  - **Chapter 2**- Example: Grouping an Aggregated Measure
  - **Chapter 2**- Example: Creating a Tabular Aggregated Measure
  - **Chapter 3**- Example: Linking to a Parameterized Report
  - **Chapter 4**- Example: Showing Top Customers
  - **Chapter 5**- Example: Ranking Top or Bottom Values

- **Customers_Loc**: This data set contains details about customers who purchased products from a fictitious sports and outdoors store, Orion Star. It has information about the customers (including the distance from purchase, satisfaction, and geographic location) and products purchased (including the brand, make, style, prices, costs, and quality). This data set is used in the following examples:
    - **Chapter 3**- Example: Linking to a File
    - **Chapter 4**- Example: Highlighting Values below a Threshold
    - **Chapter 7**- Example: Syncing Hierarchies
    - **Chapter 8**- Example: Using a Circle Packing Plot
    - **Chapter 8**- Example: Using and Modifying a Sunburst Plot

- **Employees_Clean**: This data set contains details about employees who work for a fictitious sports and outdoors store, Orion Star. It has information about the employees (including their department, job title, salary, hire date, and profits generated) and their managers. This data set is used in the following example:
    - **Chapter 2**- Example: Using a Common Filter

- **Forecast_Of_Injuries**: This data set contains a forecast of injuries from motor vehicle accidents in California. It was created from the **MVAINJURIES** data set. This data set is used in the following example:
    - **Chapter 7**- Example: Creating a Chart with Overlays

- **Honey_Prices**: This data set contains details about average honey prices by year for all states within the United States. This data set is used in the following example:
    - **Chapter 4**- Example: Grouping Values Based on a Threshold

- **Insight_Toy_Company_2017**: This data set contains details about orders for a fictitious toy company, Insight Toy Company, for the year 2017. It has information about the orders, facilities (including geographical information, number of employees, and efficiency), customers (including geographical information, distance, and satisfaction), units (including age, capacity, production, and yield), products (including brand, line, style, prices, costs, and quality), and sales reps. This data set is used in the following example:
    - **Chapter 7**- Example: Building a Custom Map

- **Jobs**: This data set contains details about jobs available in New York City. It has information about the jobs, including the title, category, career level, salary range, minimum requirements, and preferred skills, as well as a job description. This data set is used in the following example:
    - **Chapter 5**- Example: Searching for a String

- **MVAINJURIES**: This data set contains details about injuries from motor vehicle accidents in California for the 1990s and the 2000s. It has information about the injuries, the number of vehicles, the number of drivers, and the population. This data set is used in the following examples:
    - **Chapter 6**- Example: Viewing the Last Five Years of Available Data
    - **Chapter 7**- Creating a Chart with Overlays

- **Orders43K**: This data set contains details about orders placed at a fictitious sports and outdoors store, Orion Star. It has information about orders (including totals, costs, dates, and notes), vendors, facility locations, and products. This data set is used in the following examples:
  - ○ **Chapter 2**- Example: Creating a Periodic Aggregated Measure and Adding Time Filters
  - ○ **Chapter 6**- Example: Displaying Data within a Selected Range
  - ○ **Chapter 9**- Example: Returning SAS Results
  - ○ **Chapter 9**- Example: Returning SAS Results Using an HTML Form

- **Parks/National_Parks**: This data set contains details about national parks in the United States. It has information about the location of the park and the number of acres in each park. This data set is used in the following examples:
  - ○ **Chapter 3**- Example: Viewing a Map Location
  - ○ **Chapter 9**- Example: Adding Data to a Table
  - ○ **Chapter 9**- Example: Updating Data in a Table
  - ○ **Chapter 9**- Example: Deleting Data in a Table

- **PG1**: This data set contains details about courses attended by students who took the SAS Programming 1: Essentials course. It has information about training classes conducted within various SAS training centers (including the length of the course, the training center where the course was conducted, and the end date of the course). This data set is used in the following examples:
  - ○ **Chapter 2**- Example: Creating a Calculated Item and a Basic Filter
  - ○ **Chapter 3**- Example: Searching a Web Page

- **Products_Clean**: This data set contains details about products purchased from a fictitious sports and outdoors store, Orion Star. It has information about the products (including names, categories, and groups), suppliers (including geographic information), and orders (including dates, costs, and quantities). This data set is used in the following examples:
  - ○ **Chapter 3**- Example: Creating a Static URL Link
  - ○ **Chapter 3**- Example: Linking to a Parameterized Report
  - ○ **Chapter 4**- Example: Displaying Countries with Orders above a Minimum

- **SolarEclipse_2021**: This data set contains details about solar eclipses starting in 2021 and extending through the year 3000. It has information about the eclipses, including the location, date, type, catalog (or identification) number, and Terrestrial Dynamical Time. This data set is used in the following examples:
  - ○ **Chapter 4**- Example: Viewing Data for the Next N Years
  - ○ **Chapter 6**- Example: Viewing 10 Years after a Selected Year

- **Species**: This data set contains details about species found in national parks in the United States. It has information about the park and the species (including the common and scientific name, the order, the seasonality, and the conservation status). This data set is used in the following example:
  - ○ **Chapter 5**- Example: Selecting Characteristics for Indirect Filtering

- **Stocks**: This data set contains details about stock prices for three companies: IBM, Microsoft, and Intel. This data set is used in the following examples:
  - ○ **Chapter 7**- Example: Using a Data-Driven Lattice
  - ○ **Chapter 7**- Using Overlays with a User-Defined Lattice

- **Taxes2017**: This data set contains details about the number of tax returns for 2017 for various states and counties. This data set is used in the following example:
  - ○ **Chapter 5**- Example: Selecting a Region

- **VA_Dummy_Data_Body**: This data set is a dummy data set that can be used for creating new data items that contain a list of values for use with character parameters. This data set was created by Stu Sztukowski in his paper *Mastering Parameters in SAS Visual Analytics*. This data set is used in the following examples:
  - ○ **Chapter 5**- Example: Ranking Top or Bottom Values
  - ○ **Chapter 5**- Selecting a Region

You can access the example code and data for this book by linking to its author page at https://support.sas.com/ball.

We Want to Hear from You

SAS Press books are written **by** SAS Users **for** SAS Users. We welcome your participation in their development and your feedback on SAS Press books that you are using. Please visit sas.com/books to do the following:

- Sign up to review a book
- Recommend a topic
- Request information about how to become a SAS Press author
- Provide feedback on a book

About The Author

 Nicole Ball, a Principal Technical Training Consultant at SAS, teaches courses on SAS Visual Analytics, SAS Data Quality, and the SAS programming language. Nicole is also a course developer for SAS Visual Analytics, which includes writing and updating courses and preparing customized training. Before coming to SAS, Nicole was an Economic Analyst at the Federal Reserve where she learned more about SAS code and how to apply it to real-world problems. She has an MS in Economics from the University of Texas at Dallas and a BA in Economics from Trinity University in San Antonio, TX. When she's not learning about new features in SAS software and trying to come up with neat solutions to student questions, Nicole loves to crochet and design stuffed animals, read fiction books of any kind, and do CrossFit. Nicole currently lives in Celina, TX, with her husband, Keith, and their dog, Winston.

Learn more about this author by visiting her author page at http://support.sas.com/ball. There you can download free book excerpts, access example code and data, read the latest reviews, get updates, and more.

Chapter 1: Introduction

Introduction

The introduction and evolution of technology has increased the amount of time available for analyzing data and presenting those findings to others. Data visualization is a useful part of any project because it fosters a better understanding of the data, which can help with identifying future areas for analysis. Because the human brain can process information displayed in a chart or graph more easily than lists of numbers in tables and spreadsheets, data visualization has quickly become one of the more popular ways to convey messages.

Choosing the best visualization to showcase your data or tell your story is even more important. In fact, as data collection and preparation gets faster and easier, more emphasis is placed on ensuring that your reports are both nice looking and useful. Creating a beautiful, effective report is both an art and a science. Your reports must be visually appealing and easy to use. Creating user-friendly reports, however, can require extra time and effort from the report designer. Not only must the designer understand the audience and their requirements for the report, but the designer also needs to have an intimate knowledge of the reporting tool being used in order to implement the desired functionality.

This book will help you develop that knowledge. It contains a variety of examples that enable you to customize SAS Visual Analytics reports to enhance the viewer experience. Specifically, it walks you through creating interactive links to external websites, using parameters to give the viewer more control over the report, adding custom graphs and third-party visualizations, using SAS code to extend the functionality of the report, and even embedding report content in your own web pages or apps.

This book is recommended for users who are familiar with both basic and advanced functionality of SAS Visual Analytics in SAS Viya and who want to create reports that enable users to exert more control over their experience. This would be a great follow-up to *An Introduction to SAS Visual Analytics* or for students who have taken the SAS Visual Analytics 1 for SAS Viya: Basics course or the SAS Visual Analytics 2 for SAS Viya: Advanced course.

SAS Visual Analytics

SAS Visual Analytics is data visualization software that enables you to quickly identify trends and patterns in your data and use that insight to solve difficult problems, improve business performance, predict future performance, and mitigate risk.

SAS Visual Analytics is available both on SAS®9 and in SAS Viya. SAS Visual Analytics in SAS®9 uses the SAS LASR Analytic Server to store data in memory, whereas SAS Visual Analytics in SAS Viya uses SAS Cloud Analytic Services (CAS), a server that provides the run-time environment for data management and analytics with SAS. Although there are some differences in how each operates behind the scenes, the report designer is accessing data quickly and easily in both cases. In fact, a lot of the functionality between SAS Visual Analytics on SAS®9 (specifically version 7.5) and SAS Visual Analytics in SAS Viya is the same. Many of the examples in this book can be performed both in SAS®9 and in SAS Viya. However, SAS Viya does have many features that are not available in SAS®9 (for example, the examples in Chapter 8 and 10). Examples that can be implemented only in specific versions of SAS Visual Analytics are noted.

Starting in 2020, SAS Viya has been re-engineered to take advantage of the latest cloud technologies and has been designed to be delivered and updated continuously. This enables customers to access new features as they become available or even incorporate updates on their own schedule. Although this approach puts solutions into the hands of the customers more quickly, it makes it a bit challenging to differentiate between versions. Most of the examples in this book were created using SAS Visual Analytics 2020.1 but will also work in future versions and in SAS Visual Analytics 8.5.

SAS Viya

SAS Viya is a cloud-ready analytics and data management engine that uses CAS to process and analyze data. When performing analytics, CAS efficiently spreads big data processing across all nodes in the cluster, which results in very fast operations. In this configuration, CAS has a communications layer that supports fault tolerance, meaning it can continue processing requests even after losing connectivity to some nodes. It does this by distributing work to other nodes. This communications layer also enables you to dynamically delete and add nodes to the system while the server is running.

CAS is designed to run in a single-machine (symmetric multiprocessing, SMP) or multi-machine (massively parallel processing, MPP) configuration. For both configurations, the CAS server uses multi-threaded algorithms to rapidly perform analytic processing on in-memory data of any size. In fact, the CAS server can continue processing data even when the memory capacity of the server is exceeded.

In the single-machine configuration, all processing is completed on one node. The multi-machine configuration, however, consists of one controller and one or more worker nodes, and it provides optimal processing capabilities.

The following applications are available in SAS Viya and are used throughout this book (in no particular order):

- **SAS Studio**: The programming application that enables you to prepare and create SAS data sets and CAS tables using SAS code and tasks.
- **SAS Data Studio**: The data preparation application that enables you to prepare CAS tables and create CAS tables using transforms. In SAS®9, SAS Visual Data Builder enables users to prepare data and create new LASR tables.
- **SAS Visual Analytics**: The analysis and reporting application that enables you to visualize data, build statistical models, create interactive reports, and view reports in a browser.
- **SAS Graph Builder**: The custom graph application that enables you to create custom graph objects for use in building reports.
- **SAS Environment Manager**: The administration application that enables you to manage the environment.

In addition to using SAS Viya applications to access CAS, you can also use scripts via the command line interface (CLI), REST APIs, and third-party languages (such as Python, R, Lua, and Java).

Chapter 2: Creating Advanced Data Items and Filters

Introduction

Before you can begin analyzing your data and creating reports, you need to ensure that you have the correct data for your analysis. You might need to prepare the data before loading it into memory for use in SAS Visual Analytics. Part of the data preparation process can include joining the data, modifying existing data items, creating new data items, or filtering the data to focus on specific areas. Ideally, all data preparation would occur before the data is loaded into memory and ready for use in SAS Visual Analytics, but this is not always the case. Sometimes, while exploring your data, you identify a new data item that needs to be created or discover a new area that you can focus on to refine your analysis. SAS Visual Analytics enables users to easily add data items and filters for these situations.

Users can create calculated items or aggregated measures. Calculated items are created by performing an operation on unaggregated data, meaning that the expression is evaluated for every row in the data source. You can create numeric, character, date, datetime, or time data items. These types of data items can also be created before data is accessed in SAS Visual Analytics, like during the data preparation phase.

Aggregated measures, on the other hand, are created from aggregated values, meaning that the data is combined first and then the operation is performed. With aggregated measures, the calculation changes depending on other items available in the graph, which makes them very flexible. Due to their dynamic nature, these data items cannot be created outside of SAS Visual Analytics. In the following examples, you see how to create a basic calculated item along with derived, periodic, and advanced aggregated measures.

In addition to creating data items, users can also create filters in SAS Visual Analytics to subset the data to a specific group or subgroup. Two types of filters can be created: static and interactive. Static filters are created by the report designer and cannot be modified by the report viewer. Interactive filters are also created by the report designer, but they **can** be modified by the report viewer. These are also known as *actions* and *links*.

In addition to creating basic static filters, users can also create more advanced filters, like common filters, advanced static filters, and time-based interactive filters. You see how to create a basic filter and some more advanced filters in the following examples.

Example: Creating a Calculated Item and a Basic Filter

In this example, the data contains details about training classes conducted at various SAS training centers. You want to create a schedule chart that shows the courses offered, the length of the courses, and the training centers where they were conducted. However, the data contains only the end dates for courses and the length of courses, not the start dates. You can create a calculated item that computes the date on which a training class started using the end date of the class and the length of the course (in days).

To create a calculated item, in the Data pane, click **New data item** and select **Calculated item**. Then do the following:

❶ Specify a name for the new calculated item. (See Figure 2.1.)
❷ Specify the result type. It's a best practice to specify the result type before creating the expression.
❸ Specify an appropriate format.
❹ Using the Visual view, build the expression using data items and operators. As an alternative, you can use the Text view to enter the expression.

Note: Building advanced filters for an object (using the Filters pane) is similar to building new calculated items. The main difference is that, when building filters, no aggregated operators are

Figure 2.1: Creating a Calculated Item

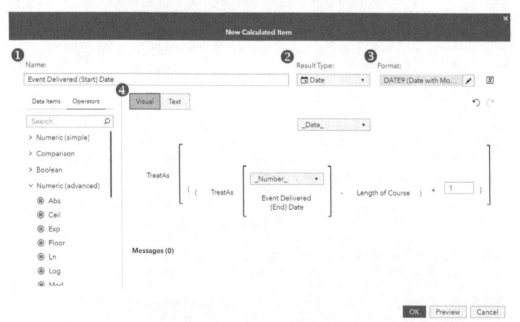

available. This is because filters created in the Filters pane use detail data. For some objects, you can create a post-aggregate report filter to subset the data in the object using aggregated values.

In this example, the embedded TreatAs operator enables **Event Delivered (End) Date** to be used as a number for the calculation. This means that it converts the date value to the underlying numeric value (the number of days since January 1, 1960). Then the **Length of Course** measure is subtracted from the end date and 1 is added to account for the start date of the class. For example, assume that **Event Delivered (End) Date** is on a Thursday (represented as R in Figure 2.2) and **Length of Course** is three days. This means that class starts on Tuesday. To get the appropriate date, you must subtract the **Length of Course** value (3) from **Event Delivered (End) Date**, which gives you Monday. Then you must add 1 to get the correct start date, Tuesday.

The result of subtracting the **Length of Course** value and adding 1 is a numeric value. This must then be treated as a date to return a Date data item. This expression is evaluated for every row in the data source. After the new Date data item is created, add it to the **Start** role for the schedule chart. For this data, there are too many values to display in the schedule chart. You need to add a filter to reduce the number of values so that the schedule chart is displayed.

Figure 2.2: Calculating the Event Delivered (Start) Date

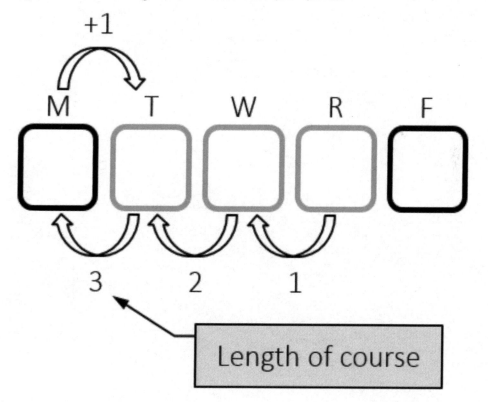

You can create a basic static filter that subsets a schedule chart to show only courses in the Texas training centers: AU (Austin), DA (Dallas), and HO (Houston). The schedule chart shows all product codes (courses) grouped by **Training Center Code**. For each course, the chart indicates the length of the course using **Event Delivered (Start) Date** and **Event Delivered (End) Date**.

To create a basic static filter, do the following:

❶ Select the object on the canvas. (See Figure 2.3.)
❷ In the right pane, click **Filters**.
❸ Click **New filter** and select **Training Center Code**.
❹ Clear any values that you want filtered out. For example, clear **Select all** and select the following training centers: **AU**, **DA**, **HO**.

While creating this report, you also made several changes to the schedule chart. (See Table 2.1.)

Table 2.1: Modifying Options for the Schedule Chart

Option	Value
X Axis Options: Axis label	<clear>
Y Axis Options: Axis label	<clear>
Y Axis Options: Axis line	<clear>
Legend: Placement	Upper, middle

Figure 2.3: Creating a Basic Static Filter

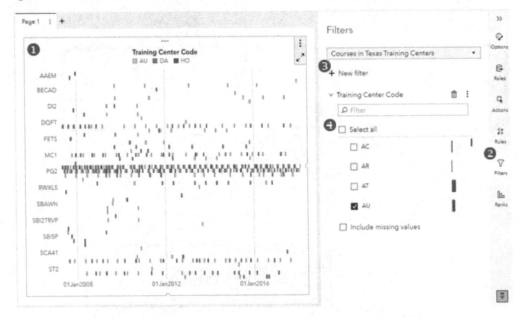

Beginning in SAS Visual Analytics 8.3 (September update), you can save the modified chart as an object template rather than make these same changes each time you use the schedule chart.

To save an object template, do the following after your chart has been modified:

❶ Right-click the chart and select **Save to Objects pane**. (See Figure 2.4.)
❷ Choose the **Include Data** (like role assignments, display rules, filters, ranks, and sorting) or **Don't Include Data** option. The option to include data was introduced in SAS Visual Analytics 8.4 and can be useful for copying objects or whole pages (using containers) between reports.
Objects that are saved without data are added to the list of object types in the Objects pane. Objects that are saved with data are added to a new group, **Objects with data**, in the Objects pane.
❸ In the Objects pane, modify the name of the object and make it shared. Only application administrators have the option to share object templates. Any object templates created by users who are not application administrators are private, meaning they can't be used by anyone else.

Now the object template can be used in other reports.

Figure 2.4: Saving an Object Template

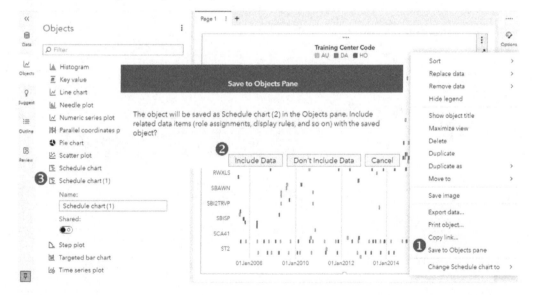

Example: Grouping an Aggregated Measure

In this example, the report displays the number of customers in each country. You want to group countries based on customer ranges: Low (0 – 499), Medium (500 – 999), High (1000 – 9000), and Very High (9001 and above). The data source does not contain a count of customers in each country. It does, however, have information about customer IDs for each customer country.

To start, you'll need to create a new aggregated measure that counts the number of customers within each country. Aggregated measures can be created using quick calculations or using the **Visual** view or **Text** view in the New Calculated Item window.

Note: Quick calculations are referred to as derived data items in SAS Visual Analytics 2020.1.4 (March 2021) and prior releases.

To create this aggregated measure as a quick calculation, do the following:

❶ In the Data pane, right-click **Customer ID** and select **New calculation**. (See Figure 2.5.)
❷ Specify a name for the new calculated item.
❸ Specify the type. Selecting **Distinct count** counts the distinct values of **Customer ID**.

The new data item appears in the Aggregated Measure group in the Data pane. You can right-click the data item and select **Edit** to view the expression. (See Figure 2.6.)

Figure 2.5: Creating an Aggregated Measure

Figure 2.6: Viewing the Expression for an Aggregated Measure

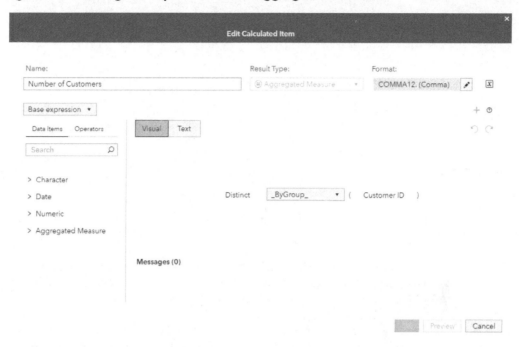

The result type of the new data item is **Aggregated Measure**. To create aggregated measures, you need to use aggregated operators. There are four groups of aggregated operators: Aggregated (simple), Aggregated (periodic), Aggregated (advanced), and Aggregated (tabular). In this case, you use the Distinct operator, which is in the Aggregated (simple) group.

Each aggregated operator requires several parameters. For Aggregated (simple) operators, you need to specify the **Aggregation context** parameter. This specifies how data is aggregated when paired with other data items in the report. **ByGroup** calculates the aggregation for each subset of data items used in the object, whereas **ForAll** calculates the aggregation for the entire data source. For example, if you pair **Number of Customers** (as calculated above) with **Continent Name**, you get a count of the distinct number of customers in each continent (the group). If you change **Aggregation context** to **ForAll**, you get a count of the distinct number of customers in *all* continents. This means that you can easily compare a local value (**ByGroup**) to a global value (**ForAll**).

Remember, aggregated measures are calculated by first aggregating values and then by performing the calculation. The values are aggregated depending on other data items in the object. In Figure 2.7, the aggregated measure was paired with **Continent Name**, so the distinct number of customer IDs in each continent were counted to return the **ByGroup** calculation.

You could pair the same data item with **Customer Country**, and the aggregation is reevaluated to return the distinct number of customers in each country.

Figure 2.7: Illustrating ByGroup and ForAll

Continent Name ▲	ByGroup	ForAll
Africa	156	68,300
Asia	295	68,300
Europe	41,228	68,300
North America	23,189	68,300
Oceania	3,432	68,300
	Total: 68,300	Total: 68,300

The dynamic nature of aggregated measures makes them very useful in many different applications. This also explains why these measures cannot be created before bringing the data into SAS Visual Analytics: The **ByGroup** value needs to be known before the calculation can be performed.

Now that you have the number of customers, you need to group each country based on customer ranges: Low (0 – 499), Medium (500 – 999), High (1000 – 9000), and Very High (9001 and above). Typically, you would do this with a custom category or a calculated item that uses the IF...THEN operator. However, aggregated measures cannot be used in custom categories or calculated items.

To accomplish this task, you can create an aggregated data source of **Customer Country** and **Number of Customers**. Beginning in SAS Visual Analytics 8.3, aggregated data sources are available to simplify visualizations and potentially shorten query times. Another use for aggregated data sources was soon discovered: They work great for grouping aggregated measures! When you create an aggregated data source of an aggregated measure, it becomes a regular measure, which you can use in custom categories and calculated items.

To create an aggregated data source, do the following:

❶ In the Data pane, view the Data source menu and select **New data from aggregation of <CAS-table>**. (See Figure 2.8.)
❷ Specify a name for the new aggregated data.
❸ Select columns to include in the aggregated data.
❹ Add a filter (optional).

Note: The list of available items includes all data items except for hierarchies, geography items, spline effects, partitions, scoped calculations, interaction effects, calculations that contain a suppressed or time-period calculation, and calculations that use the AggregateCells operator.

Figure 2.8: Creating an Aggregated Data Source

Then using the new aggregated data, you can create a custom category that groups countries by number of customers into Low (0 – 499), Medium (500 – 999), High (1000 – 9000), and Very High (9001 and above) groups.

To create the custom category, do the following:

❶ In the Data pane, select the aggregated data source. (See Figure 2.9.)
❷ In the Measure group, right-click **Number of Customers** and select **New custom category**.
❸ Specify a name for the custom category.
❹ Verify that **Number of Customers** is selected for the **Based on** field.
❺ Verify that **Intervals** is selected for the **Group by** field.
❻ Create **Value Groups** by specifying labels and ranges. (See Table 2.2.)
❼ Specify how to display remaining values (for example, values that do not fit into value groups).

Figure 2.9: Creating a Custom Category

Table 2.2: Intervals for Customer Ranges Custom Category

Customer Ranges	Interval
Low	0 <= Number of Customers <= 499
Medium	500 <= Number of Customers <= 999
High	1,000 <= Number of Customers <= 9,000
Very High	Remaining Values

The custom category (Customer Ranges) can then be used with **Customer Country** and **Number of Customers** from the aggregated data source to categorize each country as Low, Medium, High, or Very High. (See Figure 2.10.)

Remember, SAS Visual Analytics generates temporary tables in each user's personal library when the user opens a report that uses aggregated data. This means that in production reports that many users access, aggregated data can degrade performance. For these reports and for releases prior to SAS Visual Analytics 8.3, you need to prepare the data ahead of time, like in SAS Visual Data Builder (for SAS Visual Analytics 7.5) or SAS Data Studio (for SAS Visual Analytics 8.1+). You could also use the SQL code to create the aggregated data of Customer Country and Number of Customers. (See Program 2.1.)

Figure 2.10: Categorizing Countries by Number of Customers

Customer Country ▲	Customer Ranges	Number of Customers
Andorra	Low	9
Australia	High	3,420
Austria	Low	432
Belgium	High	1,394
Benin	Low	4
Bulgaria	Low	6
Canada	Medium	956
China	Low	1
Croatia	Low	12
Czech Republic	Low	9
Denmark	Medium	868

Program 2.1: Creating an Aggregated Data Source

```
libname ch2 '<path-for-data>';
proc sql;
create table ch2.AggregatedData as
select CustomerCountryLabel, count(distinct 'Customer ID'n) as
      NumberOfCustomers label='Number of Customers'
  from ch2.Customers_Clean
  group by CustomerCountryLabel;
run;
```

Note: For your LIBNAME statement, specify the path where the Chapter 2 data is located.

Note: In the **Customers_Clean** table, **Customer Country** is named **CustomerCountryLabel**.

Note: Because **Customer ID** contains an embedded blank, a SAS named literal ('*name-of-column*'n) must be used to reference the column in code.

Example: Using a Common Filter

In this example, the report displays details about profit generated by employee and by group. The report should contain two sets of objects: one set to show details for all employees and one set to show details for specific job titles. Each set consists of a key value object that displays total

Figure 2.11: Displaying Profit by Employee

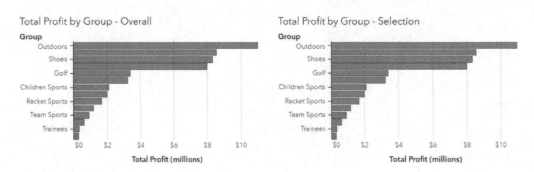

profit, a list table that lists the top five employees by total profit, and a bar chart that shows total profit by group. Currently, both sets show details for all employees. (See Figure 2.11.)

You want to filter the objects on the right (the key value object, list table, and bar chart) by **Job Title**. To do this, you can use a special type of static filter, a common filter.

Beginning in SAS Visual Analytics 8.3, common filters can be created and shared between objects in a report. When you edit the common filter, it's updated everywhere that the common filter is used. This means that you can create the filter once, apply it to any objects in the report, and modify the filter in one location.

To create the common filter, do the following:

❶ Select one of the objects in the canvas. (See Figure 2.12.)
❷ In the Filters pane, click **New filter** and select a data item.
❸ Select the values for the filter.
❹ Click the **More** icon next to the filter and select **Change to common filter**.

The common filter is added to the Common Filter group in the Data pane. You can rename the common filter and apply it to other objects in the report by either dragging the common filter to the object (See Figure 2.13.) or by clicking **New filter** and selecting the common filter in the Filters pane. (See Figure 2.14.)

Figure 2.12: Creating a Common Filter

Figure 2.13: Applying a Common Filter (Click and Drag)

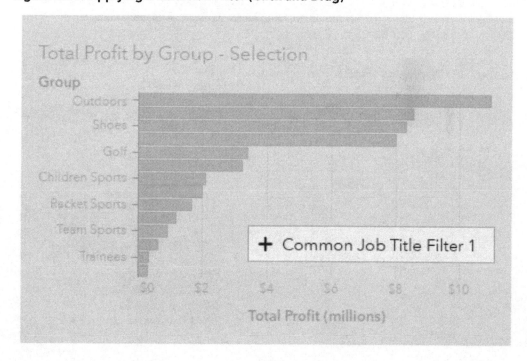

Figure 2.14: Applying a Common Filter (Filters Pane)

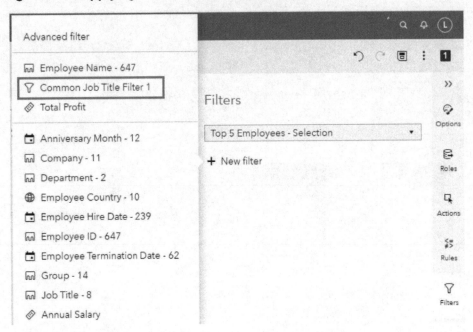

After you apply the common filter to the objects on the right, they now show details for the selected job titles: Purchasing Agent I, Purchasing Agent III, Temp. Sales Rep., Trainee, and missing values. (See Figure 2.15.)

Figure 2.15: Displaying Profit for Selected Job Titles

You could clear Purchasing Agent I and Purchasing Agent III to see details in those charts for only Temp. Sales Rep., Trainee, and missing values.

Example: Creating a Periodic Aggregated Measure and Adding Time Filters

For this example, you want to create a report that shows the one-year change in cumulative profit over time. The data source contains **TransactionDate**, **OrderTotal**, and **OrderProductCost**. Before calculating cumulative profit, you need to create a new data item for **Profit** by subtracting **OrderProductCost** from **OrderTotal**. (See Figure 2.16.)

Then you can create an aggregated measure that calculates cumulative profit for each year; that is, it consecutively adds each month's profit to the total from the previous month and it resets in January of each year.

To create this aggregated measure using aggregated (periodic) operators, in the Data pane, click **New data item** and select **Calculated item**. Then do the following:

❶ Specify a name for the new calculated item. (See Figure 2.17.)
❷ Specify the result type. It's a best practice to specify the result type before creating the expression.
❸ Specify an appropriate format.
❹ Using the Visual view, build the expression using data items and operators. As an alternative, you can use the Text view to enter the expression.

Note: Both calculated items and aggregated measures can be created by clicking **New data item** and selecting **Calculated item** in the Data pane. The result type determines whether the new data item is a calculated item (Numeric, Character, Date, Datetime) or an aggregated measure.

The CumulativePeriod operator returns aggregated values during a period of time within a larger time period (for example, the year-to-date total). Remember, each aggregated operator requires parameters. Aggregated (periodic) operators require several parameters, which differ based on the operator used. (See Table 2.3 for the parameters required for the CumulativePeriod operator.)

In this example, the CumulativePeriod operator sums profits by month over the calendar year (which starts in January). The calculation is processed for the current year before any time filters are applied (**IgnoreAllTimeFrameFilters**) for the entire period (**Full**). If you want to calculate

Figure 2.16: Calculation for Profit

```
(    OrderTotal    -    OrderProductCost    )
```

Figure 2.17: Creating a Periodic Aggregated Measure

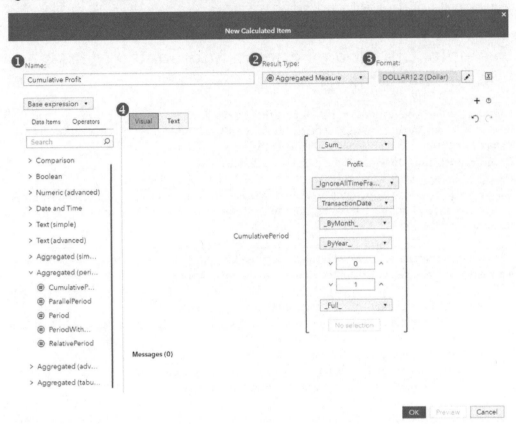

cumulative profit for a fiscal year that starts in June, then you can change the **Starting point for each new outer period** parameter to **6** (for June). Each May will show totals for the entire fiscal year, and the cumulative totals will reset every June.

If you want to calculate cumulative profit for a portion of each period (for example, the first 15 days), then you can specify **ToDate** as the **Subset period** parameter and select the 15th day of any month (for example, March15). This totals profits for the first 15 days of each month and accumulates those values for the year. The **ToToday** option updates the portion of each period based on the date on which the report is opened. For example, if you open the report on 22Dec2020, then the first 22 days of each month are totaled, but if you open the report on 02Jan2021, then the first two days of each month are totaled.

Remember, for this example we want to calculate the one-year change in cumulative profit. To do this, we also need to calculate the cumulative profit for the previous year. This data item can be easily created by duplicating the **Cumulative Profit** data item and changing the **Outer interval**

Table 2.3: Parameters Required for the CumulativePeriod Operator

Parameter	Description
Aggregation	The aggregation applied to the measure.
Measure	The data item to be aggregated.
Time filters	Specifies which time filters should be applied before processing the calculation.
Date	The date data item for the period calculation. Only data items whose formats specify a year are available.
Inner interval	The smaller time period for which the values are aggregated (for example, ByMonth).
Outer interval	The larger time period over which the cumulation occurs (for example, ByYear).
Outer interval offset	The number of outer intervals to offset from the current period, where 0 specifies the current period.
Starting point for each new outer period	The starting point for each outer period (that is, when the calculation will reset, where 1 is January).
Scope	How much of each period is aggregated, where Full aggregates values for the entire time period.
Subset period	The date used to subset each period, if ToDate is specified for the scope parameter.

offset parameter to **-1**. This enables you to look at the previous outer interval, which in this case is the previous year.

Then, to calculate the 1Y change, simply subtract **Cumulative Profit (Previous Year)** from **Cumulative Profit**.

Viewing the aggregated measures in a list table enables you to verify that the calculations are evaluated as expected. (See Figure 2.18.)

Notice that **Cumulative Profit** resets every January and shows totals for the calendar year every December, **Cumulative Profit (Previous Year)** shows values for the prior year, and **Cumulative Profit (1Y change)** shows the difference between the current month's cumulative profit and the value from the same month in the prior year.

This data can also be displayed using other chart types. The waterfall chart is a great choice for presenting periodic calculations. This chart displays how a measure increases (in green) or decreases (in red) from an initial value over a series of operations, transactions, or time. (See Figure 2.19.)

Figure 2.18: Verifying Cumulative Profit Calculations

TransactionDate ▲	Profit	Cumulative Profit	Cumulative Profit (Previous Year)	Cumulative Profit (1Y change)
Jan2010	$321,190.08	$321,190.08	.	.
Feb2010	$242,120.45	$563,310.53	.	.
Mar2010	$286,257.14	$849,567.67	.	.
Apr2010	$273,587.10	$1,123,154.77	.	.
May2010	$185,216.57	$1,308,371.35	.	.
Jun2010	$188,015.37	$1,496,386.72	.	.
Jul2010	$167,618.94	$1,664,005.66	.	.
Aug2010	$179,523.64	$1,843,529.30	.	.
Sep2010	$190,598.61	$2,034,127.91	.	.
Oct2010	$191,928.04	$2,226,055.94	.	.
Nov2010	$505,000.38	$2,731,056.32	.	.
Dec2010	$526,047.14	$3,257,103.46	.	.
Jan2011	$348,260.84	$348,260.84	$321,190.08	$27,070.76
Feb2011	$283,113.05	$631,373.89	$563,310.53	$68,063.36
Mar2011	$294,383.92	$925,757.81	$849,567.67	$76,190.14
Apr2011	$263,875.48	$1,189,633.29	$1,123,154.77	$66,478.52
May2011	$212,858.12	$1,402,491.42	$1,308,371.35	$94,120.07
Jun2011	$231,985.08	$1,634,476.49	$1,496,386.72	$138,089.77
Jul2011	$175,266.75	$1,809,743.24	$1,664,005.66	$145,737.58

Note: **Cumulative Profit (1Y change)** starts in January 2011 because the data source does not contain data prior to January 2010. A basic filter has been added to the waterfall chart to filter out all months prior to January 2011.

To make this report more interactive, you can add a button bar with a filter action to subset the waterfall chart by year. This data source already contains **TransactionYear**. However, adding it to the button bar and selecting a year returns no data. This is because date filters must use the same data item that is used in the calculation or a duplicate data item that is based on the same data item. **TransactionYear** is not the data item used to calculate **Cumulative Profit (1Y change)** and is also not a duplicate.

To apply this type of filter, you could duplicate the date data item used in the calculation (**TransactionDate**), change the format to **Year**, and use that data item in the button bar. Now the filter will work as expected. (See Figure 2.20.)

Because the **Time filters** parameter is set to **IgnoreAllTimeFrameFilters**, the calculation is evaluated first, and then all time filters are applied (static and interactive). If the **Time filters** parameter was set to **ApplyAllFilters**, all time filters (static and interactive) would be applied first, and then the calculation would be evaluated. In this example, that would result in no data because the waterfall chart contains only one year and the **Cumulative Profit (1Y change)** calculation compares two years. The final option, **IgnoreInteractiveTimeFrameFilters**, ignores interactive time filters, but not static time filters. This means any static time filters (based on

Figure 2.19: Displaying Cumulative Profit in a Waterfall Chart

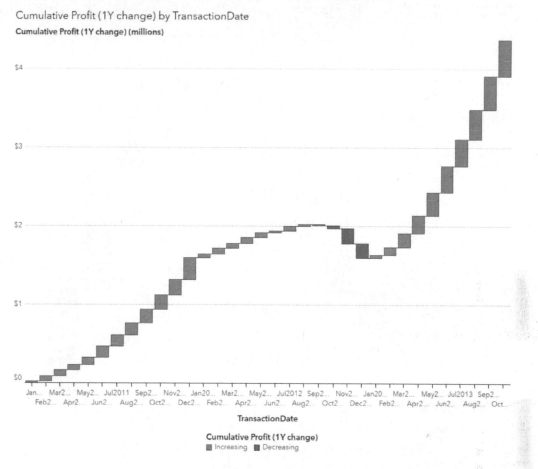

Cumulative Profit (1Y change) by TransactionDate

the same date data item used in the calculation) would be applied first, the calculation would be evaluated, and then any interactive time filters (based on the same data item used in the calculation) would be applied last. Remember, in this example, there is a static filter applied to the waterfall chart to filter out 2010. With this option, there would be missing data for 2011 in the chart because the 2010 data would be filtered out before the calculation is performed. Therefore, the first year that the **Cumulative Profit (1Y change)** data would be available is January 2012.

To finish up this example, imagine you want the grand total for **Cumulative Profit** to show the total profit for all time. Adding totals to the list table would display a grand total for **Profit**, but not for any of the aggregated measures. This is because aggregated (periodic) operators aggregate values only over a period of time. The grand total does not represent a specific period of time, so no value is displayed.

Figure 2.20: Filtering by Year

| 2010 | 2011 | 2012 | 2013 |

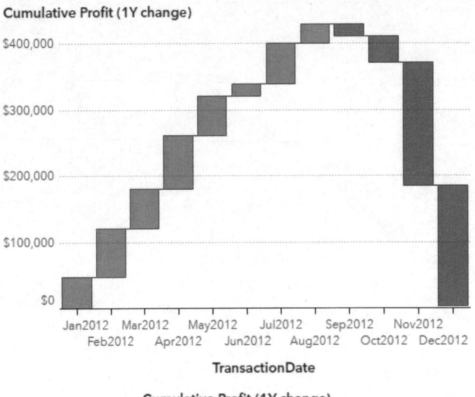

Cumulative Profit (1Y change) by TransactionDate

You can use scopes to display the total profit when totals are added to the list table. Aggregated measures can have multiple scopes, where each scope is defined by a specific intersection of categories (like a custom intersection of categories or grand total). Each scope can consist of a different expression that is evaluated whenever that specific intersection of categories is available in a chart.

To add a scope to display the total profits when totals are added to the list table, in the Data pane, right-click **Cumulative Profit** and select **Edit**. Then do the following:

❶ In the upper right corner of the window, below the **Format** field, click the **Add** icon. (See Figure 2.21.)
❷ In the New Scope window, select **Grand total** for the **Specify scope** field.
❸ Select **Blank expression** for the **Start scope with field** and click **OK**.
❹ Verify that **Grand total** is specified for the selector below the **Name** field. You can use this selector to toggle between the default expression and the scope expression.
❺ Using the Visual view, build the expression using data items and operators. As an alternative, you can use the Text view to enter the expression.

Once the scope is added, the total for **Cumulative Profit** shows the total profit for all the data.

In this example, you used only one of the aggregated (periodic) operators, CumulativePeriod. The other operators work in a similar way but can be used for different types of periodic calculations.

Figure 2.21: Adding a Scope to an Aggregated Measure

The ParallelPeriod operator returns the aggregated value for a time period that is parallel to the current period. This operator can be used to calculate the 12-month change in **Profit**. (See Figure 2.22.)

The Period operator returns the aggregated value for a time period. This operator can be used to calculate the portion of yearly profit generated each month. (See Figure 2.23.)

The PeriodWithDate operator returns the aggregated value for a specific time period. This operator can be used to compare the current monthly profit to the profit for the month in which the company went public, June2011. (See Figure 2.24.)

The RelativePeriod operator returns the aggregated value for a time period that is relative to the current time period. This operator can be used calculate the three-month change in profit. (See Figure 2.25.)

Figure 2.22: Using the ParallelPeriod Operator

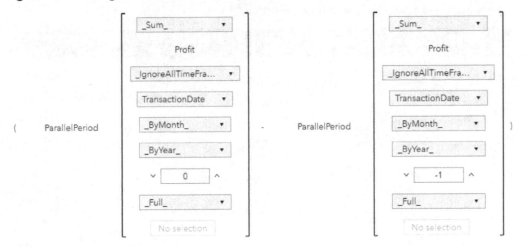

Figure 2.23: Using the Period Operator

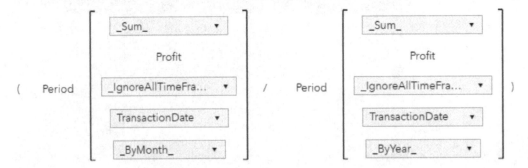

Figure 2.24: Using the PeriodWithDate Operator

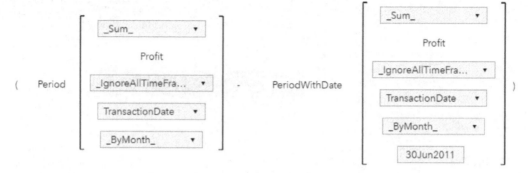

Figure 2.25: Using the RelativePeriod Operator

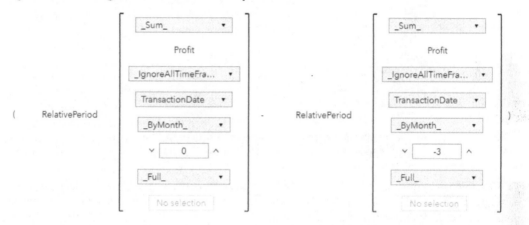

Example: Creating a Moving Average

In this example, you want a report that compares the number of animals surrendered at an Austin animal shelter to the three-month moving average. In addition, you want to calculate the total animals surrendered to date. The data source contains a column, **Animals**, that provides a count of the animals surrendered each month. You can create a quick calculation to calculate the moving average for a measure.

To create the quick calculation, do the following:

❶ In the Data pane, right-click **Animals** and select **New calculation**. (See Figure 2.26.)
❷ Specify the type.
❸ For the moving average, specify the number of cells to average. Specifying **3** takes the three-month moving average of the number of animals surrendered.
❹ Specify a name for the new calculated item. You need to select a type before changing the name.

Figure 2.26: Creating a Derived Data Item

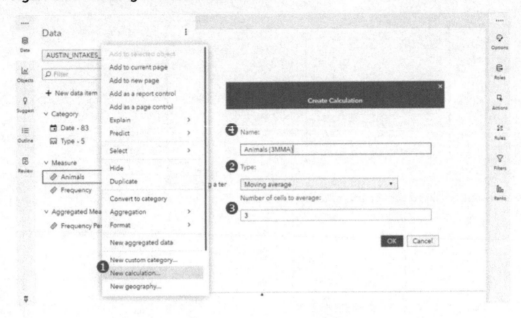

The new data item appears in the Aggregated Measure group in the Data pane. You can right-click the data item and select **Edit** to view the expression. (See Figure 2.27.)

This derived data item uses the AggregateCells operator from the Aggregated (tabular) group. This operator, introduced in SAS Visual Analytics 8.2, applies an aggregation to a range of items in a group. It requires five parameters. (See Table 2.4.)

Figure 2.27: Viewing the Expression for the Moving Average Derived Data Item

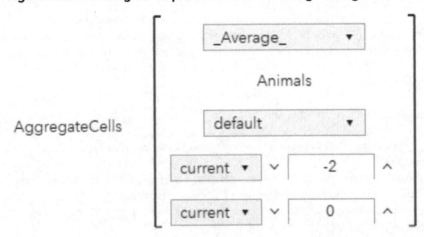

Table 2.4: Parameters Required for the AggregateCells Operator

Parameter	Description
Measure	The data item to be aggregated.
Direction	The direction in which values should be aggregated. Values are default, column, and row.
Starting point	The starting point for the aggregation. Values are start, current, and end.
Ending point	The ending point for the aggregation. Values are start, current, and end.

Both the **Starting point** and **Ending point** parameters can be offset, where 0 represents the current period, negative numbers represent prior periods, and positive number represent future periods. In this example, the AggregateCells operator averages the animal count starting three months prior to the current period (the starting point is set to the current period offset by -2) through the current period (the ending point is set to the current period offset by 0).

Plotting this in a time series plot with **Animals** by **Date** shows that the three-month moving average is not as variable as the original count, but the spikes in the three-month moving average do seem to be trailing the spikes in **Animals**. This is because the expression is currently calculating a trailing moving average: It's averaging the current month and the previous two months.

To create a moving average that more closely matches the peaks and troughs of the original data item, you can create a centered moving average by duplicating **Animals (3MMA)** and modifying the expression to start at the previous period (starting point= current with offset of -1) and ending at the next period (ending point= current period with offset of 1).

Adding **Animals (3MMA, centered)** to the time series plot shows that this value more closely aligns with changes in animals but remains less variable than the original data item. (See Figure 2.28.)

To create a moving average prior to SAS Visual Analytics 8.2, you would need to create a calculated data item that uses the RelativePeriod operator to add the number of animals from two months ago, one month ago, and the current month, and then divide that sum by 3 to get the average. (See Figure 2.29.)

In addition to calculating the moving average, you also need to calculate the total animals surrendered to date. You can't use the CumulativePeriod operator to perform this calculation because it calculates the cumulative only within a larger time period (like a month or a year) not over all time. However, the AggregateCells operator can be used to perform this calculation. (See Figure 2.30.)

This calculates the sum of the number of animals starting at the beginning and going through the current period. Showing this new aggregated measure, **Cumulative Total (All Time)**, with **Date** in a list table provides the total animals surrendered to date for each month that the Austin animal center has been in business.

Figure 2.28: Viewing Trailing and Centered Moving Averages

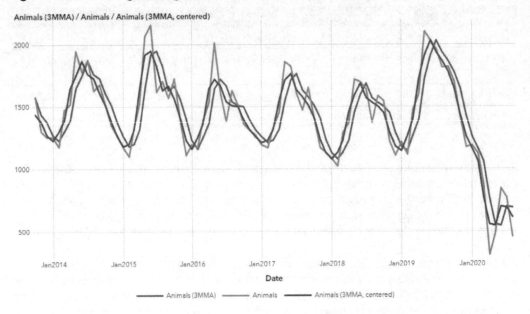

Figure 2.29: Creating a Moving Average Using the RelativePeriod Operator

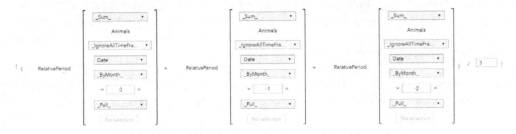

Figure 2.30: Using AggregateCells to Calculate Total Animals Surrendered to Date

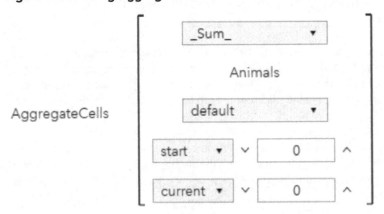

As you can see, modifying the **Starting point** and **Ending point** parameters enables you to create many different types of calculations. For example, starting at the start (with an offset of 0) and ending at the end (with an offset of 0) returns the grand total for each date. This calculation can then be used to compare a local value (like the number of animals surrendered each month) to a global value (the total number of animals surrendered for all time).

The final parameter used in the AggregateCells operator, **Direction**, specifies in which direction the values should be aggregated: column, row, or default. For example, if the **Direction** parameter is set to **columns**, the **Cumulative Total (column)** data item aggregates down each column. (See Figure 2.31.)

If the **Direction** parameter is set to **rows**, however, the **Cumulative Total (row)** data item aggregates across each row. (See Figure 2.32.)

When the **Direction** parameter is set to **default**, the type of aggregation (column or row) differs based on the chart type and the options set for the chart. (See Table 2.5.)

Note: The following chart types cannot use aggregated measures: Box plot, Correlation matrix, Heat map, Histogram, Parallel coordinates plot, Geo contour, Geo network, Slider control, Automated explanation, Automated prediction, Network analysis, Path analysis, Text topics, all the SAS Visual Statistics objects, and all the SAS Visual Data Mining and Machine Learning objects.

Note: Because the key value object shows total or top/bottom value, the **default**, **row**, and **column** values are all the same.

Figure 2.31: Aggregating by Column with AggregateCells

Type ▲	Bird		Cat		Dog		Livestock		Other	
Date ▲	Animals	Cumulative Total (column)	Animals	Cumulative Total (column)	Animals	Cumulative Total (column)	Animals	Cumulative Total (column)	Animals	Cumulative Total (column)
Oct2013	1	1	541	541	952	952	—	.	81	81
Nov2013	4	5	434	975	795	1,747	1	1	65	146
Dec2013	—	5	326	1,301	842	2,589	—	1	87	233
Jan2014	—	5	325	1,626	870	3,459	—	1	59	292
Feb2014	5	10	267	1,893	804	4,263	1	2	99	391
Mar2014	3	13	353	2,246	884	5,147	1	3	232	623
Apr2014	7	20	563	2,809	846	5,993	—	3	104	727
May2014	3	23	900	3,709	955	6,948	1	4	86	813
Jun2014	8	31	819	4,528	864	7,812	—	4	87	900
Jul2014	5	36	878	5,406	916	8,728	—	4	76	976
Aug2014	6	42	678	6,084	824	9,552	—	4	119	1,095
Sep2014	8	50	698	6,782	902	10,454	—	4	69	1,164
Oct2014	1	51	602	7,384	839	11,293	—	4	71	1,235
Nov2014	—	51	477	7,861	826	12,119	—	4	43	1,278
Dec2014	7	58	335	8,196	877	12,996	—	4	49	1,327

Figure 2.32: Aggregating by Row with AggregateCells

Type ▲	Bird		Cat		Dog		Livestock		Other	
Date ▲	Animals	Cumulative Total (row)	Animals	Cumulative Total (row)	Animals	Cumulative Total (row)	Animals	Cumulative Total (row)	Animals	Cumulative Total (row)
Oct2013	1	1	541	542	952	1,494	—	1,494	81	1,575
Nov2013	4	4	434	438	795	1,233	1	1,234	65	1,299
Dec2013	—	.	326	326	842	1,168	—	1,168	87	1,255
Jan2014	—	.	325	325	870	1,195	—	1,195	59	1,254
Feb2014	5	5	267	272	804	1,076	1	1,077	99	1,176
Mar2014	3	3	353	356	884	1,240	1	1,241	232	1,473
Apr2014	7	7	563	570	846	1,416	—	1,416	104	1,520
May2014	3	3	900	903	955	1,858	1	1,859	86	1,945
Jun2014	8	8	819	827	864	1,691	—	1,691	87	1,778
Jul2014	5	5	878	883	916	1,799	—	1,799	76	1,875
Aug2014	6	6	678	684	824	1,508	—	1,508	119	1,627
Sep2014	8	8	698	706	902	1,608	—	1,608	69	1,677
Oct2014	1	1	602	603	839	1,442	—	1,442	71	1,513
Nov2014	—	.	477	477	826	1,303	—	1,303	43	1,346
Dec2014	7	7	335	342	877	1,219	—	1,219	49	1,268

Table 2.5: Default Aggregation for Each Chart Type

Chart Type	Default=Column	Default=Row
List table	X	
Crosstab with Columns role, Measures as columns		X
Crosstab with Columns role, Measures as rows		X
Crosstab with Rows role, Measures as columns	X	
Crosstab with Rows role, Measures as rows	X	
Crosstab with Columns and Rows, Measures as columns	X	
Crosstab with Columns and Rows, Measures as rows		X
Bar chart	X	
Bubble change plot		X
Bubble plot		X
Butterfly chart		X
Comparative time series plot		X
Dot plot		X
Dual axis bar chart		X
Dual axis bar-line chart		X

(Continued)

Table 2.5: Default Aggregation for Each Chart Type (*Continued*)

Chart Type	Default=Column	Default=Row
Dual axis line chart		X
Dual axis time series chart		X
Gauge	X	
Line chart	X	
Needle plot		X
Numeric series plot	X	
Pie chart		X
Scatter plot	X	
Schedule chart	X	
Step plot		X
Targeted bar chart	X	
Time series plot		X
Treemap	X	
Vector plot		X
Waterfall chart		X
Word cloud	X	
Geo coordinate	X	
Geo region	X	
Geo region-coordinate	X	
Button bar	X	
Drop-down list	X	
List	X	
Text input	X	
Forecasting		X

Example: Creating a Tabular Aggregated Measure

For this example, you want to create a report that looks at the total and average costs by country and continent. The data source contains cost details (**Cost**) for each value of **Customer Country** and **Continent Name**.

To start, you want to calculate the contribution of cost for each country to the continent's total cost, **% of Total by Continent**. That is, you want to take the total cost for each country and divide by the total cost for each continent. While it's pretty straight forward to calculate the total cost for each country using aggregated measures, it's not so simple to compare this value to the total cost for each continent. This is because the numerator and denominator are evaluating different groups of data (country and continent, respectively). When you use the Aggregated (simple) operators you can aggregate only **ByGroup** or **ForAll**; there is no option to aggregate for different groups.

The AggregateTable operator, introduced in SAS Visual Analytics 8.3, enables you to perform aggregations on data crossings that are independent of (or changed from) the data in your objects. This means that you can use this operator to compare aggregations for different groups of data in one single object.

The easiest way to understand how these calculations are performed is to view the data in a crosstab. The crosstab should have both **Continent Name** and **Customer Country** added to the **Rows** role and **Cost** added to the **Measures** role. Subtotals and totals are added to the crosstab (after the groups) for comparison purposes.

As a first step, you calculate the numerator, **Total by Country**. Remember, when a measure is added to an object, the values are aggregated. In this case, total costs are determined for each country. To calculate this value as an aggregated measure, you use the Sum operator with the **Aggregation** parameter set to **ByGroup**. In this case, the group is **Customer Country**.

Replacing **Cost** with the calculated item **Total by Country** in the crosstab produces identical results.

Then calculate the denominator, **Total by Continent**. For this calculation, you need to use the AggregateTable operator because you want to calculate a total for a data crossing that is different from the one used in the crosstab. (See Figure 2.33.)

Figure 2.33: Using the AggregateTable Operator

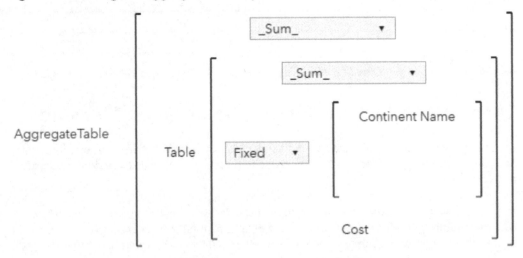

The AggregateTable operator requires five parameters. (See Table 2.6.)

The Table operator creates a table as defined by the **Type of aggregation**, **Categories**, **Measure**, and **Aggregation- Measure** parameters. In this example, because the **Type of aggregation** parameter is **Fixed**, a table of **Continent Name** and the total of **Cost** is created as a result of the Table operator. Basically, the total cost is fixed for **Continent Name**. (See Figure 2.34.)

If **Type of aggregation** was set to **Remove**, a table of **Customer Country** and the total cost is created because **Continent Name** is removed from the groupings (so only **Customer Country** is left).

If **Type of aggregation** was set to **Add**, another data item not used in the crosstab can be specified in the Categories group and a table of **Continent Name**, **Customer Country**, and the additional data item is created.

In this case, the **Aggregation- Aggregated** parameter does not matter because the number of groupings in the crosstab is not less than the number of groupings used in the expression.

Table 2.6: Parameters Required for the AggregateTable Operator

Parameter	Description
Aggregation- Aggregated	The aggregation applied to the aggregated item when it is used in an object that displays fewer group-by crossings than the table in the expression.
Aggregation- Measure	The aggregation applied to the measure in the inner table context.
Type of aggregation	The type of aggregation that is performed. Values are Fixed, Add, or Remove.
Categories	The list of categories used to alter the data crossing for the aggregation.
Measure	The measure that is aggregated. A Table operator can be added as the measure to perform a nested aggregation.

Figure 2.34: Viewing the Table Created from the Table Operator (Total Cost)

Continent Name ▲	Cost
Africa	$87,096.20
Asia	$125,983.80
Europe	$50,600,011.32
North America	$18,518,294.90
Oceania	$4,666,493.04

The totals for each continent are then added to the crosstab for each country, which makes it easy to compare the total country values to the total continent values. (See Figure 2.35.)

Notice how **Total by Continent** was determined from the table created by the Table operator. (See Figure 2.34.)

The last step is to calculate **% of Total by Continent** by dividing **Total by Country** and **Total** by **Continent**.

After adding **% of Total by Continent** to the crosstab, the contribution of each country to the total continent cost is shown. This calculation can also be used in other chart types. (See Figure 2.36.)

Figure 2.35: Comparing Total by Country to Total by Continent

Continent Name ▲	Customer Country ▲	Total by Country	Total by Continent
Africa	Benin	$464.00	$87,096.20
	Ivory Coast	$3,015.00	$87,096.20
	Morocco	$2,351.60	$87,096.20
	Mozambique	$677.80	$87,096.20
	Nigeria	$228.30	$87,096.20
	Senegal	$2,007.90	$87,096.20
	South Africa	$77,055.60	$87,096.20
	Tunisia	$1,296.00	$87,096.20
Subtotal: Africa		**$87,096.20**	**$87,096.20**
	China	$74.80	$125,983.80
	Israel	$6,940.20	$125,983.80

Figure 2.36: Viewing % of Total by Continent

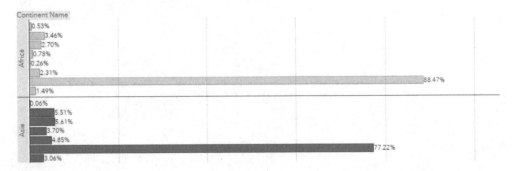

Next, you use a similar calculation to determine the difference between average cost for each country and the continent's average cost, **Difference from Continent Average**.

First, create an aggregated measure that calculates average cost for each country, **Average by Country**, using the Avg operator and specifying **ByGroup** as the aggregation context.

Then, create an aggregated measure that calculates average cost for each continent, **Average by Continent**. (See Figure 2.37.)

In this case, the Table operator produces a table that returns the average cost for each continent because the **Aggregation- Measure** parameter is set to **Avg**. (See Figure 2.38.)

Lastly, create **Difference from Continent Average** by subtracting **Average by Continent** from **Average by Country**.

Figure 2.37: Calculating Average Cost for Each Continent

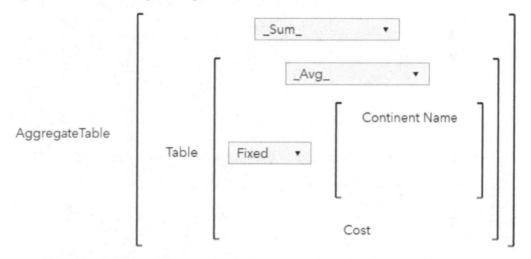

Figure 2.38: Viewing the Table Created from the Table Operator (Average Cost)

Continent Name ▲	Average Cost
Africa	$113.11
Asia	$113.50
Europe	$77.41
North America	$78.56
Oceania	$77.26

In these two examples, the value of the **Aggregation- Aggregated** parameter did not matter. This is because this parameter makes a difference only if the calculated item is used in an object with fewer group-by crossings than specified for the Table operator. To see how this works, create **Minimum by Country**. (See Figure 2.39.)

The Table operator produces a table of **Continent Name**, **Customer Country**, and the total of **Cost** with two crossings or two categories. (See Figure 2.40.)

Figure 2.39: Calculating Minimum by Country

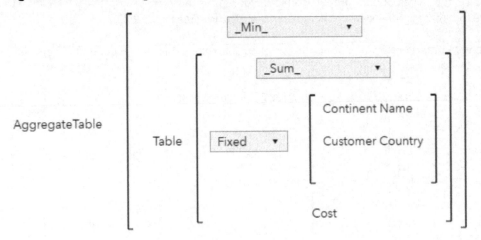

Figure 2.40: Viewing the Table Created from the Table Operator (Average)

Continent Name ▲	Customer Country ▲	Cost
Africa	Benin	$464.00
Africa	Ivory Coast	$3,015.00
Africa	Morocco	$2,351.60
Africa	Mozambique	$677.80
Africa	Nigeria	$228.30
Africa	Senegal	$2,007.90
Africa	South Africa	$77,055.60
Africa	Tunisia	$1,296.00
Asia	China	$74.80
Asia	Israel	$6,940.20
Asia	Russian Federation	$7,064.60
Asia	Saudi Arabia	$4,655.40
Asia	Singapore	$6,116.10

Figure 2.41: Viewing the Table Created from the Table Operator (Minimum)

Continent Name ▲	Minimum by Country
Africa	$228.30
Asia	$74.80
Europe	$617.10
North America	$317,149.10
Oceania	$8,717.10

If **Minimum by Country** is added to a table with fewer crossings (for example, **Continent Name**), the value shows the cost for the country within each continent that has the lowest total cost because the **Aggregation- Aggregated** parameter is set to **Min**. (See Figure 2.41.)

You could change the **Aggregation- Aggregated** parameter to **Max** to see the cost for the country with the highest total cost or to **Avg** to see the average total costs for all countries within each continent.

Chapter 3: Linking to External Websites

Introduction

SAS Visual Analytics is a powerful tool that enables you to quickly and easily create reports to satisfy the needs of your viewers. In some instances, viewers might need to take the insights that they glean from your reports and view more details on a separate web page. To satisfy these requirements, SAS Visual Analytics enables users to create links from an object to an external URL. These links can be static or interactive.

Interactive links change based on user selections. These interactive links use parameters to pass a selected value from the report to the web page.

To create these interactive links, follow four simple steps:

1. Research the structure of the URL.
2. Use a hardcoded value to test the link.
3. Parameterize the link.
4. Test the parameterized value.

Step 1: Research

Before adding interactive links to a report, you first need to understand how the target web page structures the URL. Often, this information can be determined by accessing the target web page and searching for a specific subject. In some cases, you might need to view the Developer Guide for the website to fully understand the structure (see Example: Viewing a Map Location).

Typically, URLs are constructed in one of three ways:

- **Path**: In these URLs, the subject is added at the end of the URL. For example, to view a country page on Wikipedia, you use the following URL: https://en.wikipedia.org/wiki/country, where *country* is the full name of the country of interest (see Example: Creating a Web Link).

- **Query**: In these URLs, the subject is assigned to the value of a URL parameter using a sequence of attribute-value pairs: *?parameter1=value1&parameter2=value2*. Multiple parameters can be assigned by separating the attribute-value pairs with an ampersand (&). For example, to search Etsy for a specific type of item, you use the following URL: https://www.etsy.com/search?q=item, where *item* is the specific search string (see Example: Searching a Web Page).
- **File**: In these URLs, the subject is a part of a file name at the end of the URL. For example, to view country details on www.listofcountriesoftheworld.com, you use the following URL: https://www.listofcountriesoftheworld.com/country-code.html, where *country-code* is the two-letter abbreviation of the country of interest (see Example: Linking to a File).

Step 2: Hardcode

Once you understand the structure of the URL, you can test the link using various hardcoded values. For example, when linking to Wikipedia, you can test the link for different countries: https://en.wikipedia.org/wiki/China to view details about China and https://en.wikipedia.org/wiki/Argentina to view details about Argentina.

Step 3: Parameterize

After you have tested the URL using hardcoded values, you need to replace the hardcoded value with parameters. These are values that will be passed from your report to the external URL to make the links interactive. Depending on the structure of the URL, you can use one of the examples in this chapter to replace the hardcoded value with parameters.

Step 4: Test

After the interactive link has been created, you need to ensure that the link works by testing it in the report.

Example: Creating a Static URL Link

For example, you can create a static link from your report to a web page that discusses data collection techniques or describes the characteristics of the data used in a report.

To create a static link from an image in a report to the SAS Documentation page, do the following:

❶ Add an object to the canvas and specify roles and options for the object. For example, add an **Image** object (from the Content group in the Objects pane) and select an image.
❷ Click **Actions** in the right pane.
❸ Expand **URL Links** and click **New URL Link**. (See Figure 3.1.)

Figure 3.1: Adding a Static URL Link

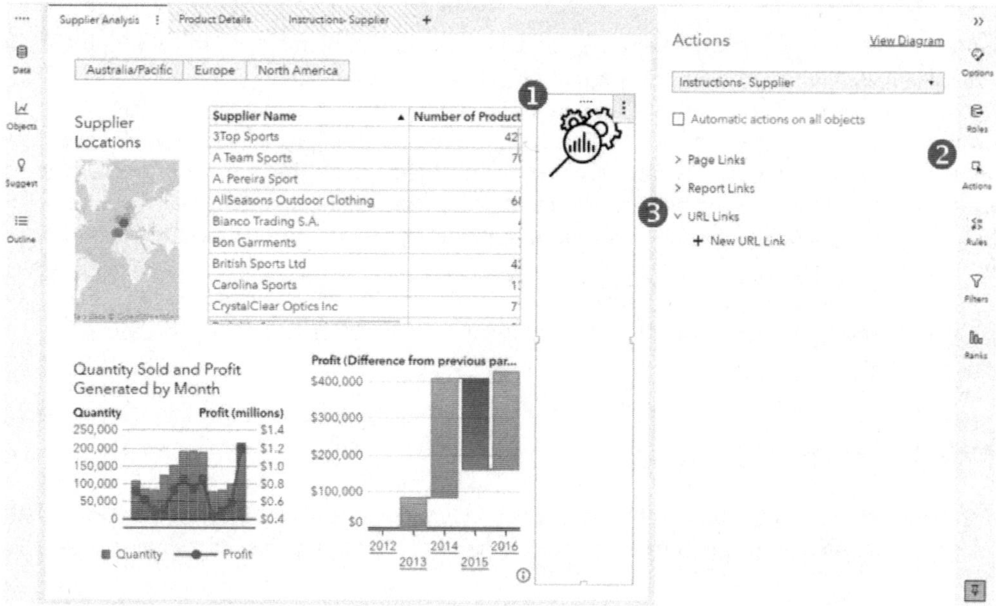

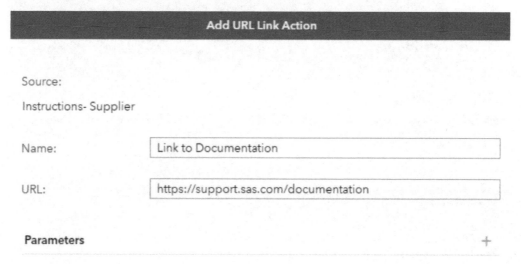

Then specify a descriptive name for the link and the URL as shown in Figure 3.2.

Now when viewers double-click the image in the report, they are taken to the SAS Documentation site.

Figure 3.2: Specifying Properties for Static URL Link

Add URL Link Action

Source:

Instructions- Supplier

Name:

Link to Documentation

URL:

https://support.sas.com/documentation

Parameters

Example: Creating a Web Link

The rest of the examples in this chapter discuss ways to add interactive links to your report. In this example, the report displays information about book ratings from Goodreads (www.goodreads.com). The data source contains a column **book** that includes the 10,000 most popular books (based on the number of ratings) on Goodreads. A page prompt enables the viewer to filter for a range of ratings. Three key value objects show the number of books, the most frequent author, and the highest average rating, respectively. A list table shows details about the book, including the title, the year of publication, the average rating, and the author or authors. (See Figure 3.3.)

You want to add an interactive link to Goodreads from the list table to see details about a selected book.

Step 1: Research

To start, select one of the books in the list, *The Complete Calvin and Hobbes*. Then on Goodreads, enter the name of the book in the search box to see a list of books with similar names. (See Figure 3.4.)

Click on a specific search result to view more details about the book, including a summary, book details, and reviews. (See Figure 3.5.)

Figure 3.3: Creating a Web Link Report

Select a rating range:

4.1 to 4.9

2.4   4.9

Number of Books	Most Frequent Author	Highest Average Rating
3,820	**J.D. Robb** 33	**4.82**

Title	Publication	average_rating	Authors
When We Were Very Young (Winnie-the-Pooh, #3)	1924	4.32	A.A. Milne, Ernest H. Shepard
Now We Are Six (Winnie-the-Pooh, #4)	1927	4.38	A.A. Milne, Ernest H. Shepard
The World of Winnie-the-Pooh (Winnie-the-Pooh, #1-2)	1926	4.43	A.A. Milne, Ernest H. Shepard
The House at Pooh Corner (Winnie-the-Pooh, #2)	1928	4.36	A.A. Milne, Ernest H. Shepard
The Complete Tales and Poems of Winnie-the-Pooh (Winnie-the-Pooh, #1-4)	1961	4.49	A.A. Milne, Ernest H. Shepard
Winnie-the-Pooh (Winnie-the-Pooh, #1)	1926	4.34	A.A. Milne, Ernest H. Shepard
Unhinged (Splintered, #2)	2014	4.25	A.G. Howard
Sleeping Beauty (Disney Princess, 5)	1974	4.32	A.L. Singer, Walt Disney Company
Wings of Fire: An Autobiography	1999	4.19	A.P.J. Abdul Kalam, Arun Tiwari
The Knowledge of the Holy	1961	4.37	A.W. Tozer
The Pursuit of God	1948	4.38	A.W. Tozer

Figure 3.4: Searching for a Book on Goodreads

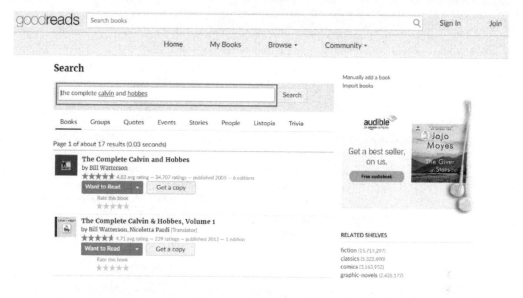

Figure 3.5: Viewing Book Details on Goodreads

In this example, the URL is constructed with the subject as part of the path: https://www.goodreads.com/book/show/book-id.title, where *book-id* is a unique ID used to identify the book and *title* is the title of the book. The data set contains both **book_id** and **Title.**

Step 2: Hardcode

Now that you understand the structure of the URL, you can test it using hardcoded values. (See Table 3.1.)

Table 3.1: Testing the Link for Goodreads

book_id	Title
7667	Airframe
228296	Rosemary's Baby
92147	Map of Bones (Sigma Force, #2)

Remember, you need to use URL encoded values for the title, meaning no spaces and no special characters (like apostrophes, commas, or parentheses). Although it is possible to create a URL encoded value in SAS Visual Analytics, Goodreads needs only the book ID to link to the appropriate page. This means that you can access a book by using the following URL: https://www.goodreads.com/book/show/book-id. Replacing *book-id* in the URL with the values from the table above displays the correct book page.

Step 3: Parameterize

Next, you need to add the link to the list table in the report and replace the hardcoded *book-id* with the **book_id** value for the selected book. Because you are passing **book_id** from the list table to the URL, you need to add the data item to one of the roles for the list table. In this case, you can add **book_id** to the **Hidden** role. (See Figure 3.6.)

Figure 3.6: Adding book_id to the Hidden Role

Data Roles

Book Details ▼

∨ Columns

⊞ Title

⊞ Publication

◈ average_rating

⊞ Authors

+ Add

∨ Hidden

⊞ book_id

+ Add

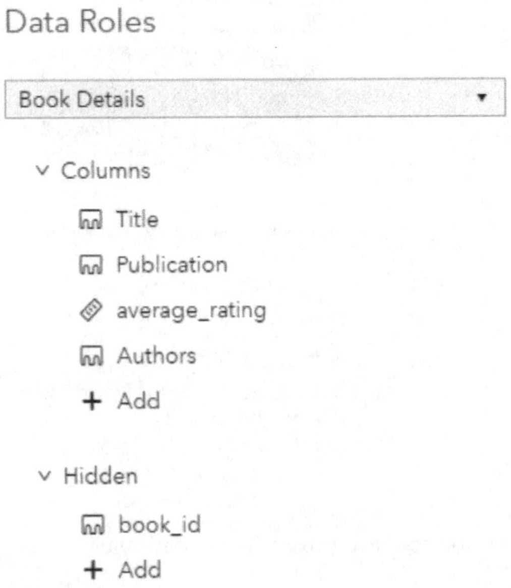

> **Tip**
>
> Data items assigned to the **Hidden** role are available for color-mapped value display rules, external links, and mapping data sources and should be assigned only if doing so does not increase the number of rows in the query. In this example, the list table shows details about books, each with a unique book_id. Adding book_id to the **Hidden** role makes the value available for the external link and does not increase the number of rows in the query.

Then, add the link by selecting the list table on the canvas, clicking **Actions** in the right pane, and expanding **URL Links**. Click **New URL Link**. In the Add URL Link Action window, do the following:

❶ Specify a descriptive name for the link. (See Figure 3.7.)
❷ For the **URL** field, enter the URL up to, but not including, *book-id*. This value will be passed from the selected book in the list table.
❸ Next to **Parameters**, click the **Add** icon.
❹ For the **Source** field, verify that **book_id** is selected, and leave the **Target** field blank. Adding nothing to the **Target** field indicates that the value of **book_id** should be appended to the end of the URL.

When a viewer selects a row in the list table for a specific book, the **book_id** value is appended to the end of the URL and details for that book are displayed.

Step 4: Test

Once the link has been created, test it by double-clicking a book in the list table. For example, double-clicking **Cutting for Stone** opens the book details page for the book by Abraham Verghese.

Figure 3.7: Adding an Interactive Link to Goodreads

Source:

Book Details

❶ Name: Link to Goodreads

❷ URL: https://www.goodreads.com/book/show

Parameters   ❸ +

❹ Source: Target:
☑ Format   📘 book_id   ▾   Optional   🗑

Example: Searching a Web Page

In this example, the report displays information about SAS courses offered in different countries. The data source contains a column **Product Code** that includes the different courses attended by students who took PG1 (SAS Programming 1: Essentials). A required page prompt enables the viewer to filter by country. A treemap displays a tile for each course and is sized by the number of students who attended that course. (See Figure 3.8.)

You want to add an interactive link from the treemap to search the SAS Training Page (https://support.sas.com/edu/) for details about a selected course.

Step 1: Research

To start, select one of the courses in the treemap, **PG1**. Then, on the SAS Training Page, enter **PG1** in the search box to see a list of courses. (See Figure 3.9.)

In this example, the URL is constructed with the course details as part of a query: https://support.sas.com/edu/search.html?searchString=PG1&ctry=us, where *searchString* is the course code and *ctry* is the country code. The data set contains both **Product Code** (course code) and **Student Country**.

Figure 3.8: Searching a Web Page Report

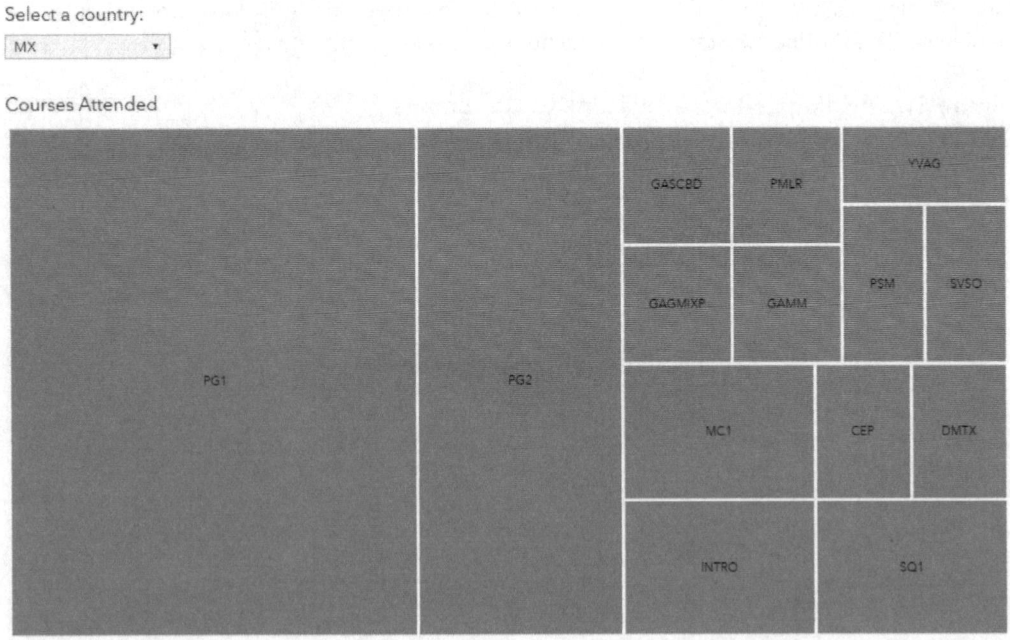

Figure 3.9: Searching for a Course on the SAS Training Page

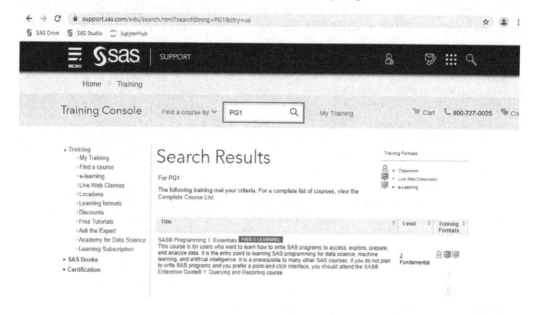

Step 2: Hardcode

Now that you understand the structure of the URL, test it using hardcoded values. In this case, you want to test the URL using hardcoded values for two parameters: *searchString* and *ctry*. (See Table 3.2.)

Note: Because the value of the parameter is used in a query, the casing of the parameter values (for the course and country code) does not matter. The casing of the parameter names, however, does matter.

Step 3: Parameterize

Next, you need to add the link to the treemap in the report and replace the hardcoded *searchString* with the **Product Code** value for the selected course, and the hardcoded *ctry* with

Table 3.2: Testing the Link for the SAS Training Page

searchString	ctry	Course
PG2	GB	SAS Programming 2: Data Manipulation Techniques (Great Britain)
st1	Ca	Statistics 1: Introduction to ANOVA, Regression, and Logistic Regression (Canada)
Mc1	us	SAS Macro Language 1: Essentials (United States)

the selected **Student Country** value. Because both **Product Code** and **Student Country** are being passed from the treemap to the URL, both data items need to be added to one of the roles for the treemap. In this case, **Product Code** is already added to the **Tile** role and **Student Country** can be added to the **Hidden** role. (See Figure 3.10.)

Then, add the link by selecting the treemap on the canvas, clicking **Actions** in the right pane, and expanding **URL Links**. Click **New URL Link**. Then, do the following:

❶ Specify a descriptive name for the link. (See Figure 3.11.)
❷ For the **URL**, enter the URL up to, but not including, the query parameters for *searchString* and *ctry* (https://support.sas.com/edu/search.html). These values will be passed from the selected course in the treemap.
❸ Next to **Parameters**, click the **Add** icon twice, once for each parameter.
❹ For the **Source** field for the first parameter, verify that **Product Code** is selected, and enter **searchString** in the **Target** field.
❺ For the **Source** field for the second parameter, verify that **Student Country** is selected, and enter **ctry** in the **Target** field.

Figure 3.10: Adding Student Country to the Hidden Role

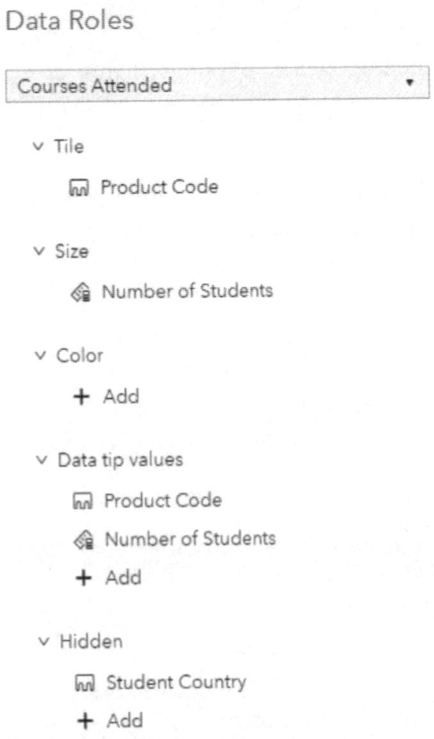

Data Roles

Courses Attended ▾

∨ Tile

    ⊞ Product Code

∨ Size

    ⊞ Number of Students

∨ Color

    + Add

∨ Data tip values

    ⊞ Product Code
    ⊞ Number of Students
    + Add

∨ Hidden

    ⊞ Student Country
    + Add

Figure 3.11: Adding an Interactive Link to the SAS Training Page

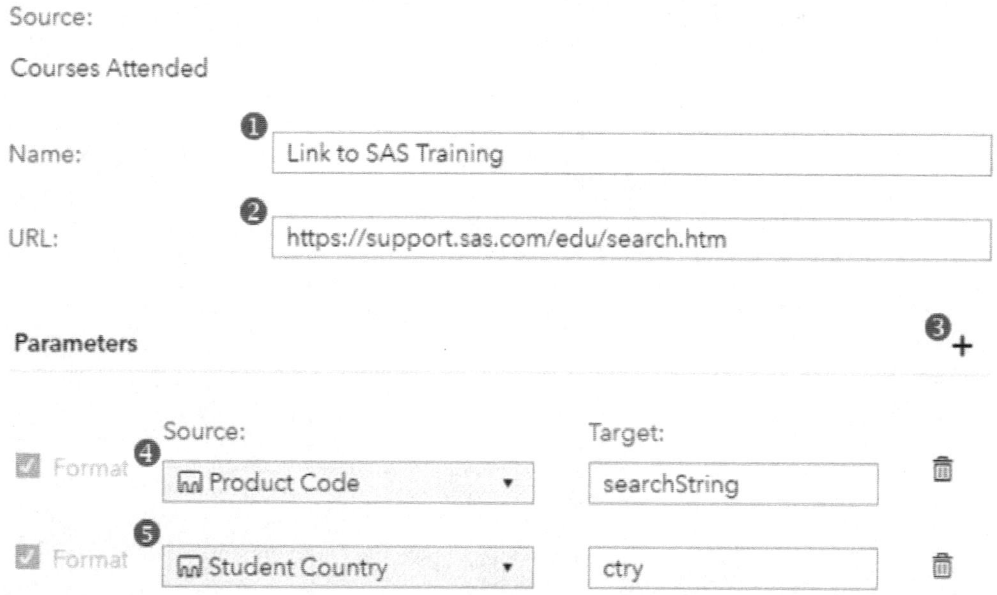

Source:

Courses Attended

Name: ❶ [Link to SAS Training]

URL: ❷ [https://support.sas.com/edu/search.htm]

Parameters ❸ +

	Source:	Target:	
☑ Format ❹	📊 Product Code ▼	searchString	🗑
☑ Format ❺	📊 Student Country ▼	ctry	🗑

When a viewer selects a tile in the treemap for a specific course, a question mark (?) followed by the ampersand-delimited (&) attribute-value pairs are appended to the end of the URL, and the values are populated with the selected **Product Code** and **Student Country** (?searchString=*course*&ctry=*country*).

Step 4: Test

Once the link has been created, test it by selecting a country in the drop-down list and double-clicking a tile in the treemap. For example, selecting **MX** in the drop-down list and double-clicking the tile for **PG2** searches Mexico's SAS Training page for the PG2 course.

Example: Linking to a File

In this example, the report displays customer satisfaction ratings by country. The data source contains a column **Customer Country** that contains the ISO two-letter codes for each country. This column has been created as a geography data item using **Country or Region ISO 2-Letter codes** for the **Geographic name or code lookup** field. A geo coordinate map shows the average customer satisfaction for each country. (See Figure 3.12.)

In addition, a display rule has been added to the geo map to show satisfaction values below 50% (or 0.5) using an orange sad face and satisfaction values above 50% (or 0.5) using a green happy face.

Figure 3.12: Linking to a File Report

Customer Satisfaction by Country

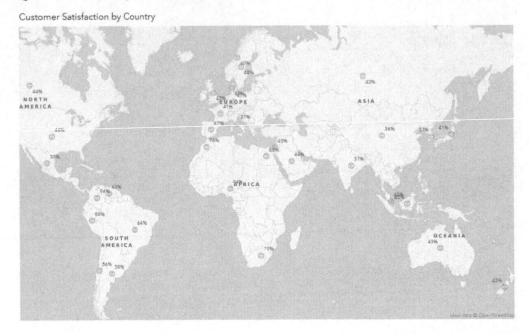

To use display rules to replace markers on a geo map with icons, do the following:

❶ Select the geo map object on the canvas. (See Figure 3.13.)
❷ Click **Rules** in the right pane.
❸ Click **New rule** and select the measure on which the rule is based (in this example, **Customer Satisfaction**).
❹ Specify the condition for the display rule.
❺ Click the **Style** color tile to select the color and icon.

Then, on the Color tab, select a basic color from the palette or select a custom color. On the Icon tab, select an icon. (See Figure 3.14.)

Note: In addition to using the basic icons, you can also use your own custom icons. Replacing markers in a geo map with icons is available only in SAS Visual Analytics 8.2 and later.

You want to add an interactive link to https://www.listofcountriesoftheworld.com from the coordinate geo map to see facts about a selected country.

Step 1: Research

To start, select one of the countries in the data: **AF** (Afghanistan). On the website, select **Afghanistan** in the countries list. (See Figure 3.15.)

Figure 3.13: Creating a Display Rule

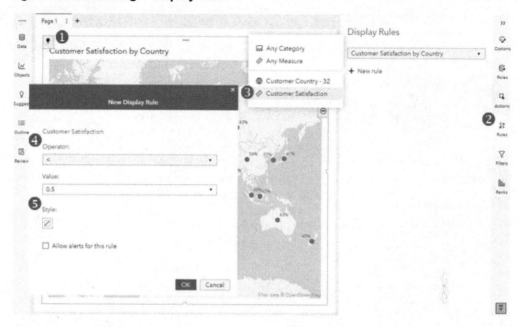

Figure 3.14: Replacing Markers with Icons

Figure 3.15: Viewing Country Details on www.listofcountriesoftheworld.com

Countries of the world in alphabetical order

Search | Google
Custom Search

This page answers the following questions:

- "Which countries are there in the world ?"
- "How many countries are there in the world ?"

View also countries of the world ordered by:

This site has information about all the countries in the world. Did you know there are only 191 countries that are not disputed? The list below has more (partially disputed) countries, a total of 257 countries with links to pages with facts about the country, the flag, maps, population, languages, birth rate, information about the land, size, death rate, animals, coordinates, other facts and additional information. Looking for a specific country? Please look in the list below, it is ordered alphabetically in two columns.

1 **Afghanistan**

2 **Akrotiri**

3 **Albania**

In this example, the URL is constructed with the country as part of a file name at the end of the link: https://www.listofcountriesoftheworld.com/code.html, where *code* is the two-letter abbreviation for the country. The data set contains **Customer Country**, which is the two-letter abbreviation for each country.

Step 2: Hardcode

Now that you understand the structure of the URL, test it using hardcoded values. (See Table 3.3.)

Note: Because the value of the parameter is used as part of the link (the file name), the casing of the country code values matters. The web page expects a lowercase two-letter abbreviation for each country.

Table 3.3: Testing the Link for The World Factbook

code	Country
in	India
nz	New Zealand
co	Colombia

Step 3: Parameterize

Next, you need to add the link to the geo coordinate map in the report and replace the hardcoded *code* with the **Customer Country** value for the selected country. In this case, however, notice that *code* is not the last part of the URL. In the previous examples, the values that were passed to the link appeared at the end of the URL. To ensure that the **.html** portion of the link is also passed to the URL, you need to create a calculated data item that contains the lowercased value of the country code and the extension for the file. (See Figure 3.16.)

Because you want to pass **Link (Character)** from the geo map to the URL, you need to add it to one of the roles for the geo map, the **Hidden** role.

Then, add the link by selecting the geo map, clicking **Actions** in the right pane, and expanding **URL Links**. Click **New URL Link**. Then, do the following:

❶ Specify a descriptive name for the link. (See Figure 3.17.)
❷ For the **URL** field, enter the URL up to but not including *code*.html (https://www.listofcountriesoftheworld.com). This value will be passed from the selected country in the geo map.
❸ Next to **Parameters**, click the **Add** icon.
❹ For the **Source** field, select **Link (Character)**, and leave the **Target** field blank. Adding nothing to the **Target** field indicates that the value of **Link (Character)** should be appended to the end of the URL.

When a viewer selects a country in the geo coordinate map, the value of **Link (Character)**, which contains the country code and the file extension, is appended to the end of the URL and facts for that country are displayed.

Step 4: Test

Once the link has been created, test it by double-clicking a country in the geo map. For example, double-clicking **IT** (for Italy) displays facts about Italy.

Figure 3.16: Creating a Character Data Item: Link (Character)

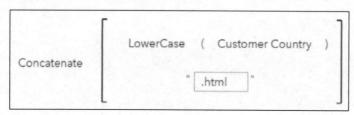

Figure 3.17: Adding an Interactive Link to The World Factbook

Source:

Customer Satisfaction by Country

❶

Name: | Link to www.listofcountriesoftheworld.com |

❷

URL: | https://www.listofcountriesoftheworld.com |

Parameters ❸ +

❹ Source: Target:

☑ Format | 🔗 Link (Character) ▾ | | Optional | 🗑

Example: Viewing a Map Location (Additional)

In this example, the report displays total acreage of each national park within the United States. The data source contains a column **Park Name** with the name of the park and columns that contain the latitude and longitude of the park. **Park Name** has been created as a geography data item using **Latitude and longitude in data**. A geo coordinate map shows the total acreage for each national park. (See Figure 3.18.)

Figure 3.18: Viewing a Map Location Report

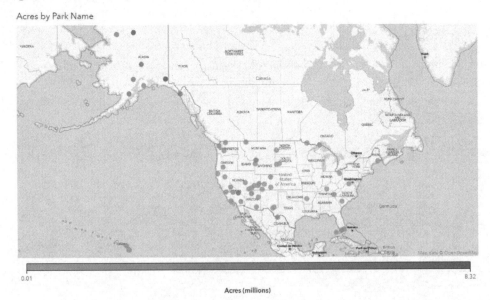

Acres by Park Name

0.01   8.32

Acres (millions)

You want to add an interactive link to Google Maps from the geo map to see a terrain map with an additional layer (bicycling routes) in Google Maps.

Step 1: Research

To start, select one of the national parks (**Glacier National Park**) and obtain the latitude and longitude of that location (**Latitude**=48.8, **Longitude**=-114).

For Google Maps, you want to start by reading the documentation for how map URLs are constructed (see https://developers.google.com/maps/documentation/urls/guide). From this, you can see the required base link (https://www.google.com/maps/@?api=1) and the different attribute-value pairs that can be combined to get the desired map.

- The **map_action=map** parameter returns a map with no markers or directions. Another option is **pano** (to display an interactive panorama image).
- The **basemap=terrain** parameter specifies that a terrain map should be displayed. Other options are **roadmap** (to display the default roadmap view) or **satellite** (to display the satellite view).
- The **zoom=10** parameter sets the initial zoom level of the map. Any whole integer between 0 (the whole world) to 21 (individual buildings) can be specified.
- The **layer=bicycling** parameter displays a bicycling layer on the map. Other options are **none** (to display the default with no extra layers), **transit** (to display a transit layer), or **traffic** (to display a traffic layer).
- The **center=lat,lon** parameter defines the center of the map using latitude and longitude coordinates as comma-separated values.

These attribute-value pairs are separated with an ampersand (&) and appended to the base link, and they can be combined in any order. Because you want the **lat** and **lon** values to be populated by the latitude and longitude for the selected park, you will add this attribute-value pair to the end of the link.

The link to show Glacier National Park should resemble the following: https://www.google.com/maps/@?api=1&map_action=map&basemap=terrain&zoom=10&layer=bicycling&center=48.8,-114. (See Figure 3.19.)

Step 2: Hardcode

Now that you understand the structure of the URL, test it using hardcoded values. (See Table 3.4.)

Step 3: Parameterize

Next, you need to add the link to the geo map in the report and replace the hardcoded **lat** and **lon** values with the latitude and longitude of the selected park. Before you do this,

Figure 3.19: Viewing a National Park on Google Maps

Table 3.4: Testing the Link for Google Maps

lat	lon	Park
44.35	-68.21	Acadia National park
41.24	-81.55	Cuyahoga Valley National Park
19.38	-155.2	Hawaii Volcanoes National Park

notice that the URL contains special characters (@, ?). In SAS Visual Analytics, you cannot include special characters in the **URL** field when creating a link to a website. What you can do instead is create a calculated data item that concatenates the portion of the base link with the special characters (@?api=1), the hardcoded attribute-value pairs (&map_action=map&basemap=terrain&zoom=10&layer=bicycling), the final attribute-value pair (&center=), and the values for **Latitude** and **Longitude** (separated by a comma). (See Figure 3.20.)

Because **Latitude** and **Longitude** are classified as measures, but you are using them to create a character column, you'll use the Format operator to convert the numeric values to character. The RemoveBlanks operator removes all blanks after the conversion.

Figure 3.20: Creating a Character Data Item: Location

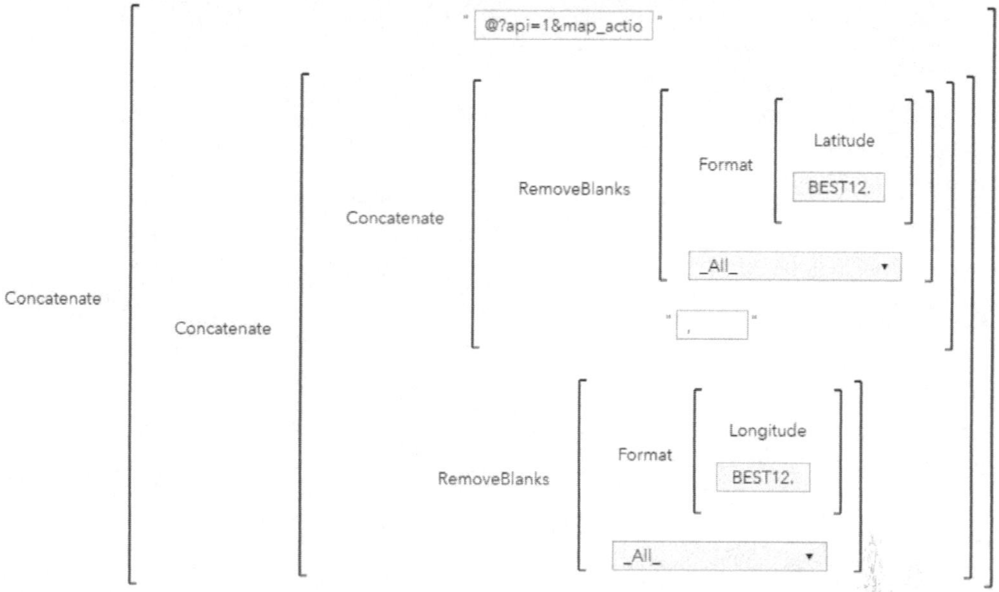

To pass **Location** from the geo map to the URL, it needs to be added to one of the roles for the geo map, the **Hidden** role.

Next, add the link by selecting the geo coordinate map, clicking **Actions** in the right pane, and expanding **URL Links**. Click **New URL Link**.

❶ Specify a descriptive name for the link. (See Figure 3.21.)
❷ For the **URL** field, enter the URL up to, but not including, the special character. The rest of the link is specified in the **Location** data item.
❸ Next to **Parameters**, click the **Add** icon.
❹ For the **Source** field, select **Location**, and leave the **Target** field blank. Adding nothing to the **Target** field indicates that the value of **Location** should be appended to the end of the URL.

When a viewer selects a national park in the geo map, the **Location** value (which includes the latitude and longitude of that park) is appended to the end of the URL and a map of that park is displayed.

Step 4: Test

Once the link has been created, test it by double-clicking a park in the geo map. For example, double-clicking **Grand Teton National Park** in Wyoming displays the terrain map and bicycle trails for the park in Google Maps.

Figure 3.21: Adding an Interactive Link to Google Maps

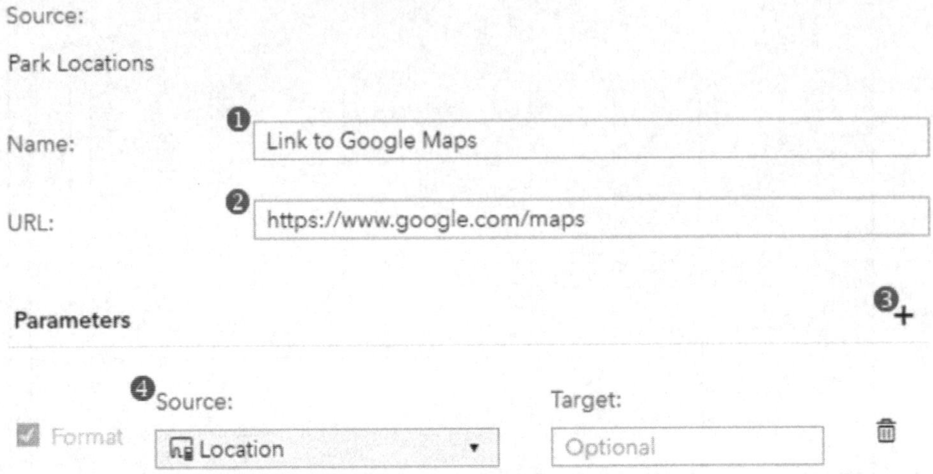

Source:

Park Locations

Name: ❶ | Link to Google Maps |

URL: ❷ | https://www.google.com/maps |

Parameters ❸₊

❹ Source: Target:

☑ Format | 📍 Location ▾ | | Optional | 🗑

Example: Linking to a Parameterized Report (Additional)

In this example, a parameterized report shows the difference in profit from a selected (or benchmark) country. A page prompt enables the viewer to filter for a specific continent, and a drop-down list control enables the viewer to select a benchmark country. A bar chart shows the difference in profit for each country in that continent when compared to the benchmark. The report uses parameters to hold the continent and country values. The parameter for the country value is then used to calculate a calculated item that returns the profit for the benchmark (or selected) country and to calculate an aggregated measure that returns the difference in profit from each country when compared to the benchmark. (See Figure 3.22.) For more information about creating reports that use character parameters, see Chapter 5, "Using Character Parameters."

You would like to create a new link report that shows the number of products by country in a geo region map. The data source contains a column **Country** that contains the full country names. This column has been created as a geography data item using **Country or Region names** for **Geographic name or code lookup**. A geo map shows the average number of products sold in each country. The continent name has been added to the **Data tip values** role, so the continent for each country is displayed. (See Figure 3.23.) This new report contains an interactive link to the parameterized report that specifies the selected country as the benchmark.

Step 1: Research

To start, you need to create the link for the parameterized report. For the parameterized report (Example: Linking to a Parameterized Report- Benchmark Country), click the **Menu** icon and select **Copy Link**. (See Figure 3.24.)

Figure 3.22: Linking to a Parameterized Report – Benchmark Country

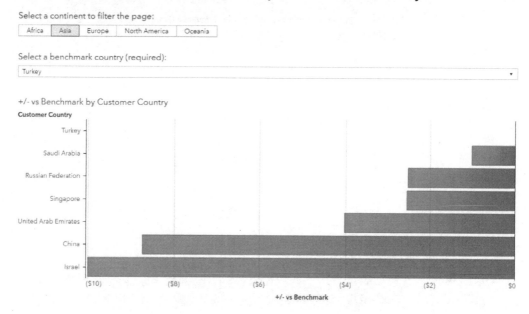

Figure 3.23: Linking to a Parameterized Report – Link

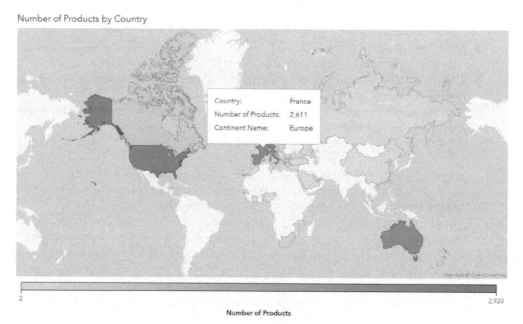

Figure 3.24: Copying the Link for a Report

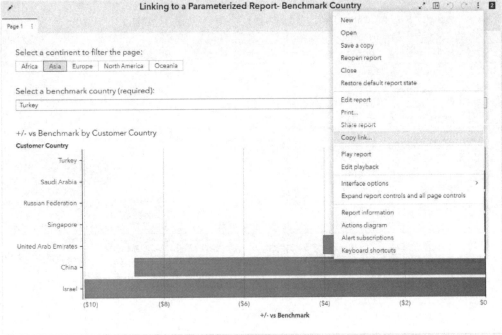

Then, do the following:

- ❶ In the Options group, specify options for the link. Specifically, hide the application bar and the report toolbar, and disable page navigation. (See Figure 3.25.)
- ❷ In the Parameters group, click **Add Parameter** and select **ContinentParameter**. Specify a default value of **Europe**.
- ❸ In the Parameters group, click **Add Parameter** and select **BenchmarkCountryParameter**. Specify a default value of **Andorra**.
- ❹ At the bottom of the window, click **Copy Link**. The link is copied to the clipboard.

In this example, the URL is constructed with the options and parameters as part of a query: http://server/SASVisualAnalytics/?reportUri=%2Freports%2Freports%2F14f9e7af-c459-4f22-b9c8-6587adf947d4&sectionIndex=0&reportViewOnly=true&reportContextBar=false&pageNavigation=false&sas-welcome=false&pr134=Europe&pr106=Andorra. Notice that each parameter is assigned an attribute value by SAS Visual Analytics. (**ContinentParameter** is assigned the attribute value **pr134**, and **BenchmarkCountryParameter** is assigned the attribute value **pr106** in this installation.)

Note: Depending on your installation, the attribute values might use the parameter names directly or they could be assigned a different numeric value after the "pr" prefix.

Figure 3.25: Specifying Options and Parameters for Link

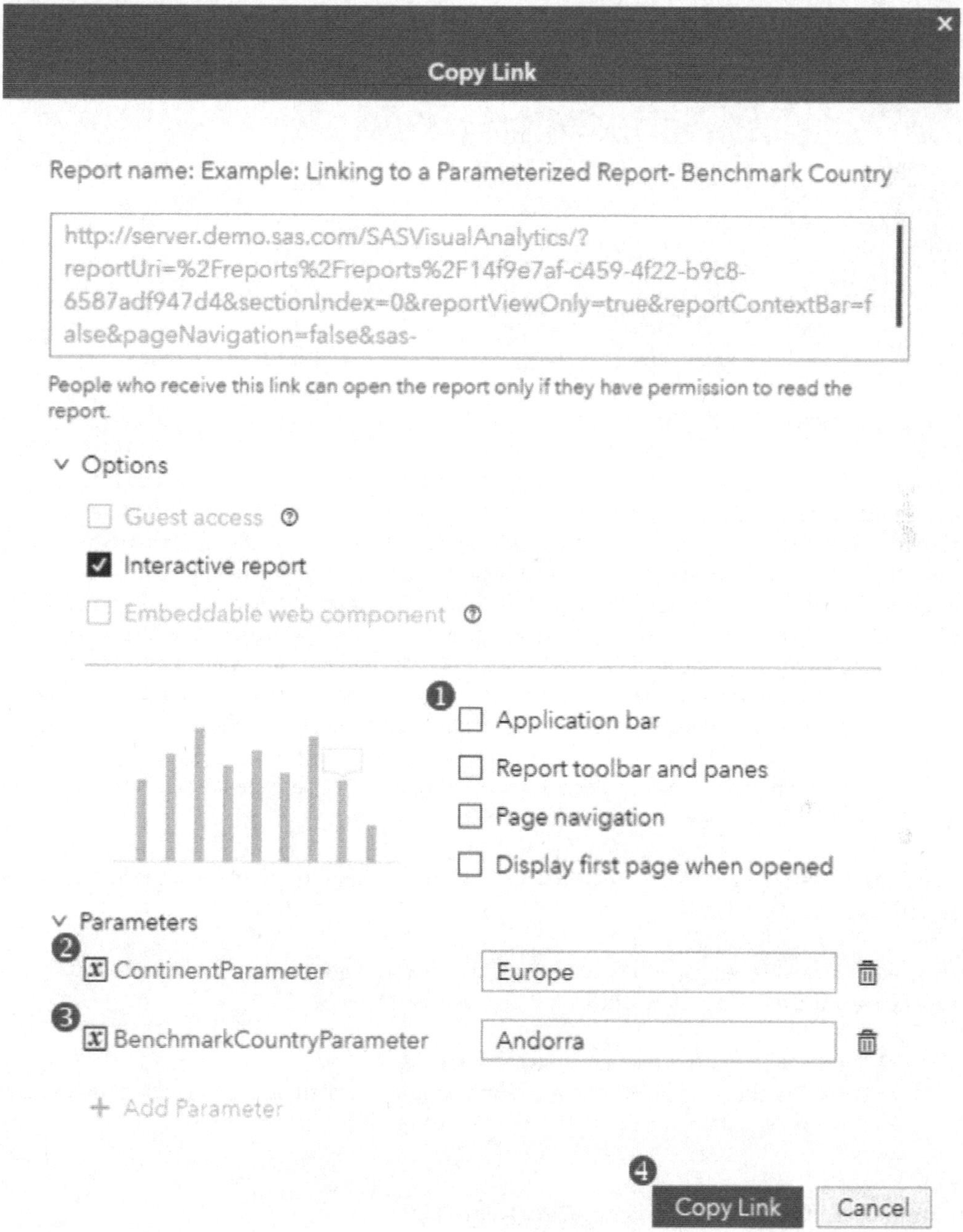

Step 2: Hardcode

Now that you understand the structure of the URL, test it using hardcoded values. (See Table 3.5.)

Table 3.5 Testing the Link for the Parameterized Report

pr134	pr106
Europe	Denmark
Africa	Morocco
Asia	Turkey

Note: In this instance, the capitalization of the parameter names and the parameter values matters.

Step 3: Parameterize

Next, you need to add the link to the geo map in the link report and replace the hardcoded **Continent Name** and **Country** values with the continent and country values for the selected country. Before you do this, notice that the URL contains special characters (?, %). In SAS Visual Analytics, you cannot include special characters in the URL field when creating a link to a website. What you can do instead is create a calculated data item that concatenates the portion of the link with the special characters (http://server/SASVisualAnalytics/?reportUri=%2Freports%2Freports %2F400fdce6-07e2-4de3-bcb4-19cec97d33f3), the hardcoded attribute-value pairs &sectionInde x=0&reportViewOnly=true&reportContextBar=false&pageNavigation=false&sas-welcome=false) and the final ampersand for the next attribute-value pair (&). (See Figure 3.26.)

The URLDecode operator returns a decoded text string using URL escape syntax. In this example, it replaces the %2F values with a forward slash (/).

To pass **Link** from the geo map to the URL, it needs to be added to one of the roles for the geo region map, the **Hidden** role.

Next, add the link by selecting the geo region map, clicking **Actions** in the right pane, and expanding **URL Links**. Click **New URL Link**. Then, do the following:

❶ Specify a descriptive name for the link. (See Figure 3.27.)
❷ Leave the **URL** field blank. The entire link will be specified by concatenating the value for the **Link** data item and the attribute-value pairs for the parameters.

Figure 3.26: Creating a Character Data Item – Link

URLDecode (" http://server/SASVisu ")

Figure 3.27: Adding an Interactive Link to a Parameterized Report

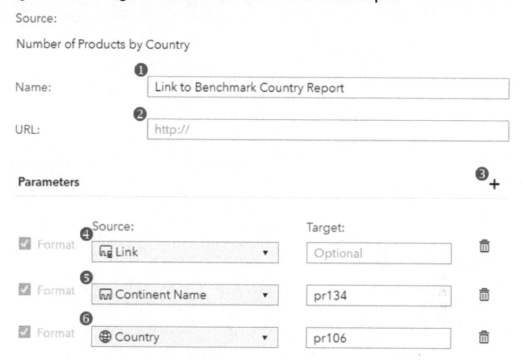

Source:

Number of Products by Country

Name: **❶** Link to Benchmark Country Report

URL: **❷** http://

Parameters   **❸** ﹢

    Source: Target:
☑ Format **❹** 🔗 Link   ▾   Optional   🗑
☑ Format **❺** 🔗 Continent Name   ▾   pr134   🗑
☑ Format **❻** 🌐 Country   ▾   pr106   🗑

❸ Next to **Parameters**, click the **Add** icon three times: once for the **Link** data item and once for each parameter.

❹ For the **Source** field for the first parameter, select **Link**, and leave the **Target** field blank. Adding nothing to the **Target** field indicates that the value of **Link** should be appended to the end of the URL (which is blank).

❺ For the **Source** field for the second parameter, select **Continent Name**, and enter **pr134** in the **Target** field.

❻ For the **Source** field for the third parameter, select **Country**, and enter **pr106** in the **Target** field.

Now when a viewer interacts with the report by selecting a country in the geo region map, the attribute-value pairs for **Continent Name** and **Country** are appended to the end of **Link**, and the report is displayed with the specified continent and country selected.

Step 4: Test

Once the link has been created, test it by double-clicking a country in the geo map. For example, double-clicking **Poland** in Europe opens the parameterized report with **Europe** selected for the page prompt and **Poland** selected as the benchmark country.

Chapter 4: Applying Numeric Parameters

Introduction

In addition to enabling you to create reports quickly and easily, SAS Visual Analytics also provides a great deal of flexibility to the report designer and the report viewer. One example of this flexibility is the ability to create and use parameters. Parameters are a special type of data item that can be created by the designer and modified by the viewer. They are like macro variables in that they are changeable and they are not tied to any specific data set. In fact, the set of acceptable values for the parameter can come from one data set and the selected value can be used in another data set.

Typically, you will add parameters to your report to give your report viewers more control over what they see. For example, you can create parameters that enable the viewer to select a value that updates a chart. This update can be in the form of a display rule that highlights values below the specified value, a filter that displays job descriptions that contain a specified string, or a rank that shows the specified number of top customers. In addition, you can create parameters that enable the viewer to specify how a data item is calculated. This calculation can be a grouping of values based on the value the viewer specifies, a specific region to display in a geo map, or a more complex calculation, like the order of a rank or a month to use for comparing values. In the next three chapters, you learn how to create different types of parameters: numeric, character, and date. You'll notice in each of these examples that parameters are required to give the report viewer more control over the data displayed in the report.

When working with parameters, it's best to build the report using hardcoded values and then modify the report to use parameters. To implement parameters, follow four simple steps:

1. Create the parameter.
2. Add an object so that the viewer can populate (or change the value of) the parameter.
3. Apply the parameter to an object.
4. Test the parameter.

Before you begin these steps, however, you need to know which type of parameter is needed for your scenario: numeric, character, or date. The easiest way to determine which type to create is to think about what report viewers need to enter for the scenario. For example, if you want them to enter a number (for example, to choose the number of years or to view a specific number of top customers), then you need to create a numeric parameter. If you want them to select or enter a value (for example, select a metric or region or enter a string to search a list of qualifications for job openings), then you need to create a character parameter. If you want them to select or enter a date (for example, highlight a selected month or display data within a range of dates), then you need to create a date parameter. The next three chapters discuss creating each type of parameter.

Step 1: Create

When using parameters in a report, the first step is to create the parameter in the Data pane. For numeric parameters, discussed in this chapter, you need to specify a minimum value, a maximum value, a format, and a current value.

Step 2: Populate

Once the parameter has been created, you need to add a control object to the canvas so that the report viewer can modify the value of the parameter. The type of control object that you add depends on your scenario and the type of parameter you created. For numeric parameters, you can add a slider control or a text input control to modify the value of the parameter. A text input control enables the viewer to enter a number directly, but that number could possibly fall outside the acceptable range., A slider control enables the viewer to see the range and select a value within it.

Step 3: Apply

When the viewer modifies the value of the parameter, you want something in the report to change. Parameters can be used in a calculation, a display rule, a filter (like detail filters, aggregated filters, and data source filters), or a rank to modify the report. Parameters can also be used in URLs (see Chapter 3) and in text objects (see Example: Viewing Data for the Next N Years).

Step 4: Test

Once the parameter has been applied, you need to ensure that it works by testing it in the report.

Example: Highlighting Values below a Threshold

In this example, the report displays the average customer satisfaction for each product style. A hierarchy (created from **Product Brand**, **Product Line**, and **Product Make**) has been added to the page prompt area to create cascading prompts, or prompts that filter values in a specific order. In this case, a user can select a product brand from the button bar to filter the list of product lines and product makes available and select a product line from the drop-down list control to filter the list of product makes available. All page prompts filter the bar chart that shows average customer satisfaction by product style.

In the Actions pane, you can view the Actions diagram to see the actions defined between the page prompts. (See Figure 4.1.) These actions were added automatically when a hierarchy was added to the page prompt area.

To start, test the actions by selecting **Novelty** as the product brand, **Gift** as the product line, and **Sweet 16** as the product make. The bar chart includes a display rule that highlights all product styles with a customer satisfaction less than 45% in dark red. (See Figure 4.2.)

Figure 4.1: Viewing Actions between Cascading Prompts

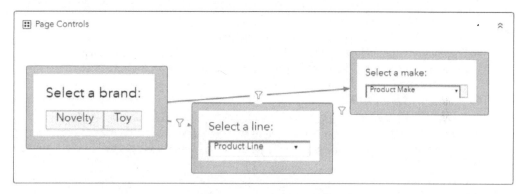

Figure 4.2: Displaying Customer Satisfaction by Product Style

For this scenario, you want to add a parameter so that the viewer can choose the minimum threshold for the display rule (instead of the hardcoded 45%).

Step 1: Create

Because you want the viewer to choose a minimum threshold for customer satisfaction (in percent), you need to create a numeric parameter.

To create the parameter, do the following:

❶ In the Data pane, click **New data item** and select **Parameter**. (See Figure 4.3.)
❷ Specify a name for the parameter. It's a best practice to give parameters a name that indicates how they will be used.
❸ Verify that **Numeric** is specified for the **Type** field.
❹ Enter a minimum value. In this example, customer satisfaction is displayed as a percentage. The acceptable range of percentages is between 0% and 100%. However, values must be entered in their decimal form (between 0 and 1).
❺ Enter a maximum value.
❻ Specify a format that will be used to display the values in the control.
❼ Enter a current value. If you enter a value that is different from the hardcoded value (in this case, 0.45), you can see exactly when the parameter is applied.

Figure 4.3: Creating a Numeric Parameter

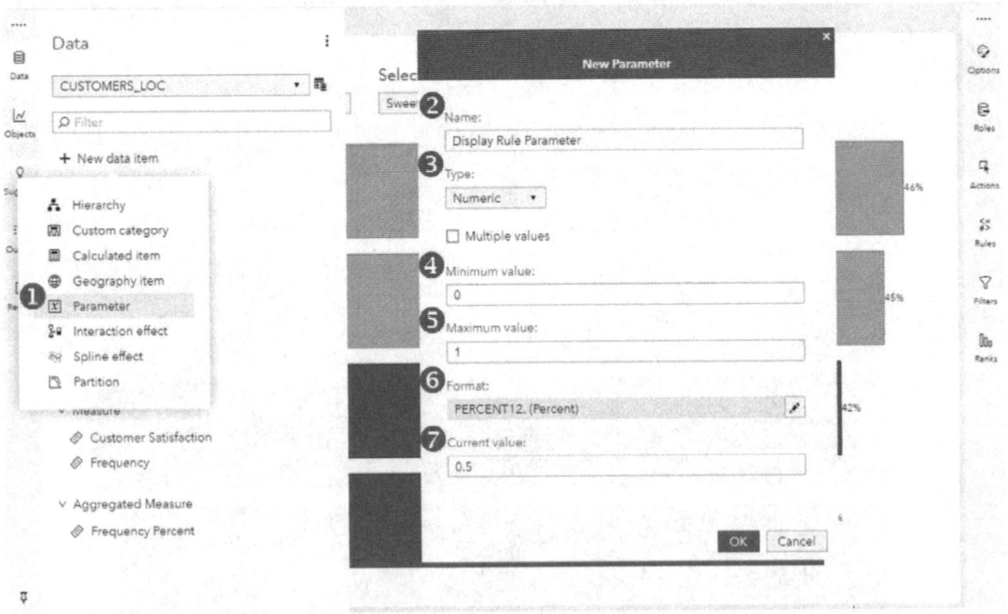

Step 2: Populate

Now that the parameter has been created, you need to add a control object to enable the viewer to populate (or modify the value) of the parameter. Because you want the viewer to see the range of acceptable values and choose an appropriate value in the range, add a slider control to the canvas above the bar chart. In the Roles pane, select **Display Rule Parameter** for the **Parameter** role. In the Options pane, add an appropriate name and title. It's a best practice to add a name that describes how the control will be used (for example, **Display Rule Selector**) and a title that includes instructions for how to use the control (for example, **Specify a value to highlight products below threshold**).

Step 3: Apply

Next, you need to apply the parameter to the report in some way. In this example, we want the display rule applied to the bar chart to update based on the value selected in the slider control.

To modify the display rule:

❶ Select the bar chart on the canvas. (See Figure 4.4.) This is the object on which the display rule is defined.
❷ In the Rules pane, edit the **Customer Satisfaction** display rule.
❸ Select **Display Rule Parameter** for the **Value** field.

Figure 4.4: Modifying the Display Rule

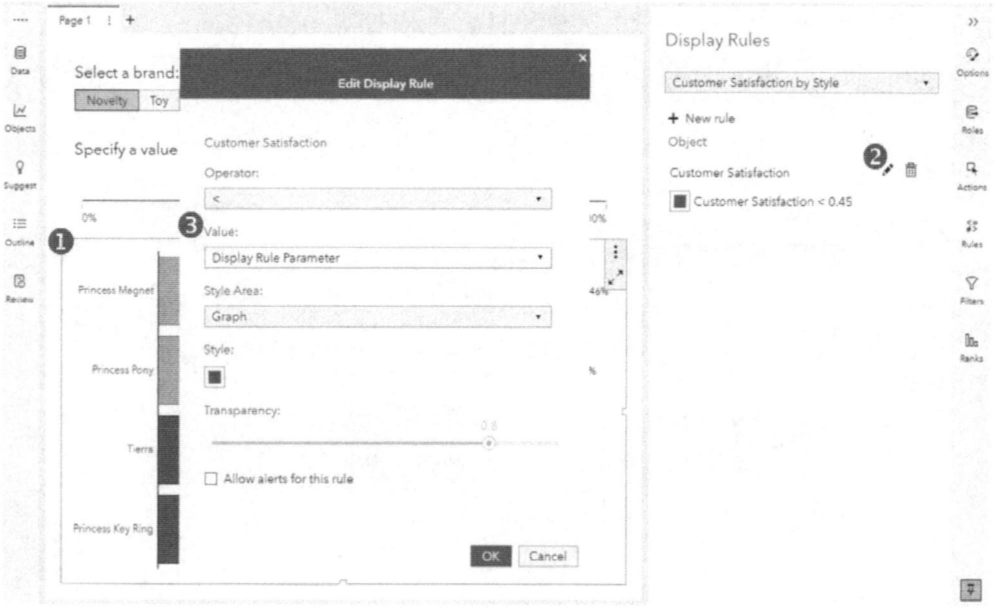

After the parameter has been applied, the Actions diagram shows how the parameter is used in the report. By default, the diagram displays filter actions, linked selection actions, page links (added from the Actions pane), parameters, and indirect filters. Parameters and indirect filters are displayed as a dashed line in the diagram. (See Figure 4.5.)

Step 4: Test

View the report to test the parameter. For example, in the page prompt, select the **Toy** product brand, the **Figurine** product line, and the **Super Hero** product make. Then select **55%** (or **.55**) as the value of the parameter. All super hero products with a customer satisfaction less than 55% are highlighted in red. (See Figure 4.6.)

Example: Displaying Countries with Orders above a Minimum

In this example, the report displays details about the number of orders by country. The list table contains a bar cell visualization to make it easy to visually compare the number of orders between countries. A post-aggregate filter has been added to the list table, but no countries are currently being filtered out. (See Figure 4.7.)

You want to add a parameter so that the viewer can specify a minimum number of orders and see only countries with orders greater than or equal to that value.

Figure 4.5: Viewing Parameter and Indirect Filter Actions

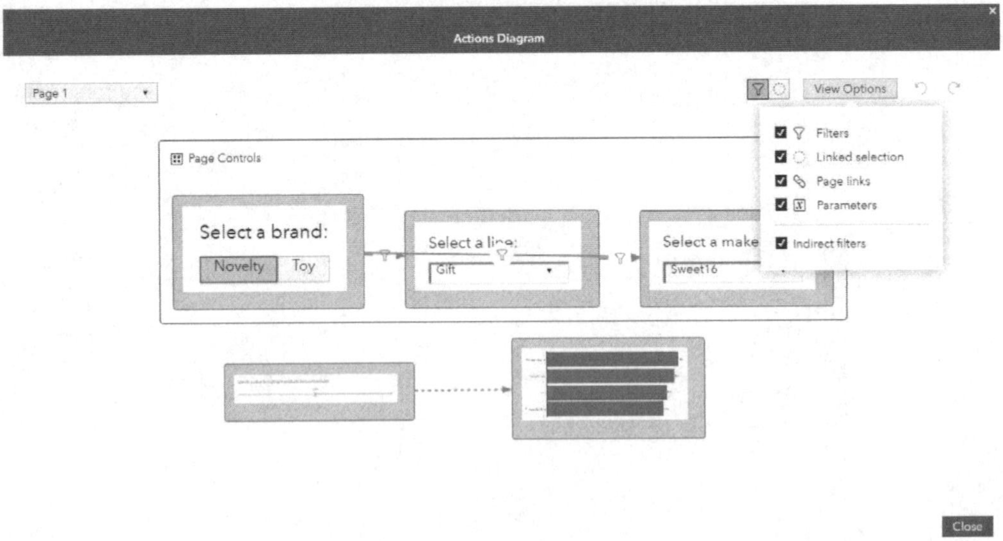

Figure 4.6: Viewing Products with a Customer Satisfaction Less than 55%

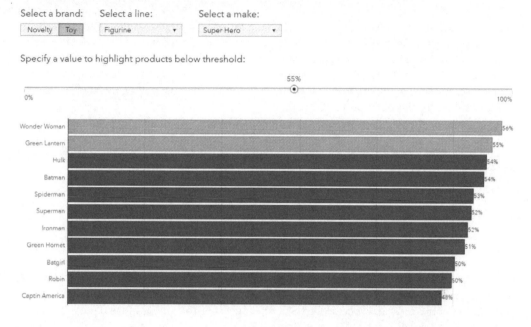

Figure 4.7: Viewing Number of Orders by Country

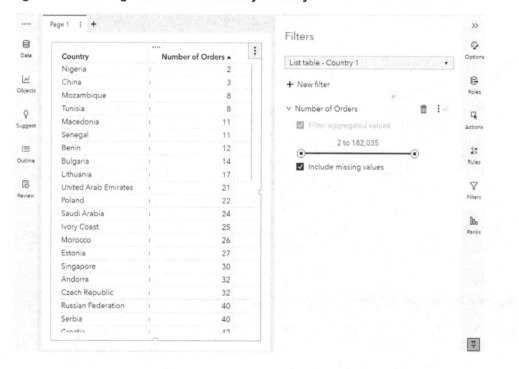

Step 1: Create

Because you want the viewer to specify a minimum number of orders, you need to create a numeric parameter. Before you can do this, you need to know the range of **Number of Orders**, an aggregated measure. Remember, aggregated measures are evaluated after they are paired with other data items (in this case, **Country**). When you filter on an aggregated measure, a post-aggregate filter is automatically created. The slider for the post-aggregate filter displays the range of values for this object: 2 to 182,035.

Now that you know the range, you can create the parameter, **Post-Aggregate Filter Parameter**. The parameter should be a numeric parameter with a minimum value of 0, a maximum value of 182,000, a format of COMMA12., and a current value of 10,000.

Step 2: Populate

Next add a control object to the canvas to populate the parameter. A text input control can be used so that the viewer can directly enter a value. In this case, the viewer can enter any number, even numbers that fall outside the minimum and maximum values specified for the parameter. If the viewer enters a number outside the range, an error is displayed. When you use text input controls to populate numeric parameters, it's a best practice to add the range of possible values, along with instructions, as the title. (See Figure 4.8.)

Step 3: Apply

Then the parameter needs to be applied to the post-aggregate filter. To modify the filter, do the following:

❶ Select the list table on the canvas. (See Figure 4.9.) This is the object that contains the post-aggregate filter.
❷ In the Filters pane, view the options menu next to the filter and select **Advanced edit**.
❸ Modify the expression to use the parameter. (See Figure 4.10.)

Step 4: Test

Finally, view the report and test the parameter with a value of 75,000. The list table displays only countries with more than 75,000 orders. (See Figure 4.11.)

Figure 4.8: Using a Text Input Control to Populate a Numeric Parameter

Enter a minimum number of orders to filter the table below (0 - 182,000):

10,000

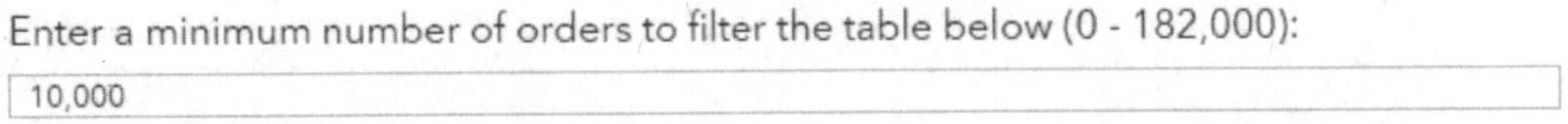

Figure 4.9: Modifying the Post-Aggregate Filter

Figure 4.10: Filtering Using the Value of a Numeric Parameter

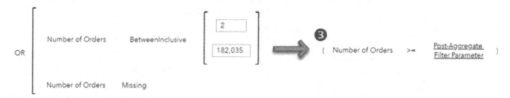

Figure 4.11: Viewing Countries with More than 75,000 Orders

Enter a minimum number of orders to filter the table below (0 - 180,000):

75,000

Country		Number of Orders ▲
Italy	▬	78K
United Kingdom	▬	85K
France	▬	89K
Germany	▬	98K
United States	▬▬▬	182K

Example: Showing Top Customers

For this example, a list table displays details (like **Customer Country** and **Customer Type Name**) for the top three customers by profit. A heat map cell visualization, totals, and a rank have been added to the list table. (See Figure 4.12.)

The rank shows the top three visible categories by profit. This means that it shows the top three values across the intersection of all categories visible in the list table. For example, a list table that shows customer orders by date is likely to have multiple orders per customer. A rank across all visible categories would show three rows, the top three total orders by date (See Figure 4.13.), whereas a rank for the top three customers would show multiple rows, all orders from the top three customers. (See Figure 4.14.)

Figure 4.12: Viewing Top Three Customers by Profit

Customer Name	Customer Country	Customer Type Name ▲	Profit
E.J. Muskens	Netherlands	Orion Club members high activity	$2,630.38
Erik Søby Rasmussen	Denmark	Orion Club Gold members high activity	$2,361.23
P.J. Van Son	Netherlands	Orion Club Gold members medium activity	$2,576.10

Sum: $7,567.71

Figure 4.13: Ranking Across All Visible Categories

Customer Name ▲	Date Order was placed by Customer	Profit
Cwyn Needham	25Dec2012	$2,121.60
E.J. Muskens	29Dec2014	$2,151.20
P.J. Van Son	06Dec2012	$2,161.20

Figure 4.14: Ranking for the Top Three Customers

Customer Name	▲ Date Order was placed by Customer	Profit
E.J. Muskens	04Jun2015	$2.80
E.J. Muskens	29Dec2014	$2,151.20
E.J. Muskens	19Sep2016	$7.40
E.J. Muskens	30Jun2014	$241.00
E.J. Muskens	24Oct2014	($4.70)
E.J. Muskens	25Mar2013	$31.20
E.J. Muskens	05Dec2012	$2.80

Another option, **Detail rank**, is available for objects that show detail data (like list tables, ungrouped bubble plots, and scatter plots). This option displays the top three rows in the entire table when looking at detail data. In this example, two of the top customers (E.J. Muskens and P.J. Van Son) placed multiple orders on the same date. (See Figure 4.15.)

Notice that all orders for E.J. Muskens on 29Dec2014 total $2,151.20 ($14.20 + $7.60 + $2,121.60 + $7.80) and all orders for P.J. Van Son on 06Dec2012 total $2,161.20 ($39.60 + $2,121.60). The **Detail rank** option displays the maximum order placed on each date. (See Figure 4.16.)

Figure 4.15: Viewing Detail Data for Top Customers

Customer Name	▲ Date Order was placed by Customer	Profit
Cwyn Needham	25Dec2012	$2,121.60
E.J. Muskens	29Dec2014	$14.20
E.J. Muskens	29Dec2014	$7.60
E.J. Muskens	29Dec2014	$2,121.60
E.J. Muskens	29Dec2014	$7.80
P.J. Van Son	06Dec2012	$39.60
P.J. Van Son	06Dec2012	$2,121.60

Figure 4.16: Viewing Detail Rank Option

Customer Name	▲ Date Order was placed by Customer	Profit
Cwyn Needham	25Dec2012	$2,121.60
E.J. Muskens	29Dec2014	$2,121.60
P.J. Van Son	06Dec2012	$2,121.60

For the list table, a rank for the top three by profit across all visible categories and a rank for the top three customers by profit are identical.

For the report, you want to use parameters so that the viewer can choose how many top customers to display.

Step 1: Create

Because you want the viewer to choose the number of top customers to display, you need to create a numeric parameter (**Rank Parameter**). For this example, you want the viewer to choose a number somewhere between 1 and 100, and you'll specify a current value of 6 so that you can tell exactly when the parameter is applied.

Step 2: Populate

Next you add a control object so that the viewer can modify the value of the parameter. A slider control enables the viewer to see the range of acceptable values and choose a value within that range.

Step 3: Apply

Then you need to apply the parameter. In this case, the parameter is used in a rank on the list table. To modify the rank, do the following:

❶ Select the list table on the canvas. (See Figure 4.17.) This is the object that contains the rank.
❷ In the Ranks pane, select **Rank Parameter** for the **Count** field.

Step 4: Test

Finally, view the report and test the parameter with a value of **12**. The list table displays only the top 12 customers by profit. (See Figure 4.18.)

Example: Grouping Values Based on a Threshold

In this example, the report displays average honey prices by year for all states within the United States. The data source contains one row for each state and each year, along with a row that represents the average price for the entire US. To plot the state averages on a map by year, a data filter is applied to filter out 'OTHER STATES' and 'US TOTAL'. In addition, the **Location** field has been converted to a geography data item using **US State Names**. The report consists of a geo map showing honey price ranges (using a display rule) animated by year. (See Figure 4.19.)

Figure 4.17: Modifying the Rank

Figure 4.18: Viewing Top 12 Customers by Profit

Specify the number of top customers to display in the table below:

Customer Name	Customer Country	Customer Type Name	Profit
Mathew Khaneka	United Kingdom	Orion Club members high activity	$2,039.90
E.J. Muskens	Netherlands	Orion Club members high activity	$2,630.36
R.M.d. Remijnse	Netherlands	Orion Club members high activity	$1,904.10
Fina Quereda Palleja	Spain	Orion Club members medium activity	$2,047.30
J.C.T. Hellendoorn	Netherlands	Orion Club Gold members high activity	$2,138.40
Jan-Reijer Hendriks	Netherlands	Orion Club Gold members high activity	$1,897.48
Erik Søby Rasmussen	Denmark	Orion Club Gold members high activity	$2,361.23
Alejandra Hierro	Spain	Orion Club Gold members high activity	$1,844.25
Raúl Pérez Laorga	Spain	Orion Club Gold members medium activity	$1,913.87
P.J. Van Son	Netherlands	Orion Club Gold members medium activity	$2,576.10
Michael Müller	Germany	Orion Club Gold members medium activity	$2,104.90
Cwyn Needham	United Kingdom	Orion Club Gold members medium activity	$2,205.30

Sum: $25,663.21

For the display rule, a new character data item (**Honey Price Ranges**) has been created to group average honey prices into *Low* or *High* based on a threshold, currently set to 100 cents/lb. (See Figure 4.20.)

A display rule based on the data item shows low honey price ranges (below the threshold) as a red bee and high honey price ranges (above the threshold) as a green bee. (See Figure 4.21.) These custom icons were uploaded from local images. It is possible to use a custom icon and select a color for the display rule, but the color is not applied to the custom icon. The icons need to be imported with the appropriate colors already applied.

Figure 4.19: Viewing Average Honey Prices by Year

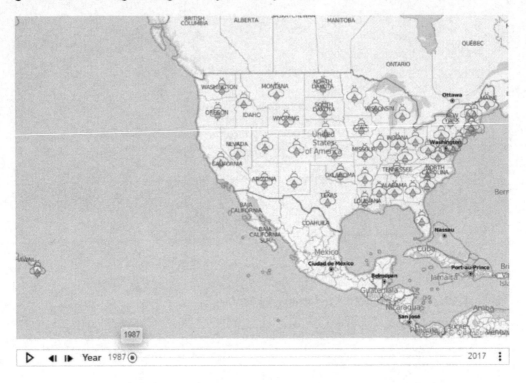

Figure 4.20: Viewing Honey Price Ranges

IF (Price (cents/lb)   <   100   )

RETURN " Low "

ELSE " High "

Figure 4.21: Using Custom Icons for Display Rules

Display Rules

Honey Prices by State   ▼

+ New rule

Object

Any Category

| 📄 | High |
| 📄 | Low |

Note: Replacing markers in a geo map with icons is available only in SAS Visual Analytics 8.2 and later.

For the display rule to work, **Honey Price Ranges** needs to be added to one of the roles for the geo map. Because **Honey Price Ranges** is a character column, it can be added to either the **Data tip values** role, the **Data labels** role, or the **Hidden** role.

For the report, you want the viewer to specify the threshold for **Honey Price Ranges**; you can do this with parameters.

Step 1: Create

Because you want the viewer to set the threshold (in cents/lb), you need to create a numeric parameter. Before you can do this, you need to know the range of honey prices. The data set has a data item that contains this information, **Price (cents/lb)**. You can create a parameter from an existing data item by right-clicking the data item and selecting **New parameter**. The **Type**, **Minimum value**, **Maximum value**, and **Format** fields are auto-populated using information about the data item. You simply need to modify the **Name** field (**Threshold Parameter**) and the **Current value** field (**50**).

Step 2: Populate

To populate the parameter, you can use a text input control. Remember that, for text input controls, it is possible for the viewer to enter a value outside the acceptable range. To prevent this from happening, it's a best practice to add the range, along with instructions, as the title for the object.

Step 3: Apply

Next you apply the parameter to the calculated item, **Honey Price Ranges**. To modify the calculated item, do the following:

❶ In the Data pane, right-click **Honey Price Ranges** and select **Edit**. (See Figure 4.22.)
❷ Modify the expression to use the parameter, **Threshold Parameter**.

Step 4: Test

After the parameter has been applied, view the report and test the parameter with a value of 300. (See Figure 4.23.) As you play the animation, notice that some states drop out in the 1990s when they stopped producing honey and that, starting in the late 2000s, some states exceed the threshold of 300 cents/lb.

Example: Viewing Data for the Next N Years

For this example, the report shows the location and type of eclipses for the next five years. A geography data item has been created for **Catalog Number** (the identification number for each eclipse) using **Latitude** and **Longitude** values. A geo map that uses the geography data item

Figure 4.22: Modifying the Calculated Item

Figure 4.23: Viewing States with Honey Prices over 300 cents/lb in 2005

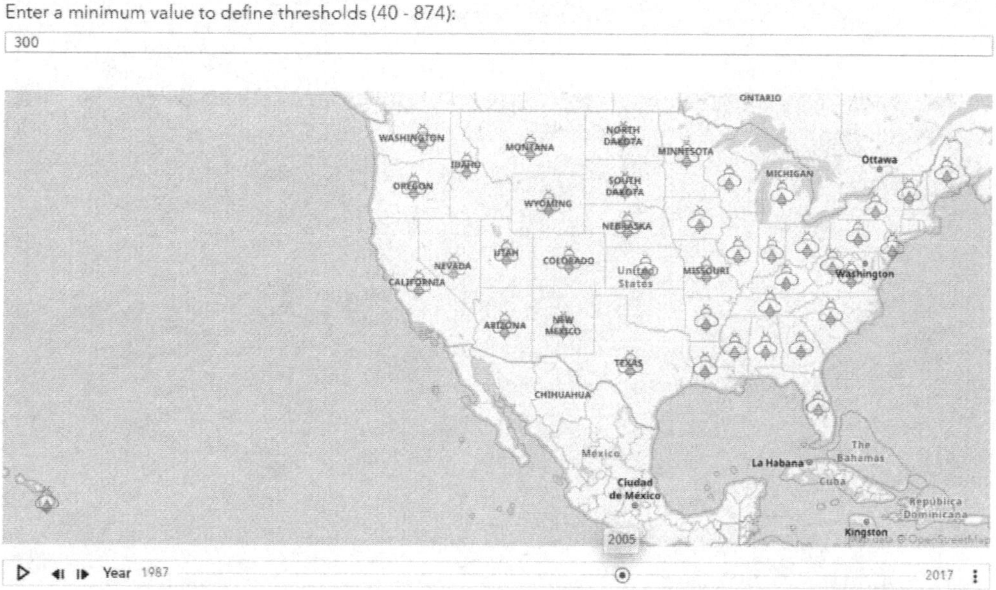

Enter a minimum value to define thresholds (40 - 874):

has been created to show the location of eclipses. In the map, each eclipse is colored by **Type** (*Annular*, *Hybrid*, *Partial*, or *Total*) and data tip values display **Date** and **TD Time** (Terrestrial Dynamical) for each eclipse. A text object has also been added as a title for the geo map. Currently, it's using static text. (See Figure 4.24.)

In addition, a data source filter has been added to show only eclipses occurring in the next five years from today's date, where today is updated each time that the report is viewed. Data source filters restrict data before it is brought into SAS Visual Analytics and the filter is applied to every object that uses the data source. To create a data source filter, do the following:

❶ In the Data pane, view the Data source menu and select **Apply data filter**. (See Figure 4.25.)

❷ Using the Visual view, build the expression using data items and operators. As an alternative, you can use the Text view to enter the expression.

The data source filter uses the Now operator to determine the date and time in which the report is opened (for example, 27Dec2020 1:08 PM). The DatePart operator returns the date portion of that value (for example, 27Dec2020). The Month operator returns the month of the date as a number between 1 and 12, where 1 is January (for example, 12). The DayOfMonth operator returns the day of the month as a number between 1 and 31 (for example, 27). The Year operator returns the year of the date as a four-digit number (for example, 2020). The DateFromMDY operator creates a date value from a month, a day, and a year. For this example, the filter returns only dates that occur between today's date and five years from today's date (for example, between 27Dec2020 and 27Dec2025). (See Figure 4.26.)

Figure 4.24: Viewing Eclipses in the Next Five Years

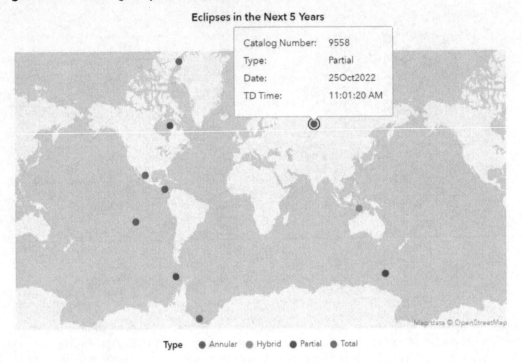

Figure 4.25: Creating a Data Source Filter

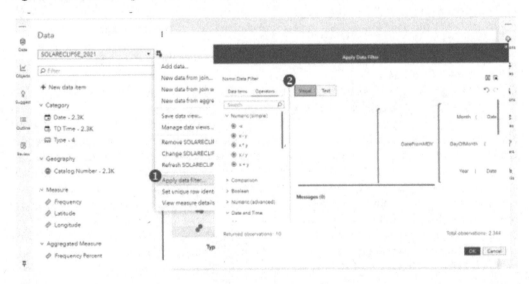

Figure 4.26: Filtering for the Next Five Years

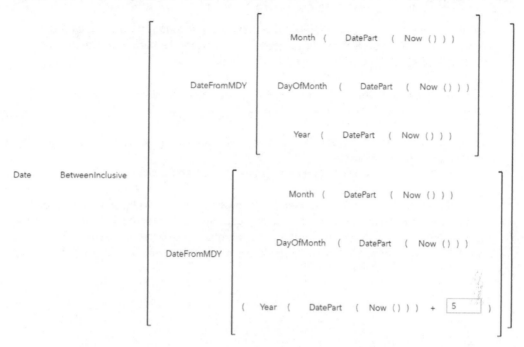

You want to use parameters so that the viewer can choose how many years to display in the geo map.

Note: This example can also be modified to look at data in the past, like orders from the past five years.

Step 1: Create

Because you want the viewer to enter the number of years, you need to create a numeric parameter (**Data Filter Parameter**). This data source contains details about solar eclipses from 2020 to the year 3000, so the range of the parameter can be from 1 to 980. However, it's unlikely that most viewers will want to view more than 100 years into the future, so you can limit the maximum value to 100. To verify the moment when the parameter is applied, enter a current value different from 5 (for example, 50).

Step 2: Populate

For this example, a slider control can be used to display the range of acceptable values and enable the viewer to choose a value within that range.

Step 3: Apply

Next you can modify the data source filter to use the parameter value instead of the hardcoded value. (See Figure 4.27.) Modify the data source filter by viewing the Data source menu and selecting **Edit data filter**.

In addition, you can modify the static text to use the value of the parameter. To display the parameter value in the text object, do the following:

❶ Double-click the text object on the canvas to edit the text. (See Figure 4.28.)
❷ Delete the hardcoded value, 5.
❸ In the Roles pane, add **Data Filter Parameter** to the **Parameters** role.

When the value of the parameter is modified, the text object automatically updates to show the new value. In addition to displaying the value of parameters, the text object can also display the value of a measure, the timestamp of the most recent update to the data source, and a description of current interactive filters. Dynamic text is available in SAS Visual Analytics 7.5 and SAS Visual Analytics 8.2 and later.

Figure 4.27: Using the Parameter in the Data Source Filter

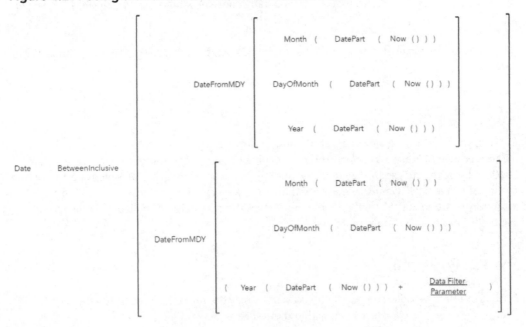

Figure 4.28: Displaying the Parameter Value in the Text Object

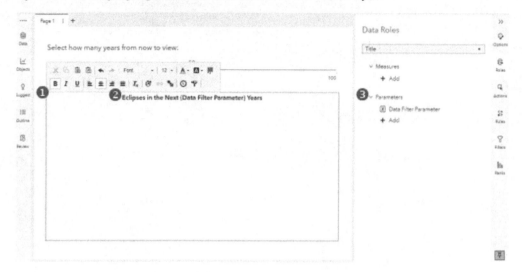

Step 4: Test

Finally, view the report and test the parameter with a value of 10. The data source filter updates to show eclipses that occur in the 10 years after today's date, the geo map is updated to show those eclipses, and the dynamic text object updates to display **10** in the title. (See Figure 4.29.)

Figure 4.29: Viewing Eclipses in the Next 10 Years

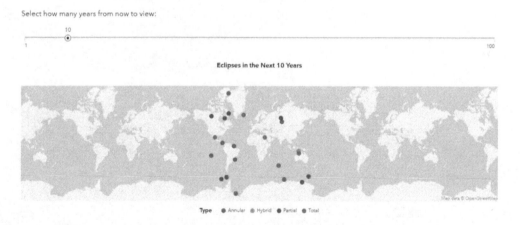

Chapter 5: Using Character Parameters

Introduction

Parameters, a special type of data item that can be created by the designer and modified by the viewer, are an easy way to put control of the report into the hands of the viewer. Parameters enable viewers to change their view of the report depending on their needs. In the previous chapter, you explored the process of creating and applying numeric parameters to make your reports more dynamic. In this chapter, you see how to create, populate, apply, and test character parameters.

Step 1: Create

For character parameters, you need to specify a name and a type, at a minimum. You also have the option of selecting **Multiple values**. A multiple values parameter can be used in conjunction with a list control so that the viewer can select more than one value at a time. This scenario is discussed in more detail in a later example (see Example: Choosing Multiple Measures). Unlike numeric parameters, which have a set range, a current value does not need to be specified when creating a character parameter. Once you populate the parameter and select a value, however, the parameter will hold the selected value.

Step 2: Populate

For character parameters, you can use a button bar, a drop-down list control, a text input control, or a list control. The list control is available for character parameters only if **Allow multiple selections** is *not* selected or if it is used in conjunction with a multiple values parameter. This control object, along with the button bar and the drop-down list control objects, show a list of possible values for the parameter. These controls are often used with a category data item that contains the list of possible values. If the category data item has fewer than 5 distinct values, a button bar is recommended. If the category data item has between 5 and 40 distinct values, a drop-down list control is recommended. If the category data item has more than 40 distinct values, a text input control is recommended.

A text input control can be used with a category data item that contains the list of possible values, or it can be used without a category data item. Using the text input control without a category data item enables users to enter free-form text and is a good choice for searching.

Step 3: Apply

Just like with numeric parameters, character parameters can be applied to a calculation, a display rule, a filter, or a rank to modify the report. They can also be used in URLs (see Chapter 3) and in text objects (see Chapter 4).

Step 4: Test

Character parameters should also be tested to ensure that they work as expected.

Example: Searching for a String

In this example, the report displays a list of jobs available in New York City. A list table contains the ID of the job, the business title, the job description, and a list of qualifications. Two page prompts enable viewers to filter the list of jobs by employment type (full-time, part-time, or unknown) and by career level (Student, Entry-Level, Experienced (non-manager), Manager, Executive, or unknown). A custom sort has been added to **Type** to display the list in a specific order and to **Career Level** to display the list by experience level. (See Figure 5.1.) Selecting a type of employment filters the list of career levels available for that specific type.

For this scenario, you want the viewer to be able to search for specific terms and return all jobs that contain those terms in the list of qualifications. This will help any job searchers identify those jobs in which they meet the requirements.

Figure 5.1: Viewing a List of Job Openings

Choose a type of employment: Choose a career level:

| Full-Time | Part-Time | Unknown | | Career Level ▾ |

ID	▲ Business Title	Job Description	Qualifications
87990	Account Manager	Division of Economic & Financial Opportunity (DEFO) Mayor Michael R. Bloomberg and SBS are committed to encouraging a competitive and diverse New York City business environment by promoting the growth and success of minority and women-owned companies. New York Cityâ™s Minority and Women-owned Business Enterprise (M/WBE) program is designed to help these historically underserved groups become more competitive. JOB DESCRIPTION The Account Manager will provide a range of supportive services to City agency purchasing personnel and private-sector prime contractors to help them comply with M/WBE utilization goals under Local Law 129. The Account Manager will oversee a portfolio of several City agencies and will be responsible for the monitoring and oversight of the strategies which have been broadly laid out for agencies to increase M/WBE utilization. The primary objective for the Account Manager is to help agencies increase the number and dollar value of contracts awarded to M/WBE at various contract levels. Specifically, the Account Manager will seek to bring agencies into compliance with the Citywide utilization goals and other metrics used for measuring agency performance. Each account manager will be responsible for procurements of all sizes and methods for their respective agencies. The Account Manager will report to the Director of Procurement Initiatives. Account Manager Model Each agency has very specific vendor requirements and needs, as well as obstacles to increasing M/WBE Utilization. The account managers will learn what is procured, by what method, how frequently, and how to get more M/WBEs participating in the process. The account manager will leverage their procurement contacts to work directly with program end users to identify needs and obstacles and create appropriate solutions. The Account Managerâ™s responsibilities will include the following: 1. Research agency procurement practices, requirements, in order to connect M/WBE firms with future procurement opportunities 2. Work with the agency senior staff to implement strategies to increase M/WBE participation 3. Introduce new M/WBE firms to agency staff 4. Assist agency staff with tools to improve performance, including monitoring prime contractor performance relating to M/WBE subcontractor utilization goals 5. Inform agency senior staff of their performance against goals on a regular basis 6. Assist	1. A baccalaureate degree from an accredite centered activities in an area related to the c years of experience in community work or c above; or 3. Education and/or experience w least one year of experience as described in and operational skills. Excellent writing and information systems desirable. Foreign lanc

Step 1: Create

Because you want the viewer to enter one (or more) search terms, you need to create a character parameter.

To create the parameter, do the following:

➊ In the Data pane, click **New data item** and select **Parameter**. (See Figure 5.2.)
➋ Specify a name for the parameter. It's a best practice to give parameters a name that indicates how they will be used.
➌ Select **Character** for the **Type** field.
➍ Verify that **Multiple values** is *not* selected. For this example, you do not need to create a multiple values parameter because you want the viewer to enter a list of search terms.
➎ You do not need to enter a current value. This value is populated when the viewer selects a value for the parameter.

Step 2: Populate

Now that the parameter has been created, you need to add a control object to enable the viewer to populate (or modify the value of) the parameter. For this type of character parameter, you can choose between button bar, drop-down list control, or text input. Because you want the viewer to enter free-form text, add a text input control to the canvas above the list table.

Figure 5.2: Creating a Character Parameter

Note: In this case, it is also possible to add the text input control to the page prompt area. The results will be identical.

In the Roles pane, select **Search Parameter** for the **Parameter** role. In the Options pane, add an appropriate name and title. It's a best practice to add a name that describes how the control will be used (for example, **Search String**) and a title that includes instructions for how to use the control (for example, **Enter a string to search qualifications**).

Steps 3 and 4: Apply and Test

Next you need to apply the parameter to the report. When a viewer enters a string, you want the list table to be filtered to show only those jobs that contain that string in the list of qualifications.

To add an advanced filter to the list table:

❶ Select the list table on the canvas. (See Figure 5.3) This is the object that will be filtered when a string is entered in the text input control.
❷ In the Filters pane, click **New filter** and select **Advanced filter**.
❸ Specify a name for the filter.
❹ Using the Visual view, build the expression using data items and operators. As an alternative, you can use the Text view to enter the expression.

Figure 5.3: Creating an Advanced Filter

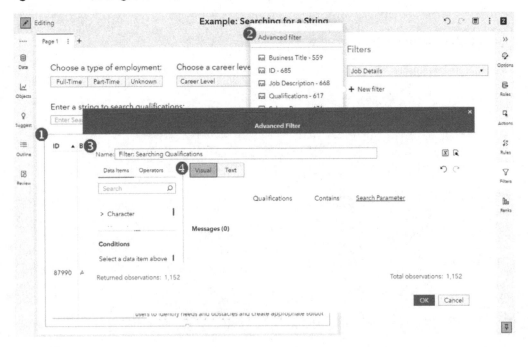

Figure 5.4: Creating a Case Insensitive Search

UpCase (Qualifications) Contains UpCase (Search Parameter)

After the parameter has been applied, enter **bachelor** in the search box to ensure that it works. Twenty-two jobs are returned, those that contain the string *bachelor* in the list of requirements. This search is case-sensitive, meaning that only jobs that contain *bachelor* are returned and any jobs that contain the string *Bachelor*, *BACHELOR*, or any other casing are filtered out. To make this search case insensitive, you can modify the filter to use the UpCase operator. (See Figure 5.4.) This operator returns the uppercase version of the string.

Note: The LowerCase operator can be used instead of the UpCase operator.

In this case, **Qualifications** is converted to uppercase values and the value of **Search Parameter** is converted to uppercase, so the casing of the search term doesn't matter. Modifying the filter to a case-insensitive search returns 69 jobs.

Now suppose that the viewer would like to search for two terms: *bachelor* and *economics*. Entering the string **bachelor;economics** (no spaces) in the search field returns no jobs. This is because the filter is looking for the literal string *bachelor;economics* and no jobs specify this string. To enable the search to use multiple terms, you can modify the filter to search for jobs that contain both terms (*bachelor* and *economics*) if the parameter contains a specific delimiter: in this case, the semicolon. (See Figure 5.5.)

Figure 5.5: Searching for Two Terms – GetWord

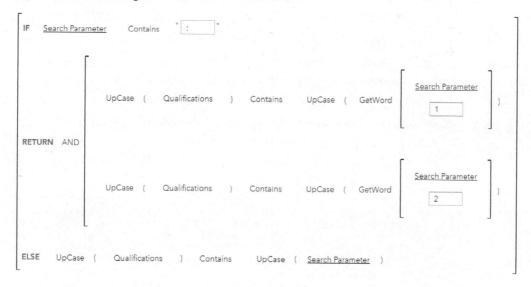

If **Search Parameter** contains a semicolon, it means that the viewer is searching for two terms. In this case, the filter returns any rows that contain both terms (using the AND operator). The GetWord operator returns the nth word based on the list of standard SAS delimiters. In this case, the first AND condition specifies to return the first word (the first search term, *bachelor*), and the second AND condition specifies to return the second word (the second search term, *economics*). If **Search Parameter** does not contain a semicolon, then the viewer is searching for only one term and the filter works as before. To enable viewers to search for more than two terms, you need to modify the expression to count the number of semicolons in **Search Parameter** and use the appropriate number of AND conditions given the number of semicolons. For example, finding two semicolons indicates there are three search terms.

When this filter is applied, two jobs are returned. Both contain the strings *bachelor* and *economics* in the list of qualifications. Because this expression requires the use of a semicolon as a delimiter, it's a good idea to add that information to the title of the text input control.

What if the viewer enters the string **labor market;projects**? The search returns 104 jobs. These are jobs that contain the strings *labor* and *market* in the list of qualifications, which is not the intended results. Remember, the GetWord operator returns words based on the list of standard SAS delimiters; a space is one of the standard delimiters. To enable the search to filter for multiple-word terms (like *labor market*), you can modify the filter to use the Substring operator instead. This operator returns a portion of the text specified by a given starting position and the number of characters to copy.

Figure 5.6 shows the first AND condition, which is modified to use the portion of **Search Parameter** starting at the beginning (position=1). The number of characters to copy is found using the FindChar operator. This operator returns the first position in the string that contains the list of characters specified (in this case, a semicolon). In this example, FindChar would return 13, and the Substring operator would return the string *labor market;*. Because we don't want to search for the semicolon, 1 is subtracted from the value returned from the FindChar operator.

Figure 5.7 shows the second AND condition, which is modified to use the portion of **Search Parameter** starting in the position after the semicolon (position=14). In this case, 1 is added to

Figure 5.6: Searching Using the Substring Operator – First AND Condition

Figure 5.7: Searching Using the Substring Operator – Second AND Condition

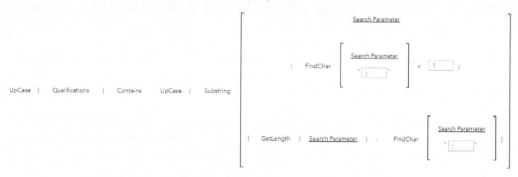

the result from the FindChar operator to find the position after the semicolon. The number of characters to copy is specified as the difference between the number of characters in the string (using the GetLength operator) and the position in which the semicolon was found. In this case, the length is 21 characters, and the semicolon is found in position 13, so this evaluates to 8, and the condition returns the 8 characters starting with the 14th character (the one after the semicolon): *projects*.

To enable viewers to search for more than two terms, the expression would need to be modified to count the number of semicolons (to determine the number of terms) and to extract each term from the list. As you can imagine, this would greatly increase the complexity of the expression.

When this filter is applied, eight jobs are returned: those that contain the strings *labor market* and *projects* in the list of qualifications.

Example: Selecting Characteristics for Indirect Filtering

In this example, the report enables a viewer to select a species and view the characteristics of that species. The unique species ID can be entered into a text input control, and the Selected Species list table is filtered to show characteristics about that species. For example, entering **YELL-1017** displays characteristics about the wolverine found in Yellowstone National Park. (See Figure 5.8.)

Figure 5.8: Viewing Characteristics for a Selected Species

Enter a unique species ID:

YELL-1017

Selected Species

Species ID ▲	Common Names	Park Name	Category	Conservation Status	Abundance	Nativeness	Occurrence	Seasonality
YELL-1017	Wolverine	Yellowstone National Park	Mammal	Not Threatened	Rare	Native	Present	Resident

Note: For this example, the table must contain one row for each **Species ID** value. If your table does not have a column to uniquely identify each row, you can use the Unique identifier transform in SAS Data Studio to create a unique ID.

Note: Because the text input control displays a list of all species, the **Override system data limit** option is set to 120,000 so that all species are displayed and can be selected. Be careful when using this option because it can degrade performance.

You want the viewer to be able to select certain characteristics from the Selected Species list (like category, conservation status, and park name) and see other species that have those same characteristics. You can use character parameters to achieve this goal.

Step 1: Create

Because you want the viewer to select certain characteristics, you need to create a character parameter – one for each characteristic. The data source already contains data items for each of these characteristics: **Category**, **Conservation Status**, and **Park Name**. You can create a parameter from an existing category by right-clicking the data item and selecting **New parameter**. When a parameter is created in this fashion, **Type** is automatically determined based on the type of the data item. For this example, create three parameters – one from each characteristic – and give them appropriate names (like **Category Parameter**, **Conservation Status Parameter**, and **Park Name Parameter**).

Step 2: Populate

Next add a control object to the canvas for each parameter. Remember, when a viewer selects a species, the control should display the specific characteristic of that species. Because only one value will be displayed in each control, a button bar is a good choice for this scenario.

For each button bar, the category data item should be added to the **Category** role, the associated parameter should be added to the **Parameter** role, and an appropriate name should be specified. For example, for the Conservation Status characteristic, **Conservation Status** is added to the **Category** role, **Conservation Status Parameter** is added to the **Parameter** role, and **Conservation Status Display** is entered as the name.

For these button bars to display the characteristics of the selected species (and not the list of characteristics for all species), a filter action needs to be added from the text input control to each button bar. This can be accomplished in the Actions pane. (See Figure 5.9.)

Note: The filter action to the Selected Species Characteristics list table was added when the report was created.

Figure 5.9: Filtering the Controls when a Species Is Selected

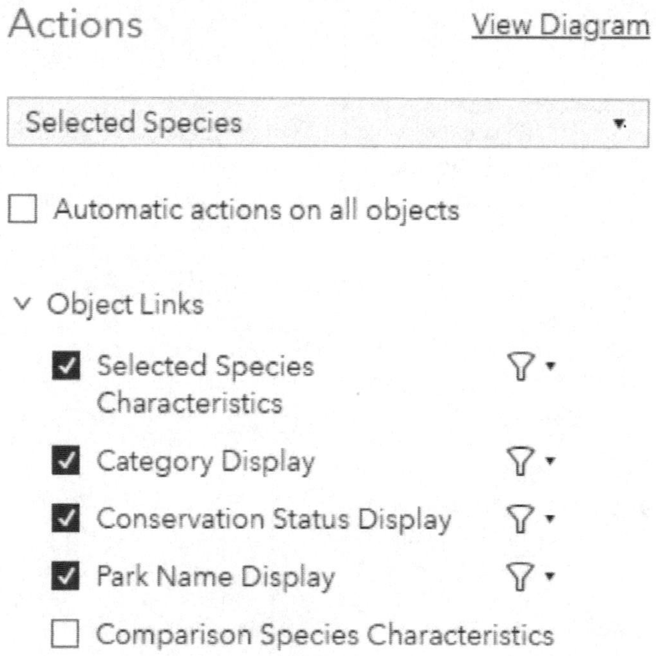

Actions   View Diagram

Selected Species   ▾

☐ Automatic actions on all objects

∨ Object Links

    ☑ Selected Species   ▽ ▾
       Characteristics

    ☑ Category Display   ▽ ▾

    ☑ Conservation Status Display   ▽ ▾

    ☑ Park Name Display   ▽ ▾

    ☐ Comparison Species Characteristics

Note: If a filter action is added to the Comparison Species Characteristics list table, this filters the table to show characteristics of only the selected species, which isn't the intended result. You want the Comparison Species Characteristics list table to be filtered by any characteristics that are selected in the three button bars. This can be accomplished by adding an object filter to the list table. (See step 3.)

Step 3: Apply

When a viewer selects one (or more) of the characteristics in the button bars, the Comparison Species Characteristics list table should be filtered to show only species that have those characteristics. To do this, create an advanced filter on the list table. (See Figure 5.10.)

Because the viewer can select up to three characteristics, the filter must include three conditions. By default, the AND operator allows for only two conditions. You can add more conditions by right-clicking the operator and selecting **Add** and **New Condition**.

Each condition filters based on a specific characteristic. For example, the first condition filters the table if **Category Parameter** is set (that is, the Category button bar is selected). The IsSet operator returns **true** if the parameter has a value and returns **false** if it does not have a value. If **Category Parameter** has a value, then the list table is filtered to show species where **Category** is equal to

Figure 5.10: Filtering for Selected Characteristics

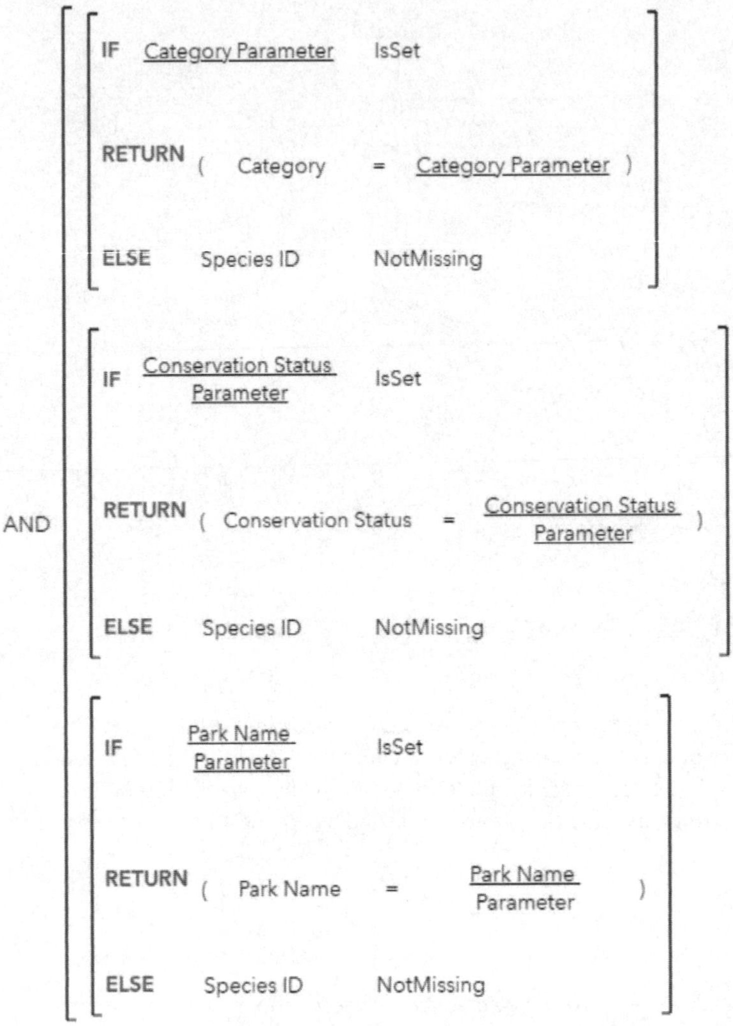

$$
\text{AND}
\begin{bmatrix}
\begin{bmatrix}
\text{IF} \quad \underline{\text{Category Parameter}} \quad \text{IsSet} \\
\\
\text{RETURN} \quad (\quad \text{Category} \quad = \quad \underline{\text{Category Parameter}} \quad) \\
\\
\text{ELSE} \quad \text{Species ID} \quad \text{NotMissing}
\end{bmatrix} \\
\\
\begin{bmatrix}
\text{IF} \quad \underline{\text{Conservation Status Parameter}} \quad \text{IsSet} \\
\\
\text{RETURN} \quad (\quad \text{Conservation Status} \quad = \quad \underline{\text{Conservation Status Parameter}} \quad) \\
\\
\text{ELSE} \quad \text{Species ID} \quad \text{NotMissing}
\end{bmatrix} \\
\\
\begin{bmatrix}
\text{IF} \quad \underline{\text{Park Name Parameter}} \quad \text{IsSet} \\
\\
\text{RETURN} \quad (\quad \text{Park Name} \quad = \quad \underline{\text{Park Name Parameter}} \quad) \\
\\
\text{ELSE} \quad \text{Species ID} \quad \text{NotMissing}
\end{bmatrix}
\end{bmatrix}
$$

the value of **Category Parameter** (which is the category for the selected species). If **Category Parameter** does not have a value (that is, the button bar is not selected), then the list table shows all species where **Species ID** is not missing. (This is all species because every species in the data set has a species ID.) The same logic is applied for the conservation status and the park name.

Viewing the Actions diagram for the report shows that when a species ID is entered, the Selected Species Characteristics list table and the three button bars are directly filtered, as indicated by the solid lines with the filter icon. When a button is selected, the Comparison Species Characteristics list table is indirectly filtered using parameters, as indicated by the dashed lines. (See Figure 5.11.)

Figure 5.11: Viewing Direct and Indirect Filters in the Actions Diagram

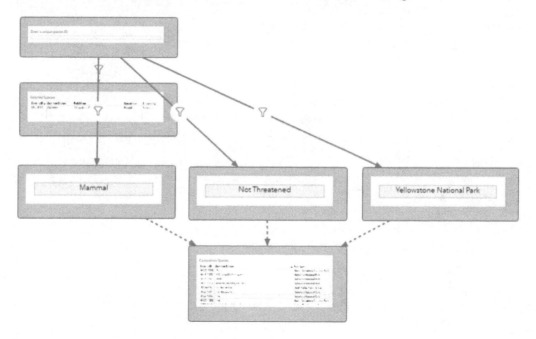

Step 4: Test

Finally, view the report and test the parameter by entering **PEFO-1552**. The selected species is the Navajo Pincushion Cactus, a vascular plant (category) that is endangered (conservation status) and can be found in Petrified Forest National Park (park name). Selecting the buttons for **Endangered** and **Petrified Forest National Park** shows all animals in that park that are considered endangered. (See Figure 5.12.)

Figure 5.12: Viewing Endangered Species in Petrified Forest National Park

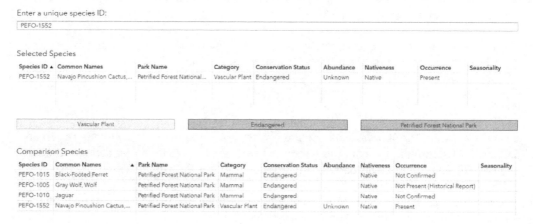

Figure 5.13: Viewing Top 10 Customers by Profit

Customer Name	Customer Country	Customer Type Name ▲	Profit
R.M.d. Remijnse	Netherlands	Orion Club members high activity	$1,904.10
Mathew Khaneka	United Kingdom	Orion Club members high activity	$2,039.90
E.J. Muskens	Netherlands	Orion Club members high activity	$2,630.38
Fina Quereda Palleja	Spain	Orion Club members medium activity	$2,047.30
Erik Søby Rasmussen	Denmark	Orion Club Gold members high activity	$2,361.23
J.C.T. Hellendoorn	Netherlands	Orion Club Gold members high activity	$2,138.40
Michael Müller	Germany	Orion Club Gold members medium activity	$2,104.90
Raúl Pérez Laorga	Spain	Orion Club Gold members medium activity	$1,913.87
P.J. Van Son	Netherlands	Orion Club Gold members medium activity	$2,576.10
Cwyn Needham	United Kingdom	Orion Club Gold members medium activity	$2,205.30
		Sum:	$21,921.48

Example: Ranking Top or Bottom Values

For this example, a list table displays details (like **Customer Country** and **Customer Type Name**) for the top 10 customers by profit. A heat map cell visualization, totals, and a rank have been added to the list table. (See Figure 5.13.)

For the report, you want to use parameters so that the viewer can choose whether to view the top 10 customers by profit or the bottom 10 customers by profit.

Step 1: Create

Because you want the viewer to choose the way to rank (top or bottom), you need to create a character parameter. To create this parameter, you need a data item that contains the two choices: top and bottom. This data set does not contain any data items with those two values.

One way to create this data item is by importing a small table to CAS that contains one column, **Ranking**, and two rows: *Top* and *Bottom*. (See Table 5.1.)

Table 5.1: Importing a Small Table to CAS

Ranking
Top
Bottom

When working with character parameters, however, this is a common scenario. You need to create a category that contains the set values for the parameter (see Example: Choosing Multiple Measures and Example: Selecting a Region (Additional)). If the designer must load a small table to CAS every time that a category data item needs to be created from scratch, the CAS server could become unmanageable. Just think of all the small tables that would need to be verified, updated, and managed!

Another way, as suggested by Stu Sztukowski in his paper *Mastering Parameters in SAS Visual Analytics*, is to create a utility data set (**VA_DUMMY_DATA_BODY**) that consists of a column of dummy data (**dummy_data_body**) with values between 1 and 25. This data set can then be used to construct your list of values and to create your character parameter. Remember, a parameter is not tied to a specific data set. It can be created from the utility data set and applied to your report data set.

To create the custom category with the ranking choices (top and bottom), do the following:

❶ In the Data pane, select the utility data set. (See Figure 5.14.)
❷ Right-click **dummy_data_body** in the Measure group and select **New custom category**.
❸ Specify a name for the custom category.
❹ Create a value group for each choice.
❺ Split the values of **dummy_data_body** between each choice created in step 4.

Then create a parameter (**Ranking Parameter**) from the custom category by right-clicking **Ranking** and selecting **New parameter**. Notice that the parameter appears in the list of data items for the utility data set (**VA_DUMMY_DATA_BODY**) and for the data set used in the report (**CUSTOMERS_CLEAN**). The parameter is independent of the data set and can span across multiple data sets.

Step 2: Populate

Next, add a control object so the viewer can select the direction of ranking. A button bar enables the viewer to see the choices and select one. Remember, the list of choices (**Ranking**) is in the utility data set (**VA_DUMMY_DATA_BODY**). To use this data in the button bar, you need to select the data set in the Data pane before assigning data to the control. Assign **Ranking** to the **Category** role. This displays the two choices (*Top* or *Bottom*). Then assign **Ranking Parameter** to the **Parameter** role. This updates the parameter with the selected value. Specify an appropriate name, add instructions as the title, and make the button bar required. This means the user must choose a direction in which to rank the list table.

Figure 5.14: Creating a Custom Category with Ranking Choices

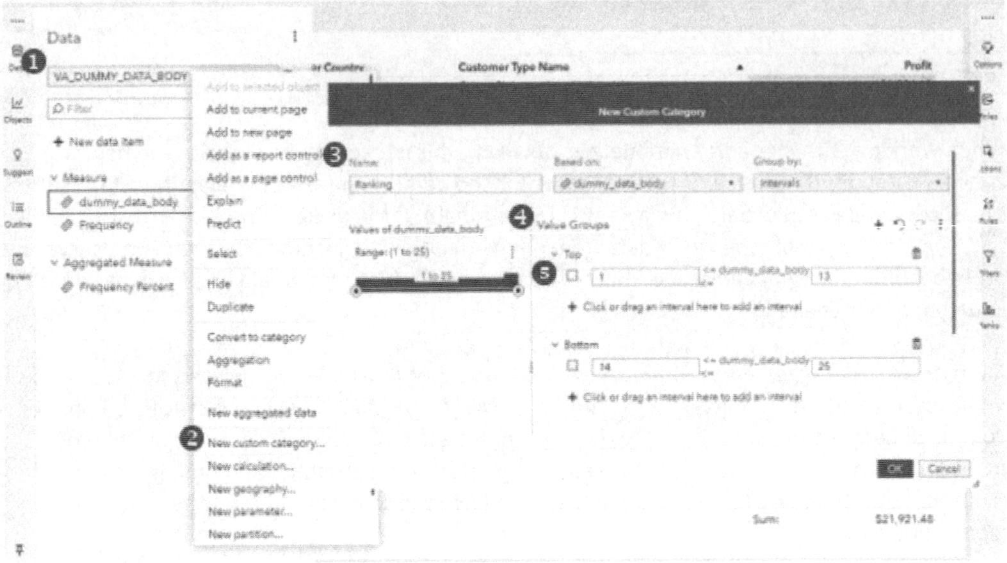

Step 3: Apply

Then you need to apply the parameter. In this case, the direction of ranking is determined by the viewer's selection. Only four types of ranks are available to choose from: Top count, Bottom count, Top percent, and Bottom percent. None of these really work for our scenario. Ideally, we want the value of the parameter to be used as the type of rank.

We can create a calculated item that will do the same thing. Leaving the rank at **Top count**, if the viewer selects **Top**, then the list table will show the top 10 customers by **Profit**. On the other hand, if the viewer selects **Bottom**, then the list table will show the top 10 customers by the negative of **Profit**. (This is equivalent to showing the bottom 10 customers by **Profit**.)

To accomplish this, you can create a calculated item (**Ranking Values**) that uses this logic. (See Figure 5.15.) Remember, **Profit** appears in the report data set (**CUSTOMERS_CLEAN**), so the new data item should be created on that table.

You can test the logic by clicking the **Preview** button in the New Calculated Item window. Because the calculation uses parameters, a Parameter Configuration area appears that enables you to modify the value of the parameter and check the results on the right.

Then modify the rank on the list table to rank by the new calculated item. (See Figure 5.16.)

Figure 5.15: Creating a Calculated Item for Ranking

$$\left[\begin{array}{l} \text{IF} \quad (\quad \underline{\text{Ranking Parameter}} \quad = \quad " \boxed{\text{Top}} " \quad) \\[2em] \text{RETURN} \quad \text{Profit} \\[2em] \text{ELSE} \quad - \quad \text{Profit} \end{array} \right]$$

Step 4: Test

Finally, view the report and test the parameter by selecting **Bottom**. The list table displays the bottom 10 customers by **Profit**. (See Figure 5.17.)

Figure 5.16: Ranking for Top or Bottom

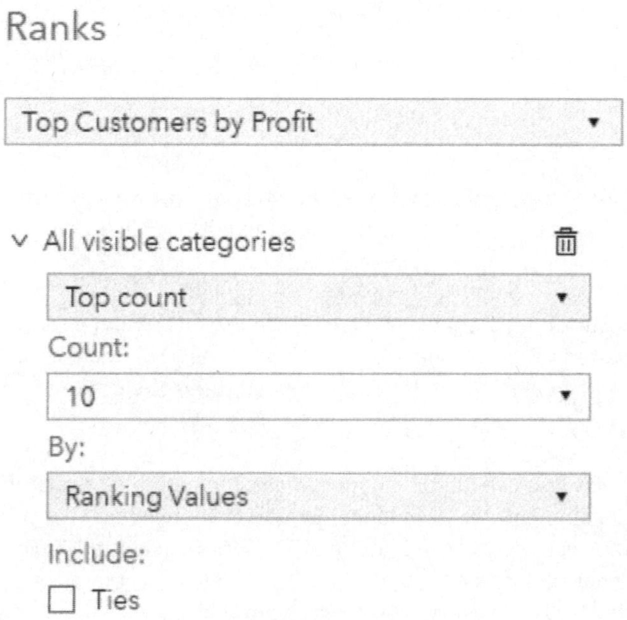

Ranks

| Top Customers by Profit ▾ |

∨ All visible categories 🗑

| Top count ▾ |

Count:

| 10 ▾ |

By:

| Ranking Values ▾ |

Include:

☐ Ties

Figure 5.17: Viewing Bottom 10 Customers by Profit

Select the direction to rank the list table:

Bottom	Top

Customer Name	Customer Country	Customer Type Name ▲	Profit
Andy Butchart	United Kingdom	Orion Club members high activity	($697.94)
J.P. Polderman	Netherlands	Orion Club members high activity	($687.20)
Yi-Lin Rodgers	United States	Orion Club members high activity	($1,152.21)
William Ohiaeri	United States	Orion Club members medium activity	($690.80)
M.M.J. Flipsen	Netherlands	Orion Club Gold members high activity	($796.30)
Zoe Roberts	United Kingdom	Orion Club Gold members low activity	($714.64)
Richard Gobeli	United States	Orion Club Gold members medium activity	($1,153.15)
Katja Lakeit	Germany	Orion Club Gold members medium activity	($705.35)
Mark Sammartino	France	Orion Club Gold members medium activity	($1,092.70)
Pedro Taboas	Spain	Orion Club members low activity	($706.99)

Sum: ($8,397.28)

Alternate Solution

For this example, instead of using parameters, you could use a stacked container with two list tables: one that displays the top 10 customers and one that displays the bottom 10 customers. (See Figure 5.18.)

Choosing **Buttons**, **Links**, or **Tabs** for **Button type** enables the viewer to interact with the report in the same fashion as the report created using parameters. The report using a stacked container, however, is much simpler to design and create. When deciding between these two options, make sure you consider the following:

- *Performance*: Typically, reports that use multiple data sources and multiple calculated items (especially those with complex logic) take longer to load than those that use a single data source and fewer calculated items. Starting in SAS Visual Analytics 2020.1.1, you can use the Report Review pane to see suggestions for improving performance. For earlier versions, you can access performance information from the SAS Visual Analytics Diagnostics window (available by clicking Ctrl+Alt+P). This gives you statistics about the

Figure 5.18: Viewing Top and Bottom Customers Using a Stacked Container

<   Top 10 Customers   Bottom 10 Customers   >

Customer Name	Customer Country	Customer Type Name	▲	Profit
Andy Butchart	United Kingdom	Orion Club members high activity		($697.94)
J.P. Polderman	Netherlands	Orion Club members high activity		($687.20)
Yi-Lin Rodgers	United States	Orion Club members high activity		($1,152.21)
William Ohiaeri	United States	Orion Club members medium activity		($690.80)
M.M.J. Flipsen	Netherlands	Orion Club Gold members high activity		($796.30)
Zoe Roberts	United Kingdom	Orion Club Gold members low activity		($714.64)
Richard Gobeli	United States	Orion Club Gold members medium activity		($1,153.15)
Katja Lakeit	Germany	Orion Club Gold members medium activity		($705.35)
Mark Sammartino	France	Orion Club Gold members medium activity		($1,092.70)
Pedro Taboas	Spain	Orion Club members low activity		($706.99)

Sum: ($8,397.28)

time it takes to load the application, the report, and the data used in the report. You can create two separate reports (one for each method) and use these performance statistics to determine which report renders at a quicker speed.

- *Maintenance*: In this example, the viewer had two choices (*Top* and *Bottom*). The report using a stacked container has only two graphs to maintain. However, consider a scenario where the viewer has 10 choices. This means more graphs to maintain if a change needs to be made. Using parameters in this scenario might simplify your maintenance because you'll need to maintain only one graph.
- *Complexity*: In these examples, the report was very simple. It contained only a few objects with limited interactivity. However, if you have a report that contains actions with other objects or other pages in the report, the stacked container report can become very complex. For example, if a user selects a value from one chart in the stack container and that filters another object, the viewer needs to remember that they made that selection when viewing other charts in the container. This report can easily become a complex puzzle. In this scenario, it might be easier to build a more complex report using parameters to make it easier on the user. For more great tips on designing reports, see *Insightful Data Visualization with SAS Viya* by Schulz and Murphy.

Figure 5.19: Viewing the Animal Intakes at a Shelter

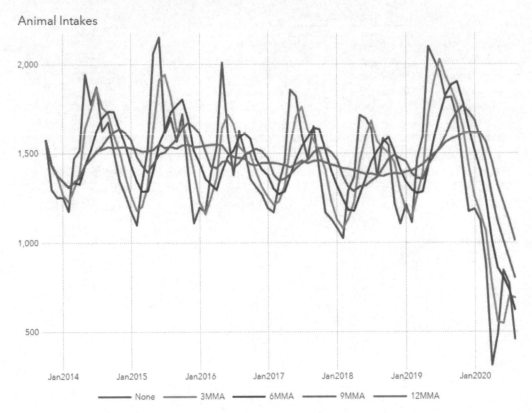

Example: Choosing Multiple Measures

In this example, a report displays the number of animals surrendered to an animal shelter by date in a time series plot. The **3MMA** (three-month moving average), **6MMA**, **9MMA**, and **12MMA** values are also displayed. (See Figure 5.19.)

Note: **None** represents that no transform has been applied to the measure. This line is simply showing the number of animals surrendered at each date.

The moving averages were calculated using the AggregateCells operator. (See Figure 5.20.) For more information about this operator, see Chapter 2.

For the report, you want the viewer to choose which data to display in the time series plot; you can do this with parameters.

Figure 5.20: Calculating Moving Averages

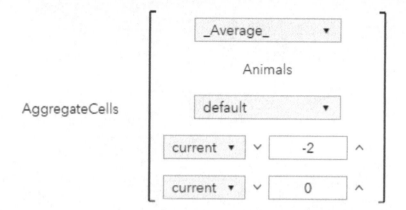

Step 1: Create

Because you want the viewer to choose one (or more) series to display in the time series plot, you need to create a multiple values character parameter. Before you can do this, you need a data item that contains the possible choices: *None* (data that has not been transformed), *3MMA*, *6MMA*, *9MMA*, and *12MMA*.

The data set does not contain any data items that contain these values. You can use a utility data set (as seen in the previous example) to create a custom category (**Moving Averages**) that contains these values. Then you can create a multiple values parameter (**Moving Averages Parameter**) from this custom category. To create a multiple values parameter, select **Multiple values** in the New Parameter window.

Note: A multiple values parameter enables the viewer to select more than one option. This works well for this example because you want the viewer to be able to compare the series as needed.

Step 2: Populate

To populate a multiple values parameter, you need to use a list control. This is the only control object that enables viewers to select multiple values. For the list control, add the **Moving Averages** custom category (from the utility data set) to the **Category** role and **Moving Averages Parameter** to the **Parameter** role. Specify an appropriate name and add instructions for the title as established.

Figure 5.21: Calculating the Data Item None

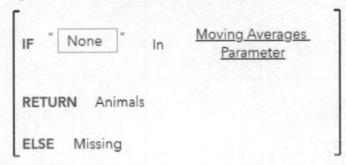

Step 3: Apply

Next modify the calculated items in the report data set (**AUSTIN_INTAKES_BY_TYPE**) to check the value of the parameter: *None, 3MMA, 6MMA, 9MMA,* and *12MMA*. For this scenario, if the name of the data item is in the list of parameter values, then the series is returned. Otherwise, missing values are returned. You want to specify missing values and not zero because if a series is not selected, a line at zero is displayed in the time series plot. Missing values are not shown on the plot. (See Figures 5.21 and 5.22.)

Figure 5.22: Calculating the Data Item 3MMA

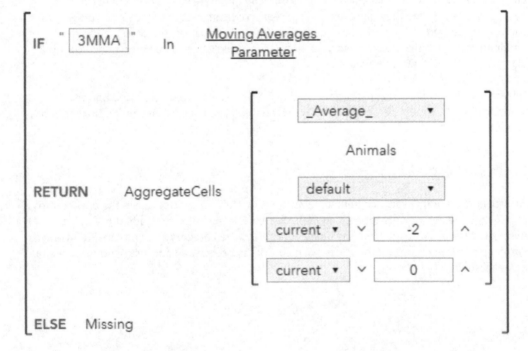

Figure 5.23: Viewing the Animal Intakes for the Selected Series

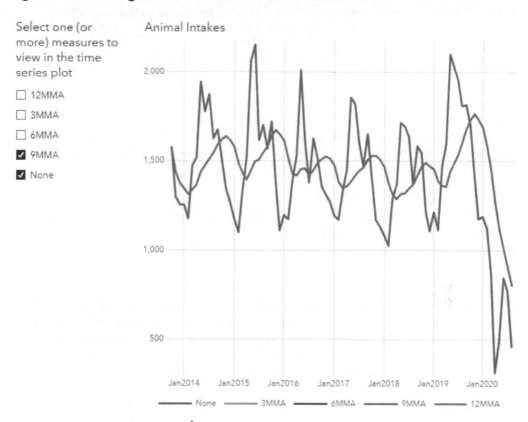

When you use a multiple values parameter in an expression (for either a filter or calculated item), you can use only the In, NotIn, or IsSet operators.

Step 4: Test

After the parameter has been applied, view the report and test the parameter by selecting **None** and **9MMA**. **Moving Averages Parameter** contains *None* and *9MMA*, so those series are displayed in the time series plot. The other series are not listed in the parameter, so missing values are returned for those series. That is, they are not shown in the plot. (See Figure 5.23.)

Example: Selecting a Region (Additional)

For this example, you want to create a report that shows the number of tax returns at different geographical levels: county, state, and US. To display this data as a region map, you need to define a custom polygon provider that references a CAS table that contains polygon information.

In this example, a CAS table (**COUNTIES_STATES_US**) is used to create a geographic data provider (County-State-US). For more details about how to create a geographic data provider, see Appendix A: Loading Geographic Polygon Data to CAS.

You want to use parameters so that the viewer can choose which level to display in the geo map.

Step 1: Create

Because you want the viewer to choose a level (county, state, or US), you need to create a character parameter. Before you can do this, you need a data item that contains the possible choices: *County*, *State*, and *US*.

The data set does not contain any data items with these values, but you can use a utility data set to create a custom category (**Levels**) with these values. Then you can create a parameter (**Levels Parameter**) from this custom category.

Step 2: Populate

Next add a button bar above the geo map so that the viewer can easily see the available levels and select a level to view in the geo map. For the button bar, add the **Levels** custom category (from the utility data set) to the **Category** role and **Levels Parameter** to the **Parameter** role. Specify an appropriate name, add instructions as the title, and make the button bar required. This means that the user must choose a level to display in the geo map.

Step 3: Apply

Next you need to apply the parameter in some way. When a level is selected, a calculated data item returns values for the selected level. (For example, when **State** is selected, the number of tax returns by state is returned).

On the Table page of this report, you can see the state FIPS code, county FIPS code, and county ID (a calculated data item). To identify each level (county, state, and US), use the following conditions:

- *US*: state FIPS code = 0
- *State*: county FIPS code = 0 and state FIPS code not equal to 0
- *County*: county FIPS code not equal to zero

Because you are using data items from the report data set (**TAXES2017**), make sure that the table is selected in the Data pane before creating the new character calculated item (**County-State-US**).

This expression contains the following pieces: (See Figure 5.24.)

Figure 5.24: Creating County-State-US

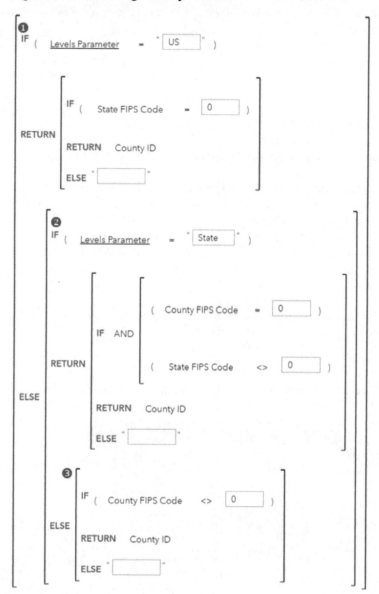

❶ *US*: If **US** is selected in the button bar and the state FIPS code = 0, then this data item equals the county ID for the US. Otherwise, it is a missing value.

❷ *State*: If **State** is selected in the button bar, the county FIPS code= 0, and the state FIPS code is not equal to zero, then this data item equals the county ID for each state. Otherwise, it is a missing value.

❸ *County*: If any other value is selected in the button bar (*County*) and the county FIPS code is not equal to zero, then this data item equals the county ID for each county. Otherwise, it is a missing value.

To create a geo map, this data item needs to be classified as a geographic data item using a geographic data provider. To create a geographic data item using a geographic data provider, do the following:

❶ In the Data pane, view properties for the data item. (See Figure 5.25.)
❷ For the **Classification** field, select **Geography**.
❸ In the Edit Geography Item window, for the **Geography data** field, select **Geographic data provider**.
❹ In the **Geographic data provider** field, select **County-State-US**. For more details about how to define a geographic data provider so that it appears in this list, see the Appendix A: Loading Geographic Polygon Data to CAS.
❺ For the **Region ID** field, select **County ID**. This is a calculated data item in the **TAXES2017** data set that contains the two-digit state FIPS code and the three-digit county FIPS code. This data item contains values that match the ID column in the geographic data provider.

Then add the new geographic data item to the **Geography** role for the geo map and add a filter to the geo map to filter out rows where **County-State-US** is missing. (See Figure 5.26.) Remember, missing values represent values from other geographic levels.

Figure 5.25: Creating a Geographic Data Item Using a Geographic Data Provider

Figure 5.26: Filtering Out Missing Values

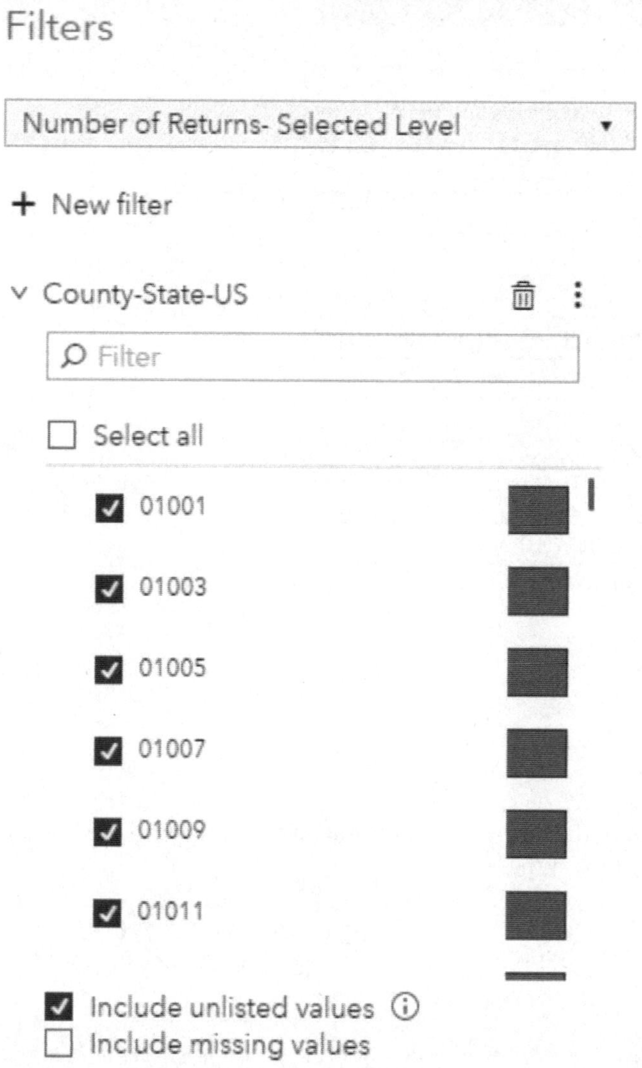

The report also contains a list control that enables the viewer to filter the map by regions. (See Table 5.2 for a list of states within each region.)

The list of choices should change depending on the level selected in the button bar. If **US** is selected in the button bar, the list control should show only the US region. If **State** or **County** is selected in the button bar, the list control should show all regions except the US region.

To accomplish this, you can add an advanced filter to the list control. (See Figure 5.27.)

Table 5.2: States within Each Region

Region	States
Texas/Louisiana	TX, LA
Florida	FL
Southeast	AL, GA, MS
Carolinas	NC, SC
Mid-South	AR, KY, TN
West Virginia	WV
Mid-Atlantic	DE, MD, DC, VA, NJ, PA
Northeast	CT, MA, ME, NH, VT, NY, RI
Northwest	AK, ID, MT, OR, WA
Great Lakes	MI, IN, OH
Upper Midwest	IA, MN, ND, SD, WI
Lower Midwest	KS, IL, MO, NE, OK
Southwest	AZ, CO, NM, UT, WY
West Coast	CA, HI, NV
US	US

Step 4: Test

Finally, view the report and test the parameter.

Start by selecting **US** in the button bar. The Regions list control should show only US, and the map should display the number of tax returns at the US level.

Then select **State** in the button bar. The Regions list control should show all regions (minus) the US. Select **Carolinas**, **Southeast**, and **Texas/Louisiana** in the list control to view the number of tax returns for states in those regions.

Finally, select **County** in the button bar to view the number of tax returns for each county in the selected regions. (See Figure 5.28.)

Figure 5.27: Creating an Advanced Filter

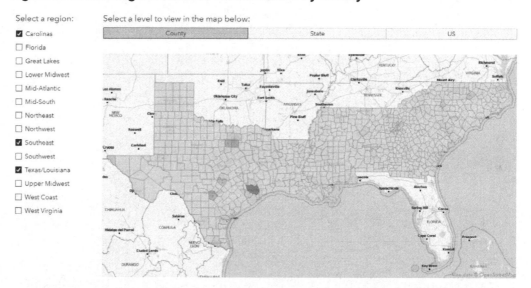

IF (<u>Levels Parameter</u> = " US ")

RETURN (Regions = " US ")

ELSE (Regions <> " US ")

Figure 5.28: Viewing the Number of Tax Returns by County

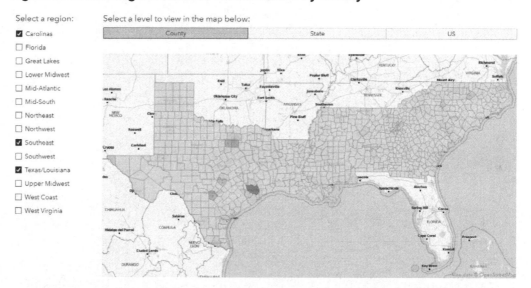

Note: You might get a warning and no data will be displayed in the geo map depending on which regions are selected in the list control for the County level. SAS Visual Analytics can render up to 250,000 points, and the County-level data has more than this number in the polygon data provider. You can either filter the map to show fewer counties (using the list control) or reduce the level of detail in the polygon data provider using the GREDUCE procedure. The **%SHPIMPRT** autocall macro also provides an option to reduce the density of the polygon data, REDUCE=1. For more details about the **%SHPIMPRT** autocall macro, see the Appendix A: Loading Geographic Polygon Data to CAS.

Chapter 6: Working with Date Parameters

Introduction

In the previous two chapters, you've seen how to make your reports more dynamic by using numeric and character parameters. In this chapter, you see how to create, populate, apply, and test date parameters. A fourth type of parameter can also be created, datetime. Datetime parameters are identical to date parameters except that they add a time interval. The steps for creating and using datetime parameters are the same as the steps for creating and using date parameters.

Date parameters, like date data items, take on some of the characteristics of numeric parameters and some of the characteristics of character parameters. Because dates are stored in SAS as numbers, they can function in the same way as numeric data items. However, when dates are used in graphs, they act more like categories because they are used to group and aggregate measures. You'll see that this blending of characteristics makes date parameters unique.

Step 1: Create

For date parameters, like numeric parameters, you need to specify a minimum value, a maximum value, a format, and a current value. In fact, date parameters are created in the same way as numeric parameters.

Step 2: Populate

Because date parameters can function like a numeric parameter and like a character parameter, you can use any control object to populate the parameter: drop-down list, list control (with a multiple values parameter), button bar, text input, or slider control (single-point only). The control you choose depends on whether you want the viewer to see the range of possible dates (slider control), see a list of possible dates (button bar, drop-down list), enter a free-form date (text input), or choose multiple dates (list control).

Step 3: Apply

Date parameters can be applied to a calculation, a display rule, or a filter. They can also be used in URLs (See Chapter 3.) and in text objects. (See Example: Viewing Last Five Years of Available Data.) However, unlike numeric and character parameters, date parameters do not work with well with ranks.

Step 4: Test

Once the parameter has been created, populated, and applied, you need to ensure that it works by testing it in the report.

Example: Highlighting a Selected Month

In this example, the report displays locations (using latitude and longitude) of accidental drug-related deaths in Connecticut. A geo map contains a display rule that shows a red marker for deaths that occurred in January and a gray marker for deaths that occurred in any other month. (See Figure 6.1.) For the display rule to work properly, **Date** needs to be added to one of the roles for the geo map. In this case, it's been added to the **Hidden** role. Therefore, it's not displayed in the map, but it is included in the query results for the graph so that the values can be used for the display rule.

This geo map uses an Esri map background (Canvas Base) that uses a neutral palette with minimal colors, labels, and features. This map background is used so that the markers stand out and are the focus of the graph. To use background maps from Esri ArcGIS Online Services, you need to read and accept the terms and conditions.

In addition to using background maps, you can also enable additional geographic mapping features, like using travel-distance and travel-time geographic selections in geo maps and importing Esri data for geoenrichment and geocoding. This option is available only if your organization has an ArcGIS Online account and if you are a member of the Esri Users group in SAS Viya. To access this functionality, you need to enable Esri Premium Services and enter your ArcGIS credentials.

If your organization provides map services on an Esri server, you can access additional background maps or custom polygons from that server by specifying your Esri Custom Services credentials.

For this scenario, you want the viewer to be able to choose a month and see all deaths that occurred in that month highlighted in the geo map.

Figure 6.1: Viewing Accidental Drug-Related Deaths in Connecticut

Step 1: Create

Because you want the viewer to select a month, you need to create a date parameter. The table contains a data item, **Date**, that has a list of all months.

To create a parameter from this data item, do the following:

❶ In the Data pane, right-click **Date** and select **New parameter**. (See Figure 6.2.)

❷ Specify a name for the parameter. It's a best practice to give parameters a name that indicates how they will be used.

❸ Verify that **Date** is specified for the **Type** field.

❹ Select a minimum value. This value is automatically populated using the minimum value of the **Date** data item.

❺ Enter a maximum value. This value is automatically populated using the maximum value of the **Date** data item.

❻ Specify a format that will be used to display the values in the control.

Figure 6.2: Creating a Date Parameter

❼ Enter a current value. If you enter a value that is different from the hardcoded value (in this case, *January*), you will be able to see exactly when the parameter is applied. Because the **Date** data item used to create this parameter shows only monthly values, when you select a current value, the year selection does not matter.

Step 2: Populate

Now that the parameter has been created, you need to add a control object to enable the viewer to select a month and modify the value of the parameter. For this type of date parameter, you can choose between button bar, drop-down list control, or text input. The list control could be chosen if the **Allow multiple selections** option is cleared, but the slider control is not available because the date values show only months and not daily or yearly data. Because you want the viewer to select a month from a list of months (and there are 12 months in a year), add a drop-down list control to the canvas above the geo map.

In the Roles pane, select **Date** for the **Category** role and **Display Rule Parameter** for the **Parameter** role. In the Options pane, add an appropriate name and title. Remember, it's a best practice to add a name that describes how the control will be used (for example, **Month Selector**) and a title that includes instructions for how to use the control (for example, **Select a month to highlight locations in the map below**). Because you want the viewer to always select a month, you want to make the control required; this means that the viewer can't clear the value.

Figure 6.3: Updating the Display Rule to Use the Parameter

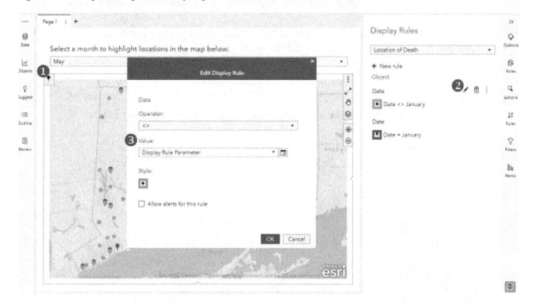

Note: In this case, you want to ensure that the control is added to the canvas and not the page prompt area or report prompt area. When a control is added to the page or report prompt areas, an automatic filter is applied. Because the control uses **Date** (a data item in the table), selecting a month would filter the data in the geo map to show deaths only from that month. For this scenario, we want to see all deaths and have those that occurred in the selected month highlighted.

Step 3: Apply

Next you need to apply the parameter to the report. When a viewer selects a month, we want the display rules on the map to update to show all deaths that occurred in the selected month in red and those that occurred in other months in gray.

To update the display rules:

    ❶ Select the geo map on the canvas. (See Figure 6.3.) This is the object with the display rules defined.
    ❷ In the Rules pane, click **Edit** next to each rule.
    ❸ For the **Value** field, select the parameter. Be sure to modify both display rules.

Step 4: Test

After the parameter has been applied, select **September** in the drop-down list control. All accidental drug-related deaths that occurred in September are highlighted in red.

Example: Choosing a Month to Compare Values

In this example, the report contains a targeted bar chart that compares the number of animals of each type surrendered at an animal shelter in February (selected month) to the number surrendered in January (prior month). This helps the shelter compare the number of animals surrendered for any two consecutive months. (See Figure 6.4.)

Figure 6.4: Comparing the Number of Animals in February and January

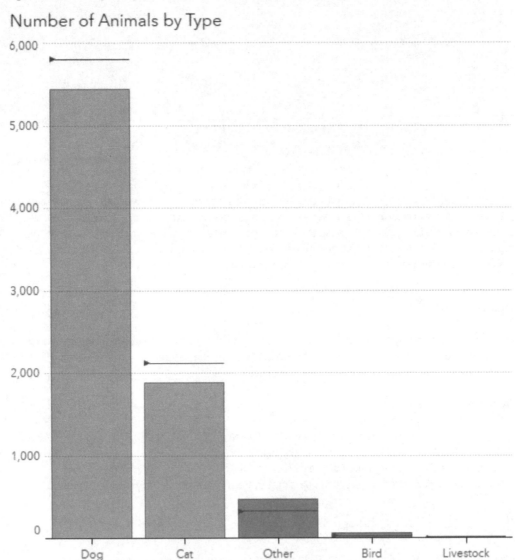

Note: A display rule has also been added to the targeted bar chart to highlight in blue animal types that exceed the prior month's count.

Selected Month (See Figure 6.5.) and **Prior Month** (See Figure 6.6.) are calculated items that return the number of animals if the month is February and January, respectively, and return missing values for all other months.

Note: The calculation used for **Prior Month**, Month(Date) = 2 – 1, is set up in this manner to make it easier to implement parameters later. You will simply replace 2 in both expressions with the parameter. For **Prior Month**, this expression is equivalent to Month(Date)=1 (for January).

A list table has also been included in the report to help with understanding the logic of the calculations and for testing purposes.

Figure 6.5: Number of Animals in February

$$\begin{bmatrix} \text{IF} \ (\ \text{Month} \ (\ \text{Date} \ ) \ = \ \boxed{2} \ ) \\ \\ \text{RETURN} \quad \text{Animals} \\ \\ \text{ELSE} \quad \text{Missing} \end{bmatrix}$$

Figure 6.6: Number of Animals in January

$$\begin{bmatrix} \text{IF} \ (\ \text{Month} \ (\ \text{Date} \ ) \ = \ (\ \boxed{2} \ - \ \boxed{1} \ ) \ ) \\ \\ \text{RETURN} \quad \text{Animals} \\ \\ \text{ELSE} \quad \text{Missing} \end{bmatrix}$$

You want the viewer to choose a month to view the number of animals in that month to compare it with the prior month. You can use date parameters to achieve this goal.

Step 1: Create

Because you want the viewer to select a month, you need to create a date parameter. The data source already contains a date data item with month values, **Date**. You can create the parameter by right-clicking the data item and selecting **New parameter**. The type is automatically determined from the type of the data item. For the name, enter **Selected Month Parameter**. For the minimum value, choose **February**. You don't want to choose January because there is no prior month for January. Later, you'll limit the months that the viewer can choose so that January is not available. Leave the default values for the maximum value and format and choose a current value of **March**. You want to choose something other than February (the value currently used to calculate **Selected Month** and **Prior Month**) so that you can see precisely when the parameter is applied.

Step 2: Populate

Next add a text input control object to the canvas to populate the parameter. If you include **Date** in the **Category** role for the text input control, when the viewer starts to enter a month name, the list of available values is displayed.

Notice that when the viewer enters **J**, the months January, July, and June are all available. If the viewer selects **January**, there is nothing to compare to (because there is no prior month of data). To ensure that **January** cannot be entered, add a filter to the text input control to filter out **Date=January**. Now, when the viewer enters **J**, only July and June are available.

Step 3: Apply

When a viewer selects a month, the **Selected Month** and **Prior Month** calculated items should update to display animals for the selected month and the prior month, respectively. To implement this, edit both calculated items to replace the hardcoded value (2) with **Selected Month Parameter**. (See Figure 6.7.)

Remember, **Date** and **Selected Month Parameter** are both date data items. The Month operator returns a number between 1 and 12 that represents the month of the date (with 1 being January). For the **Selected Month** expression, if the month of the date (in the data source) is equal to the month of the date selected for the parameter, then the number of animals is returned; otherwise, missing value are returned. For the **Prior Month** expression, if the month of the date (in the data source) is equal to the month *before* the date selected in the parameter, then the number of animals is returned; otherwise, missing values are returned.

Figure 6.7: Updating Prior Month to Use the Parameter

$$IF \; (\; Month \; (\; Date \;) \; = \; (\; Month \; (\; \underline{Selected \; Month \; Parameter} \;) \; - \; \boxed{1} \;) \;)$$

$$RETURN \quad Animals$$

$$ELSE \quad Missing$$

Step 4: Test

To verify that the parameter works as expected, verify that **March** is entered in the text input control. The targeted bar chart uses bars to show the number of animals surrendered at the animal shelter in March and horizontal lines to indicate the number of animals surrendered in the prior month (February). The list table shows values for **Selected Month** in March and values for **Prior Month** in February. (See Figure 6.8.)

Suppose the viewer clears the text input control. **Selected Month Parameter** has no value, so **Selected Month** and **Prior Month** are missing for all dates, and the targeted bar chart shows no data.

Figure 6.8: Comparing the Number of Animals in March and February

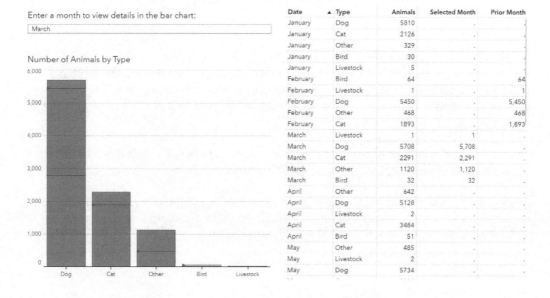

Figure 6.9: Calculating Selected Month when Parameter Is Not Set

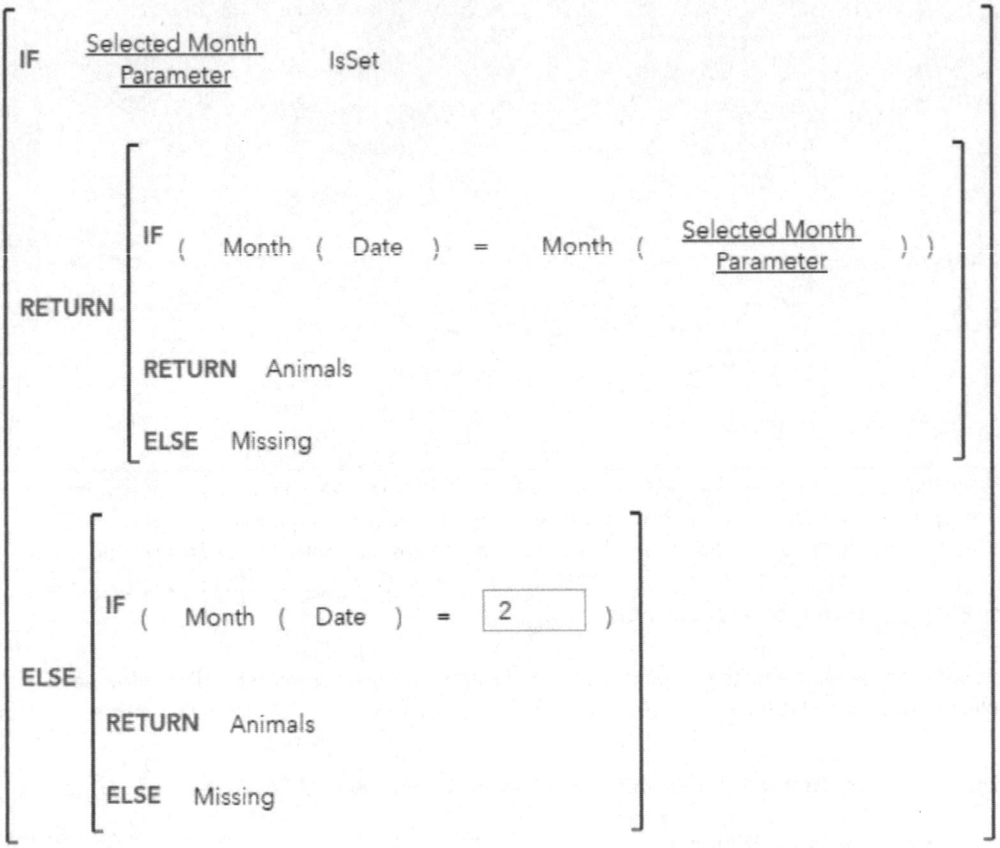

IF   Selected Month Parameter   IsSet

RETURN
   IF (Month (Date) = Month (Selected Month Parameter))
   RETURN Animals
   ELSE Missing

ELSE
   IF (Month (Date) = 2)
   RETURN Animals
   ELSE Missing

As the report designer, you have a couple of choices for preventing this situation. First, you can modify both expressions to use the IsSet operator, which returns **true** if the parameter has a value and returns **false** if the parameter does not have a value. If the parameter is set, then you can calculate the values as before. If the value is not set, you can specify a default month or enter a constant value. (See Figure 6.9.)

For this example, if the viewer does not enter a month, then **Selected Month** is set (by default) to February, and **Prior Month** is set (by default) to January.

Another option is to choose another control object, mainly one that includes the **Required** option (like a button bar or a drop-down list control). This option ensures that viewers always select a value because they will not be able to clear the control.

Figure 6.10: Calculating Prior Month for Multiple Years

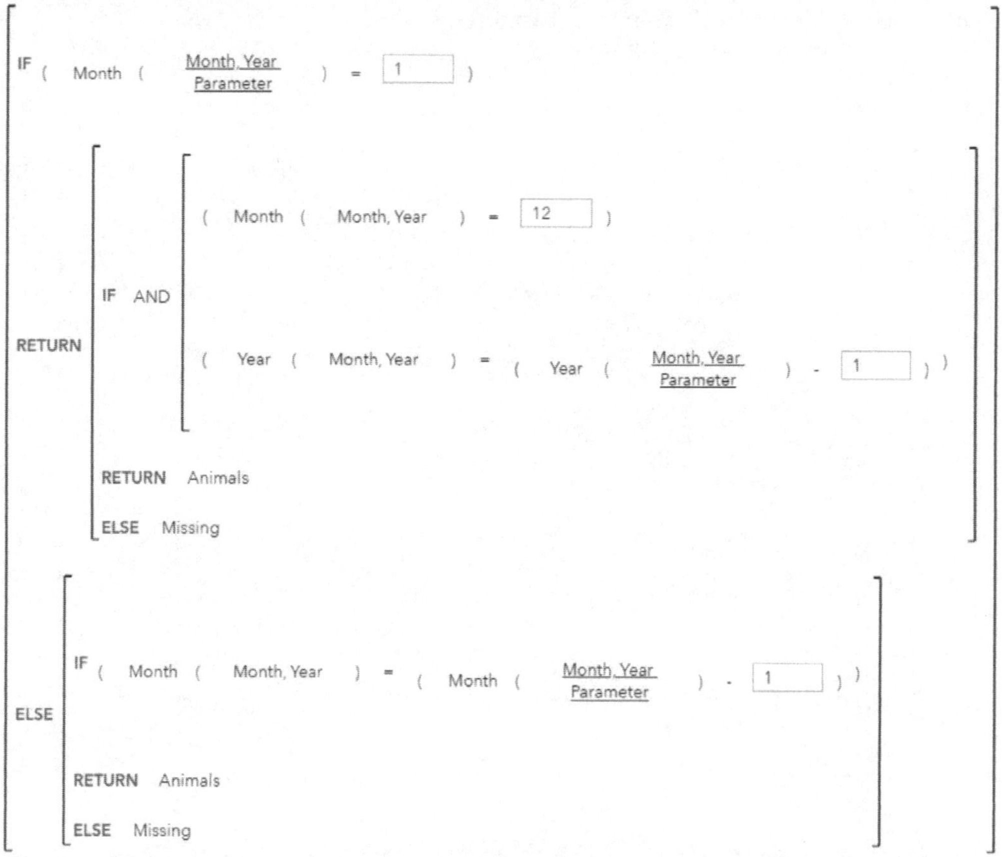

Because the **Date** value in this example contains only months (and not years), the logic used to calculate **Selected Month** and **Prior Month** is not complex. If you have dates with both months and years, however, the logic becomes a bit more difficult. This is because when the viewer selects **January**, the earlier expressions return a 0 value for **Prior Month**, and 0 is not a valid month value. In this case, you would need to add additional logic to return the value from December of the previous year for the prior month. (See Figure 6.10.) The **Selected Month** expression would not change.

Notice that if the date selected for the parameter (**Month, Year Parameter**) is in January, the RETURN condition executes. The RETURN condition returns the number of animals for the 12th month (December) in the year before the year selected for the parameter (the previous year). If the date is in any other month, the ELSE condition executes. This is identical to the expression used in the previous example.

Figure 6.11: Forecast of Injuries from Motor Vehicle Accidents

Injuries from Motor Vehicle Accidents for Last 5 Years

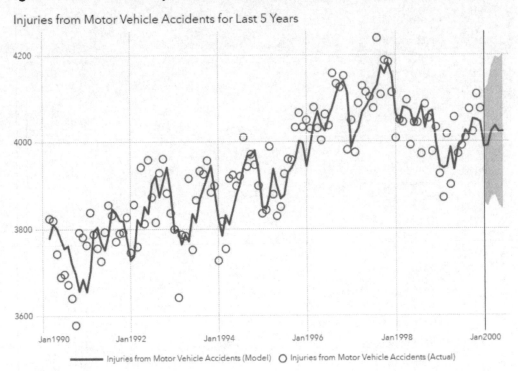

—— Injuries from Motor Vehicle Accidents (Model) ○ Injuries from Motor Vehicle Accidents (Actual)

> About this forecast

Example: Viewing the Last Five Years of Available Data

In this example, the report contains a forecasting object that forecasts the next six months of injuries from motor vehicle accidents using data from the California Highway Patrol. The current forecast, however, is using data from only the 1990s. (See Figure 6.11.)

For the report, you want to show data from the last five years (in this case, January 1994-December 1999) and use that data to create the forecast. Later, when more information is available, the forecast should automatically update (with no viewer intervention) to show the last five years of available data. To do this, you need to determine the last day of the data (or the maximum date) and use parameters to create the filter.

Step 1: Create

Because you want to filter based on the last day of available data (or the maximum date in the table), you need to create a date parameter. This process requires several steps.

First, you need to determine the maximum date. You can do this by creating an aggregated measure (**Max Date**) that looks for the maximum date over the entire table. Aggregated measures, however, can return only numeric values (not dates). Remember that, internally, SAS Visual Analytics stores dates as numbers. The TreatAs operator can be used to change the data type for the purposes of calculation. In this expression, the TreatAs operator converts the date value to a number (the number of days since January 1, 1960) and the Max operator, with the **_ForAll_** aggregation context, determines which date value in the entire data set has the highest number. That is, it determines the day farthest away from January 1, 1960, or the last day of available data. (See Figure 6.12.)

Now you need to create a parameter from this value, but you cannot create parameters from aggregated measures. (Remember, they don't hold a value until they are paired with other data items in the table.) Starting with SAS Visual Analytics 8.3, you can create an aggregated data source to transform an aggregated measure into a regular measure, which can be used to create a parameter.

To create an aggregated data source, do the following:

❶ In the Data pane, view the Data source menu and select **New data from aggregation of <CAS-table>**. (See Figure 6.13.)
❷ Specify a name for the new aggregated data.
❸ Select columns to include in the aggregated data.
❹ Add a filter (optional).

The value of **Max Date** (14,579) represents the number of days between January 1, 1960, and December 1, 1999 (the last date of data in the table).

In the aggregated data source, **Max Date** now appears as a measure. You can easily convert this measure into a date by creating a new calculated item (**Maximum Date**) using the TreatAs operator.

Then you can create a date parameter from this data item.

In this example, the minimum value, maximum value, and current value all have the same date; this represents the maximum date in the table. Later, when the table is updated to include more data with a later date, the minimum and maximum values won't matter.

Figure 6.12: Calculating Maximum Date

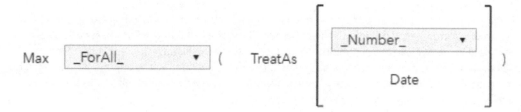

Figure 6.13: Creating an Aggregated Data Source

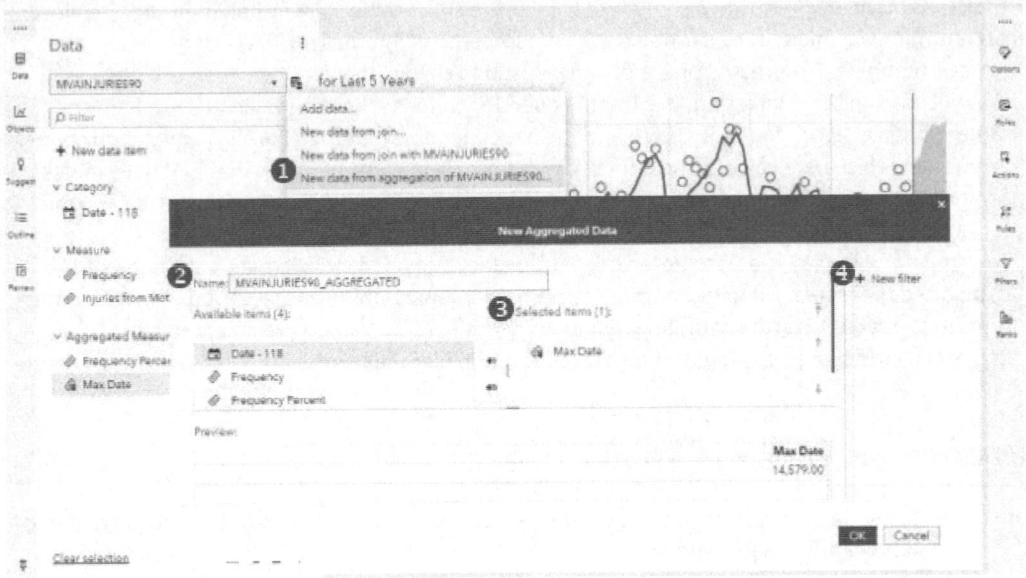

Step 2: Populate

For this example, you want to use a control that doesn't show maximum and minimum values (because those will change as more data is added to the table), that doesn't require the viewer to enter or choose a value (because the value should automatically come from the table), and that has the required property (so that the maximum date value can always be selected without requiring viewer interaction). This leaves only one choice: the button bar. Remember, the filter should update automatically using the last date of available data, so the viewer doesn't really need to see or interact with the control object. It's just used for determining where the filter should end. However. the control object still needs to be included in the report because when the data updates, the control object also updates. And because it's required, the value of the parameter updates.

Add the button bar to the top of the canvas. In the Data pane, select the aggregated data source and assign **Maximum Date** to the **Category** role and **Maximum Date Parameter** to the **Parameter** role. Specify an appropriate name and title and make the button bar required.

Note: For this example, the button bar needs to update automatically when viewing the report. When the button bar updates with the maximum date, the value of the parameter updates with that date value, which causes the filter to update to show the last five years of available data. To ensure that the button bar updates automatically when viewing the report, it must be located on the page of the object that you want to filter. When the viewer views the page, the button bar updates, and the remaining steps are completed.

Figure 6.14: Filtering for the Last Five Years of Available Data

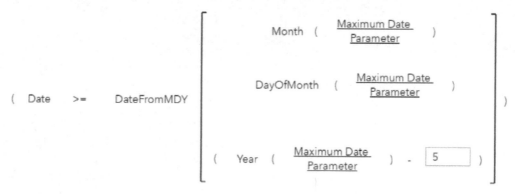

Note: For this example, you can place the button bar on the canvas, in the page prompt area, or in the report prompt area. Because the button bar uses a data item from the aggregated data source, placing the control in the page prompt area or report prompt area does not automatically filter the data. You do not want an automatic filter because that would filter the data displayed in the forecasting object to show only the last day.

Step 3: Apply

Then you need to apply the parameter. For this example, you want to add a filter to the forecasting object to show the five years of data before the maximum date, or all dates greater than or equal to the date five years before the last day of available data. (See Figure 6.14.)

The DateFromMDY operator creates a date value from a month value (1-12), a day value (1-31), and a four-digit year. The Month operator returns the month of a date as a number between 1 and 12, where 1 is January. The DayOfMonth operator returns the day of month as a number between 1 and 31. The Year operator returns the year as a four-digit number.

Note: For a more dynamic report, you can also replace the hardcoded value (5) with a numeric parameter that enables the viewer to specify how many years of data to view. (See Chapter 4.)

Step 4: Test

To test, add data from the 2000s to the data set and view the report. The report now shows the forecasted values of injuries from motor vehicle accidents using the five years of data ending December 1, 2006. (See Figure 6.15.)

Figure 6.15: Viewing Last Five Years of Available Data

Last day of data available:

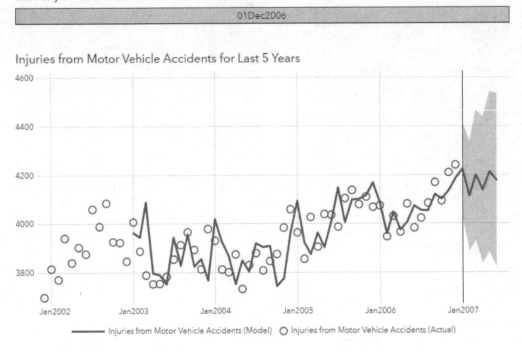

> About this forecast

Example: Viewing 10 Years after a Selected Year

For this example, the report shows the location and type of eclipses between now and the year 3000. A geography data item has been created for **Catalog Number** (the identification number for each eclipse) using **Latitude** and **Longitude** values. A geo map that uses the geography data item has been created to show the location of eclipses. In the map, each eclipse is colored by **Type** (*Annular*, *Hybrid*, *Partial*, or *Total*) and data tip values display **Date** and **TD Time** (Terrestrial Dynamical) for each eclipse. (See Figure 6.16.)

You want to use parameters so that the viewer can choose a year to see the eclipses that occur 10 years after that year.

Note: This example can also be modified to look at data in the past, like orders for the 10 years **before** a selected year.

Figure 6.16: Viewing Eclipses until the Year 3000

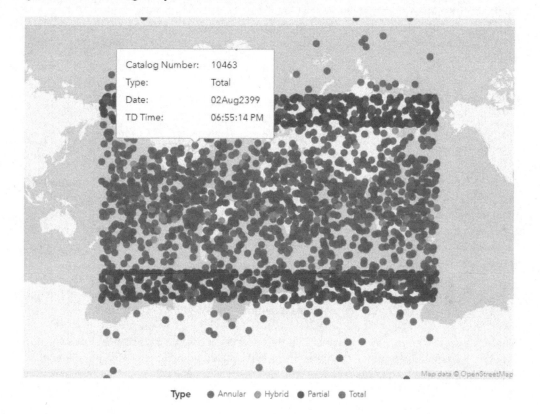

Step 1: Create

Because you want the viewer to select a year, you need to create a date parameter. The **Year** data item has been created, as a duplicate from **Date** with format modified to YEAR, for this purpose. To create the date parameter (**Data Filter Parameter**), right-click **Year** and select **New parameter**. The type, minimum value, maximum value, format, and current value are determined from the data item.

Step 2: Populate

To populate the parameter, a slider control can be used to display the range of acceptable values and enable the viewer to choose a year within that range. Make sure that the slider control is added to the canvas and not to the page prompt area or report prompt area. Because an automatic filter is applied from any control added to the page prompt area or report prompt area, the geo map would be filtered to show only the selected year, not the next 10 years.

For the slider control, add **Year** to the **Measure/Date** role and **Data Filter Parameter** to the **Parameter** role. Then specify an appropriate name and instructions as the title.

Note: When a parameter is added to the slider control, it automatically becomes a single-input slider control.

Step 3: Apply

Next add a data source filter to filter the report to show only the 10 years after the selected year. (See Figure 6.17.)

The data source filter includes years that fall between the year selected (**Data Filter Parameter**) and 10 years after that year. The date parameter needs to be converted to a number to add 10 years. Remember, dates are stored as the number of days since January 1, 1960. To add 10 years to the date parameter, you need calculate to the number of days in 10 years (365*10). The result of this is a number, which then needs to be converted to a date value to use in the BetweenInclusive operator.

Because a parameter is used in a data source filter, a warning appears at the bottom of the Apply Data Filter window: **This data filter contains a parameter**.

Typically, a data filter applies to all objects in the report that use the data source. However, if the data filter contains a parameter, then the filter is not applied to the control that populates the parameter. This enables the viewer to use the control to select the value of the parameter used for the filter.

Note: For a more dynamic report, you can also replace the hardcoded value (10) with a numeric parameter that enables the viewer to specify how many years of data to view. (See Chapter 4.)

In addition, you can add dynamic text as a title to the geo map that uses the value of the parameter. (See Figure 6.18.)

Figure 6.17: Adding a Data Source Filter Using a Parameter

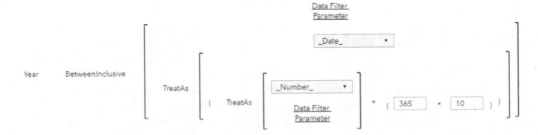

Figure 6.18: Viewing Eclipses for 10 Years After 2060

Select a year to view the next 10 years of available data:

Eclipses 10 Years After January 1, 2060

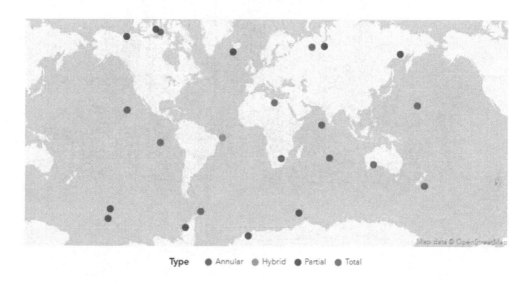

Type   ● Annular ● Hybrid ● Partial ● Total

Step 4: Test

After the parameter has been applied, view the report and test the parameter by selecting the year **2060** in the slider control. The geo map now shows eclipses 10 years after January 1, 2060. (See Figure 6.18.)

Example: Displaying Data within a Selected Range

In this example, the report contains a forecasting object that forecasts the next 30 days of order totals. Two possible underlying factors have been added to the forecast to try to improve its accuracy: **Product Cost** and **Marketing Cost**. The current forecast is using data from the entire data set (January 1, 2010 – October 30, 2013). For this range of data, **Product Cost** is identified as an underlying factor. That is, adding it to the forecasting algorithm improves the accuracy of the forecast. (See Figure 6.19.)

Figure 6.19: Forecasting Order Totals

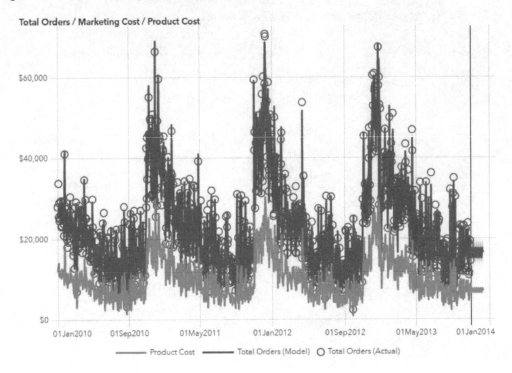

> About this forecast

You want to use parameters so that the viewer can choose which range of data (month and year) to use in the forecasting object.

Step 1: Create

Because you want the viewer to choose a range of dates, you need to create two date parameters: one for the start date of the range (**Start Date Parameter**) and one for the end date of the range (**End Date Parameter**). The forecasting object is using daily data, but the report viewer wants to be able to select data by month and year. The table contains a data item (**TransactionMonthOfYear**) that has dates formatted in this manner. Both parameters can be created from this item. Doing this will automatically specify the appropriate values for the type, the minimum value, the maximum value, and the format.

Step 2: Populate

To populate these parameters, add two drop-down list controls to the canvas above the forecasting object, one for each parameter. Make sure the controls are added to the canvas and

Figure 6.20: Filtering the Start Date Selector

$$(\quad \text{TransactionMonthOf Year} \quad < \quad \underline{\text{End Date Parameter}} \quad)$$

Figure 6.21: Filtering the End Date Selector

$$(\quad \text{TransactionMonthOf Year} \quad > \quad \underline{\text{Start Date Parameter}} \quad)$$

not to the page prompt area or report prompt areas. Because an automatic filter is applied from any control added to the page prompt area or report prompt area, the forecasting object would be filtered to show only the selected date, not the specified range of dates.

For the drop-down list controls, add **TransactionMonthOfYear** to the **Category** role. This populates the control with values from this data item. Then add the appropriate parameter to the **Parameter** role (**Start Date Parameter** or **End Date Parameter**). Specify an appropriate name and add instructions as the title.

Currently, it's possible for the viewer to choose a start date that occurs after the end date. When the parameter is applied, this breaks the filter, and no data is shown. To prevent this from happening, add a filter to the Start Date Selector to display only dates that occur before the value selected for **End Date Parameter**. (See Figure 6.20.)

It's also possible for the viewer to choose an end date that occurs before the start date. To prevent this, add a filter to the End Date Selector to display only dates that occur after the value selected for **Start Date Parameter**. (See Figure 6.21.)

To test the filters, select **May2010** as the start date. Only dates that occur after May 2010 should be available to select as the end date. Select **Jan2011** as the end date. Only dates that occur before January 2011 should be available to select as the start date.

Step 3: Apply

Next add an advanced filter (**Filter: Between Selected Dates**) to the forecasting object to show only data between the start date and end date. (See Figure 6.22.)

Step 4: Test

Finally, view the report and test the parameter. With **May2010** selected as the start date and **Jan2011** selected as the end date, both **Marketing Cost** and **Product Cost** are identified as underlying factors. (See Figure 6.23.)

Figure 6.22: Filtering for Dates between the Start Date and End Date

TransactionDate BetweenInclusive [Start Date Parameter

End Date Parameter]

Figure 6.23: Forecasting between May 2010 and January 2011

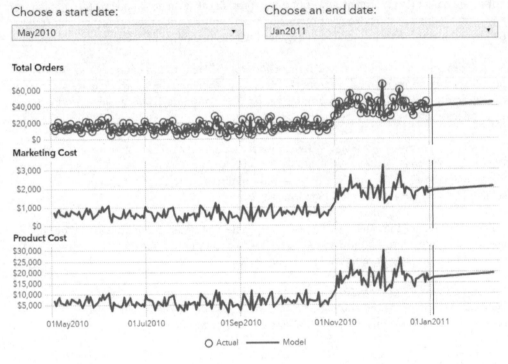

> About this forecast

If no date is selected for the start date (the filter is cleared), then the first day of available data is used. This is also true for the end date: If no date is selected, then the last day of available data is used. Using data between January 2010 and January 2011, only **Product Cost** is identified as an underlying factor.

Chapter 7: Using SAS Graph Builder to Create Custom Graphs

Introduction

SAS Visual Analytics provides a great deal of customization to the report designer. One example of this customization is the ability to create custom graph templates using SAS Graph Builder and use those templates when building your reports. These templates look and function like other report objects, meaning that you can create numerous templates with special features for showcasing your data. To create a custom graph in SAS Graph Builder, follow five simple steps:

1. Choose graph elements.
2. Layout elements.
3. Configure roles.
4. Adjust appearance.
5. Save and use.

Note: Administrators can use the **/SASGraphBuilder/**** URI as a rule target to control access to SAS Graph Builder features.

Step 1: Choose Graph Elements

First, you need to select the elements, or chart types, that will be used to build the graph template. Several elements are available for creating your template: band plots, bar charts, bubble plots, contour plots, geo map, line charts, needle plots, pie charts, region maps, scatter plots, schedule charts, series plots, step plots, time series plots, treemap, vector plots, and waterfall charts. The list of elements depends on the version of SAS Visual Analytics implemented at your site.

As an alternative, you can create a graph template from the list of charts in the Graph Gallery. Most of these charts are available, as is, in SAS Visual Analytics, but some are unique (like the stock high-low plot and the stock volume and volatility plot).

Step 2: Lay Out Elements

After you determine which elements to use in your graph template, you need to decide how these elements will be arranged in the template. You can overlay elements on top of each other, create a user-defined lattice of cells in rows and columns in the template, or use some combination of these layouts.

Step 3: Configure Roles

Next you need to define, add, and configure roles for each element. By default, each element contains required roles, but some elements enable you to add additional roles to further customize your template. You can also create shared roles to identify roles that can be shared by two or more elements or data-driven lattice roles to generate a dynamic layout. It's a best practice to give all roles meaningful names that are easy for the report designer to understand.

Step 4: Adjust Appearance

Then specify the visual attributes of the graph elements. Various options are available for different levels: the graph template, the cell, each individual element in the template (like a line chart or a geo map), each axis for each cell (the X axis, left Y axis, and right Y axis), the legend display, and legends for various elements. Some options can be modified when the graph template is used in SAS Visual Analytics, and others cannot.

Step 5: Save and Use

Finally, save the template. Before the template can be used to create reports in SAS Visual Analytics, it needs to be imported. To import a custom graph:

  ❶ In SAS Visual Analytics, click the **Objects** icon. (See Figure 7.1.)
  ❷ View the objects menu and select **Import custom graph**.

Then navigate to the folder where the custom graph was saved, select the graph, and click **OK**. The graph template appears in the Graphs group and is available to use in your reports.

Note: If the graph template is saved to a shared folder, then other users who can access that folder can also use the templates when building reports. However, each user will need to import the custom graph for it to be visible in SAS Visual Analytics.

Note: If a graph template is used in a report and then the template is modified, the changes are not applied to any reports created using the original graph template. However, new reports that use the template will reflect the changes made to the graph template.

Figure 7.1: Importing a Custom Graph into SAS Visual Analytics

Example: Using a Data-Driven Lattice

For this example, you want to create a time series plot that displays different series over time for each distinct value in a group. Specifically, you have daily data on stock market prices between 1986 and 2006 for three stocks: IBM, Intel, and Microsoft. You would like to view the prices over time for each stock as a lattice of graphs displayed in rows.

A typical time series plot in SAS Visual Analytics does not contain the **Lattice Rows** role. However, you can create a custom graph template in SAS Graph Builder that uses a data-driven lattice to accomplish this task. A data-driven lattice is a multi-cell graph in which each lattice (row or column) contains the same graph elements, but the data in each lattice is determined by the values of one or more categorical variables. You can create a data-driven lattice using lattice rows (rows of charts are created for each distinct value of the categorical variable), using lattice columns (columns of charts are created for each distinct value of the categorical variable), or using both (rows of charts are created for the distinct values of one categorical variable and columns of charts are created for the distinct value of another categorical variable).

Step 1: Choose Graph Elements

You want to display data over time, so you'll use a time series plot.

Step 2: Lay Out Elements

The charts should be displayed in rows, where the number of rows is determined by the distinct values of the categorical variable. To begin creating the template, do the following:

❶ In SAS Graph Builder, click the **Elements** tab in the left pane. (See Figure 7.2.)
❷ Drag **Time Series Plot** to the canvas. When only one element is added to the canvas, the template contains one cell (A1). As you begin adding more elements, they can be placed in the same cell (to create an overlay), to the left or right of the cell (to create a user-defined column lattice), or on top of or below the cell (to create a user-defined row lattice).

Data-driven lattices are available only when the graph template contains one cell.

Step 3: Configure Roles

Next you need to configure roles for the template. This includes modifying any required roles for the time series plot, adding additional roles, creating shared roles, or adding data-driven lattice roles.

For this example, you want to add a data-driven lattice role for rows. To add data-driven lattice roles, do the following:

❶ In the Roles pane, click **Add Role** for the Data Driven Lattice Roles group. (See Figure 7.3.)
❷ Choose the role type: **Lattice Row** or **Lattice Column**.
❸ Specify a name for the role.

Figure 7.2: Adding Elements to the Graph Template

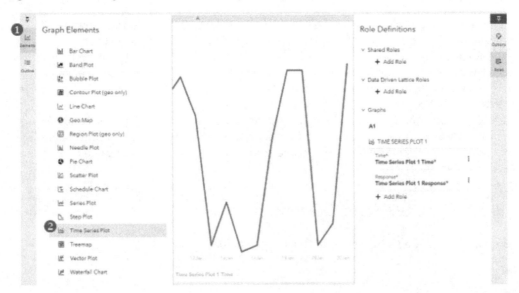

④ Select the appropriate classification. If **Category** is chosen as the classification, both category and datetime data items can be assigned to the role in SAS Visual Analytics. If **Datetime** is chosen as the classification, however, only datetime data items can be assigned to the role.

⑤ Select **Required** (optional). If this is not selected, then the designer can choose whether the chart contains a lattice.

⑥ Select **Allow multiple data assignments** (optional). If this selected, then the designer can assign more than one data item to the role.

The time series plot has two required roles: **Time** and **Response**. It's a best practice to give these roles meaningful names. To rename and modify these roles, click the **More** icon next to each role and select **Edit Role**. For the **Time** role, specify a name of **Date**. For the **Response** role, specify a name of **Measure** and select **Allow multiple data assignments**. This enables the designer to select more than one measure to display in the time series plot.

Two other roles are available for the time series plot: **Group** and **Data Tip**. To add one of these optional roles, click **Add Role** under **Time Series Plot 1** in the Roles pane. For this example, the default roles are sufficient.

Step 4: Adjust Appearance

The Options pane enables you to modify the appearance of the graph template. Remember, different levels of options are available to modify. Add markers to the time series plot by

Figure 7.3: Adding Data-Driven Lattice Roles

selecting **Time Series Plot 1** at the top of the Options pane and clicking **Markers**, and remove the X-axis label by selecting **X Axis** at the top of the Options pane and clearing **Axis label**.

As you make changes, the canvas updates to reflect those changes. (See Figure 7.4.) The charts on the canvas use sample data. To apply actual data, you need to use the graph template in a report.

Step 5: Save and Use

Finally, save the graph template and import the custom graph in SAS Visual Analytics. Add **Date** (from the **STOCKS** table) to the **Date** role, **Close** to the **Measure** role, and **Stock** to the **Lattice Row** role. Notice that multiple measures can be added to the **Measure** role because you selected **Allow multiple data assignments** for that role when building the template.

Figure 7.4: Viewing Sample Data

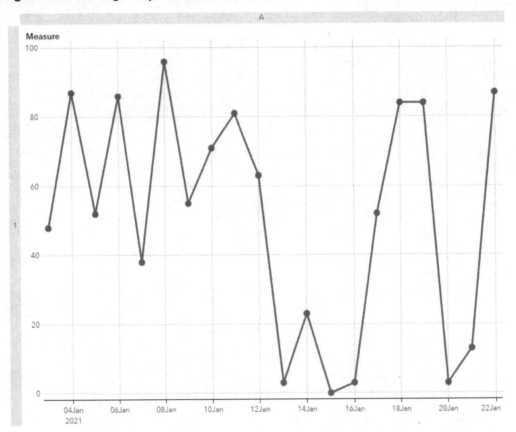

Each stock appears as a separate row in the time series plot, markers are used, and the X-axis label is not displayed. (See Figure 7.5.) For this particular template, the only options that can be modified in SAS Visual Analytics are display options (like the Style, Layout, and Graph Frame options) and legend options.

Example: Syncing Hierarchies

In this example, a report contains a time series plot and a bubble plot that use the same hierarchy (**Product Hierarchy**). This hierarchy displays details for product brand, product line, and product make. The time series plot shows sales over time for each product brand. The bubble plot displays a bubble for each product brand. The location of the bubble in the chart represents the average product quality and average customer satisfaction for that brand, and the size of the bubble represents the sales for that brand. Double-clicking a specific product brand in either chart displays details for each product line within that product brand.

Figure 7.5: Viewing Stocks Using a Data-Driven Lattice

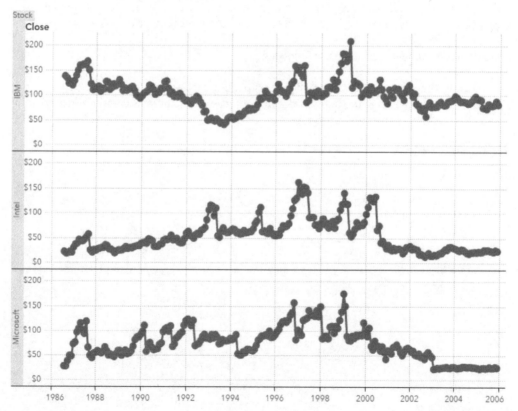

Currently, the viewer must drill through the hierarchy on each chart separately to view details at each level.

You want to create a graph template that syncs the hierarchy drill-downs in both charts so that when the viewer double-clicks a bubble in the bubble plot or a line in the time series plot, both charts show details for product lines in that product brand.

Step 1: Choose Graph Elements

For this example, you use a time series plot and a bubble plot to match the objects used in the report.

Step 2: Lay Out Elements

The charts should appear side by side, with the time series plot on the left and the bubble plot on the right. To do this, you need to create a user-defined lattice. A user-defined lattice is a graph template with more than one cell in which the cells are arranged in rows and columns. Each cell is created independently and can contain different graph elements. Cells are defined by letters (to identify columns) and numbers (to identify rows). By default, all graph templates have one cell called A1.

To create a user-defined lattice, do the following:

❶ Drag **Time Series Plot** from the Elements pane to the canvas. (See Figure 7.6.)
❷ Drag **Bubble Plot** to the right border of the time series plot. This creates a new column to the right of the time series plot.

Figure 7.6: Creating a User-Defined Lattice

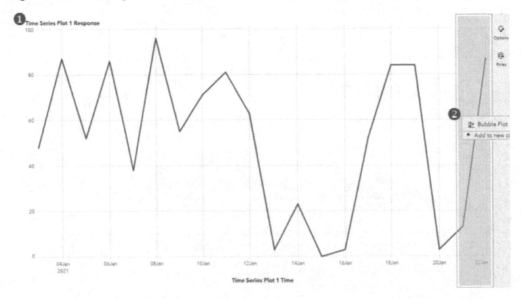

Figure 7.7: Creating a Shared Role

It is possible to sync hierarchy drill-downs for more than two charts by adding additional columns or rows to the template.

Step 3: Configure Roles

By default, the time series plot has two required roles (**Time** and **Response**) and the bubble plot has three required roles (**X**, **Y**, and **Size**). The current report has the hierarchy assigned to the group role of both charts. To create the graph template, add the **Group** role to Time Series Plot 1 (with the default name) and make the role required. Then add the **Group** role to Bubble Plot 1 (with the default name) and make the role required as well. Because you want both these roles to use the same data (the hierarchy), you can make them shared. To do this:

❶ Click the **More** icon next to **Time Series Plot 1 Group**. (See Figure 7.7.)
❷ Select **Create Shared Role With Another Role**.
❸ Choose **Bubble Plot 1 Group**.
❹ Specify a name for the shared role (for example, **Hierarchy**). By default, this role is required because the two roles that made up the shared role were required.

Shared roles can be viewed and modified under the Shared Roles group in the Roles pane.

In addition, the **Response** role for the time series plot and the **Size** role for the bubble plot should also use the same data source. Create another shared role for these two roles called **Measure-Size**.

As before, give the other required roles more meaningful names: **Date** for the **Time Series Plot 1 Time** role, **X Axis** for the **Bubble Plot 1 X** role, and **Y Axis** for the **Bubble Plot 1 Y** role. For the **X Axis** and **Y Axis** roles, any type of data item can be used (category, datetime, or measure).

Step 4: Adjust Appearance

Next modify the appearance of the graph template. For **Time Series X Axis**, clear **Axis label** (so that the date label isn't displayed below the X axis) and for **Discrete Legend**, clear **Bubble Plot 1**. The discrete legend, by default displays details for the group roles (for both charts). Because the group roles are shared between the charts, displaying the discrete legends for both is redundant. The bubble plot **Size** role is also displayed in the legend; options for that can be found under **Bubble Plot 1 Size Legend**.

Step 5: Save and Use

Save the graph template and import it into SAS Visual Analytics. Delete the existing charts and replace them with the new graph template. Assign **Transaction Date** (from the **CUSTOMERS_LOC** table) to the **Date** role (for the time series plot), **Product Quality** to the **X Axis** role (for the bubble plot), **Customer Satisfaction** to the **Y Axis** role (for the bubble plot), **Product Hierarchy** to the **Hierarchy** role (for both plots), and **Product Sale** to the **Measure-Size** role (for both plots). Now when the viewer navigates through the hierarchy on one chart, the other chart is automatically updated to show the same level of the hierarchy. (See Figure 7.8.)

Example: Creating a Chart with Overlays

For this example, the next 60 months of injuries from motor vehicle accidents have been forecast in SAS Visual Analytics. The actual data, the forecasted data, and the confidence intervals have been downloaded as a Microsoft Excel file and reimported to SAS Visual Analytics.

You want to be able to filter a graph to show only the forecasted values and bands that show the confidence intervals over the forecasted period. To do this, you need to create a custom graph in SAS Graph Builder so that you can filter the range of values without the forecasted values and confidence intervals changing. If you add a filter to the original forecasting plot, the forecast algorithm will update (to choose the best method for the data displayed in the chart), and the forecasted values and confidence intervals will update as well. For this example, you want to add a filter to the forecasting plot to view only the forecasted values and confidence intervals *without* recalculating the forecast.

Step 1: Choose Graph Elements

To display data over time with bands that show the confidence interval, you will use a time series plot and a band plot.

Figure 7.8: Navigating through Both Hierarchies Simultaneously

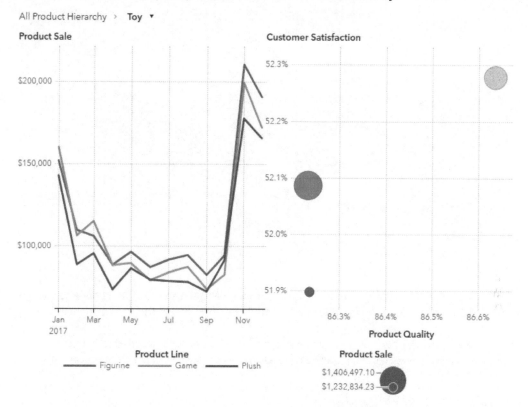

Note: In this example, a time series plot or a line chart would work. Use a line chart if you want to be able to assign category data items to the X axis.

Step 2: Lay Out Elements

The charts should be overlaid or superimposed in the same cell, one on top of the other. Because the focus is the forecasted values, the time series plot should be on top of the band plot. To overlay charts, do the following:

❶ Drag the bottom chart (the band plot) from the Elements pane to the canvas. (See Figure 7.9.)

❷ Drag the top chart (the time series plot) directly onto the chart on the canvas. This overlays the charts and automatically creates a shared role for graph elements that are compatible.

Figure 7.9: Creating an Overlay Chart

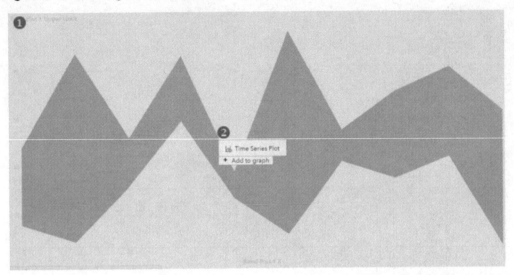

Note: If you did not add the graphs in the correct order, you can use the Outline pane to change the order. For this example, Time Series Plot 1 should be listed first in the Outline pane.

It is possible to overlay multiple charts in a single cell and create user-defined lattices in conjunction with overlay charts. (See Example: Using Overlays with a User-Defined Lattice.)

Step 3: Configure Roles

When two compatible charts are overlaid, a shared role is automatically created for the X axis. In this case, the **Time** role from the time series plot and the **X** role from the band plot were automatically shared, which works for this scenario. Edit the shared role to give it a more meaningful name (**Date**).

Then change the name of the **Response** role for the time series plot to **Forecast**, the **Upper Limit** role for the band plot to **Upper Confidence Interval**, and the **Lower Limit** role for the band plot to **Lower Confidence Interval**.

Step 4: Adjust Appearance

Next modify the appearance by doing the following:

- **Time Series Plot 1**: Change **Line color** from **Automatic (default)** to **Data line color 1**.
- **Band Plot 1**: Change **Transparency** to **75%** (0.75) and **Fill color** from **Automatic (default)** to **Data color 1**. This ensures that both the time series plot and the band plot use matching colors.

- **X Axis**: Clear **Axis label**. You don't need to see the name of the date variable in the chart.
- **Legends**: Change **Visibility** to **Hide All**. A legend is not needed for this scenario.

Step 5: Save and Use

After the graph template has been saved and imported into SAS Visual Analytics, use it to display the forecasted values. Add the graph template to the Forecasted Values page. Then,assign **Date** (from the **FORECAST OF INJURIES** table) to the **Date** role, **Injuries from Motor Vehicle Accidents (Model)** to the **Forecast** role, **Upper Confidence Interval** to the **Upper Confidence Interval** role, and **Lower Confidence Interval** to the **Lower Confidence Interval** role.

The nice thing about this chart, compared to the original forecasting chart, is that you can filter the range of values without the forecasted values and confidence intervals changing. For example, a filter can be added to view only the forecasted values and the confidence interval. (See Figure 7.10.)

Example: Using Overlays with a User-Defined Lattice

For this example, you need to create a stock plot that shows the close price of stocks over time along with bands that show the low and high price for each day. In addition, a volatility plot

Figure 7.10: Viewing Forecasted Values and Confidence Intervals

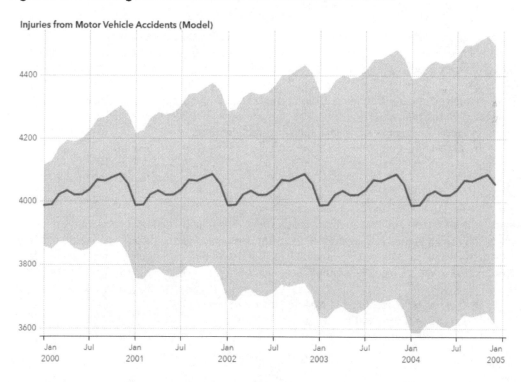

that uses a needle plot should be displayed below the stock prices to show volatility. To do this, you create a custom graph template that uses overlaid charts combined with a user-defined lattice.

Note: One of the custom graph templates available in SAS Graph Builder is a stock volume and volatility plot. This chart uses a scatter plot to show the close price, a vector plot to show high and low prices, a time series plot to show the moving average of the stock price, a band plot to show the Bollinger upper limit and Bollinger lower limit, and a needle plot to show volatility. Although this does use the elements required for this example, it has extra elements that are not necessary.

Step 1: Choose Graph Elements

To display the close price of stocks over time, you use a time series plot. Use a band plot to depict the low and high prices for each day, and use a needle plot to show volatility.

Step 2: Lay Out Elements

The band plot and time series plot are overlaid (in a similar fashion as the previous example) with the time series plot on top. Add the needle plot as a user-defined lattice to the row below the overlay plot. You can resize each cell to ensure that the overlay chart is the main focus by using the handlebars between cells. The needle plot should take up approximately one-fourth to one-third of the canvas. (See Figure 7.11.)

Note: As an alternative, you can specify an overview axis for the time series-band plot and choose a needle plot as the content of the overview axis. This would be extremely useful if you have data over a long time span. To use a needle plot as the overview axis, do the following:

❶ In the Options pane, select **Graph Template** from the drop-down list. (See Figure 7.12.)
❷ Click **Overview axis**.
❸ For the **Contents** field, select **Specify graph elements**.
❹ Drag **Needle Plot** (from the Elements pane) to the Overview axis area.

Step 3: Configure Roles

By default, when the time series plot and band plot are overlaid, the X-axis roles for these charts are automatically shared (into **Shared Role 1**). The X axis for the needle plot should use the same data item as well, so this role should also be included with the shared role. To add the **Needle Plot 1 X** role to the shared role, do the following:

❶ Click the **More** icon next to **Needle Plot 1 X**. (See Figure 7.13.)
❷ Select **Use Shared Role**.
❸ Choose **Shared Role 1**.

Figure 7.11: Resizing the Needle Plot

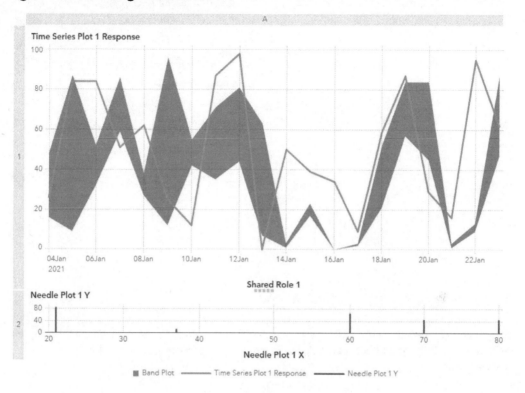

Then change the name of **Shared Role 1** to **Date**, **Time Series Plot 1 Response** to **Close**, **Band Plot 1 Upper Limit** to **High**, **Band Plot 1 Lower Limit** to **Low**, and **Needle Plot 1 Y** to **Volume**.

Step 4: Adjust Appearance

Next modify the appearance by doing the following:

- **Band Plot 1**: Change **Transparency** to **75%** (0.75).
- **Cell A1- X Axis**: Clear **Axis label** so that the label for date doesn't show in the chart.
- **Needle Plot 1**: Set a fixed baseline of **0** so that the Y axis always starts at 0.
- **Cell A2- X Axis**: Set **Grid lines** to **Off**. Clear **Axis label**, **Axis line**, and **Tick marks**. This removes unnecessary detail from the horizontal axis of the volatility chart.
- **Cell A2- Left Y Axis**: Set **Grid lines** to **Off**. Clear **Axis line** and **Tick marks**. This removes unnecessary detail from the vertical axis of the volatility chart.
- **Discrete Legend**: Clear **Band Plot 1** so that details about the band plot are not displayed in the legend.

Figure 7.12: Using a Needle Plot as the Overview Axis

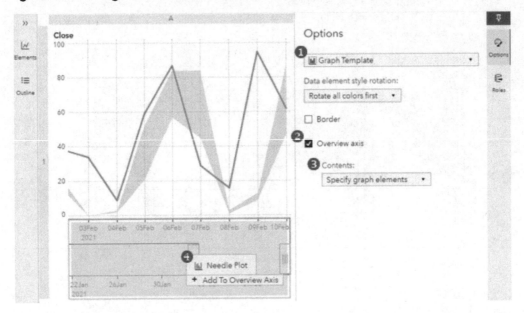

Note: If you created an overview axis for the needle plot, you don't need to specify options for **Cell A2- X Axis** and **Cell A2- Left Y Axis**. These features are turned off by default for the overview axis.

Step 5: Save and Use

After the graph template has been saved and imported into SAS Visual Analytics, use it to display daily details for IBM stock. Assign **Date** (from the **STOCKS** table) to the **Date** role, **Close** to the **Close** role, **Low** to the **Low** role, **High** to the **High** role, and **Volume** to the **Volume** role. (See Figure 7.14.)

Example: Building a Custom Map

For this example, the data source contains locations of customers and the facilities where they made a purchase. Each row has details about customers and details about facilities. You want to create one map that shows the customer using one type of marker (for example, a circle) and the facility using a different type of marker (for example, a star). To do this with the predefined geo map objects, you would need to restructure your current table so that there are separate rows for customers and facilities and a column that identifies those locations as **Customer** and **Facility**, respectively. Alternatively, you can create a custom geo map that allows for two types of geographical information (one for customers and one for facilities).

Figure 7.13: Adding a Role to a Shared Role

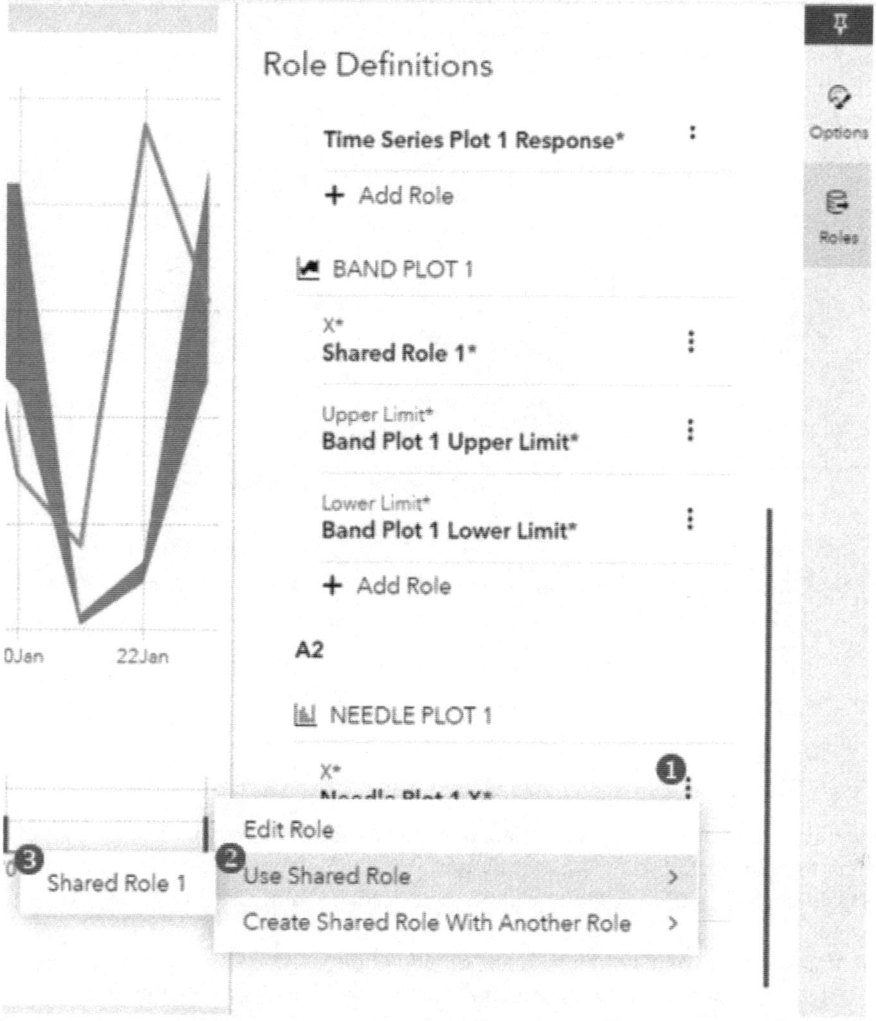

Step 1: Choose Graph Elements

Because you want to show the locations of customers and facilities, you need to use a geo map with two scatter plots (one for customers and one for facilities).

Note: Geographical map templates are available starting with SAS Visual Analytics 8.5.

Figure 7.14: Viewing Stocks Prices Using the Custom Graph

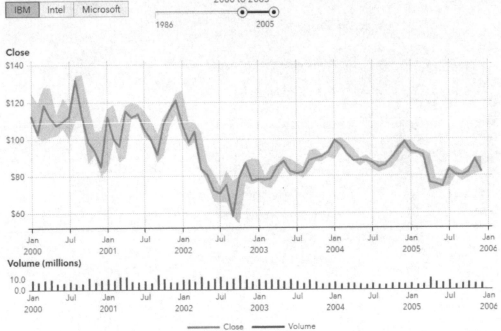

Step 2: Lay Out Elements

The geo map and two scatter plots will be overlaid in one cell. Add the geo map first (so that it appears in the background) and the two scatter plots on top. Remember, if you add the elements in the incorrect order, you can use the Outline pane to rearrange them.

Note: Map templates consist of two or more layers of elements: a geo map layer that provides the base map and a graph layer that represents the data displayed on the map. Bubble plots, contour plots, region plots, and scatter plots can all be used as the graph layer.

Step 3: Configure Roles

For this example, both scatter plots should have **Geographic ID** roles (that should not be shared). Remember, you want one scatter plot to show facility locations and one to show customer locations. Change the name of **Scatter Plot 2 Geographic ID** to **General** (this will be used to display facility locations) and **Scatter Plot 1 Geographic ID** to **Specific** (this will be used to display customer locations).

Step 4: Adjust Appearance

Next modify the appearance by doing the following:

- **Scatter Plot 2**: Set **Marker style** to **Star-filled**, adjust the size to **20**, and specify a color of **Data marker color 3**. This plot displays details about facilities.
- **Scatter Plot 1**: Set **Marker style** to **Circle-filled**, adjust the size to **10**, and specify a color of **Data marker color 4**. This plot displays details about customers.

Step 5: Save and Use

After the graph template has been saved and imported into SAS Visual Analytics, use it to display the locations of customers and facilities in Italy. Assign **Facility** (from the **INSIGHT_TOY_COMPANY_2017** table) to the **General (Coordinate 1)** role and **Customer** to the **Specific (Coordinate 2)** role.

Note: For **Facility** and **Customer** to be assigned to the custom map, both data items need to be classified as geographic data items.

Facilities are represented as a purple star, and customers are represented as an orange circle. (See Figure 7.15.)

For custom maps, more options can be modified within SAS Visual Analytics: coordinate options (like clustering adjacent markers, setting marker size and marker shape, and setting data labels), map options (like map background, map service, and transparency), and legend options. Notice that the legend displays the name of the latitude data item used to create the geography data items. To avoid confusion with viewers, change the visibility of the legend to **Off**.

Example: Building a Custom Map with Polygon Layers

For this example, the table contains location information for accidental drug-related deaths in Connecticut. Specifically, it has information about the state (Connecticut), the county, and the exact location of death (using latitude and longitude coordinates). You want to create a map that shows all three levels of data: state and county as regions and location of death as markers. In addition, you want to enable the viewer to select which counties to show on map using a list control. SAS Visual Analytics only contains a geo map object that supports two layers. Because you want to show three layers, you need to build a custom map using SAS Graph Builder.

Step 1: Choose Graph Elements

Because you want to show the locations of deaths at three levels (state-county-exact location), you need to use a geo map with three levels: two region plots (one for state and one for county) and one scatter plot (for exact location).

Figure 7.15: Viewing Facilities and Customers in a Custom Map

Select a continent:

| Africa | Asia | Europe | North America | Oceania | South America |

Select a country:

| Italy ▼ |

Geo Map of Customer

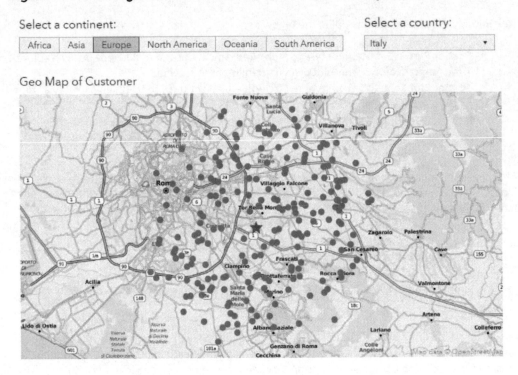

Step 2: Lay Out Elements

The geo map, the two region plots, and the scatter plot will be overlaid in one cell. Add the geo map first (so that it appears in the background), then the two region plots, and finally the scatter plot on top. The first region plot is used to show state, the second region plot to show county, and the scatter plot to show the exact location. Remember, if you add the elements in the incorrect order, you can use the Outline pane to rearrange them.

Step 3: Configure Roles

For this example, each region plot and the scatter plot should have **Geographic ID** roles (that should not be shared). Remember, you want **Region Plot 1** to display state-level information, **Region Plot 2** to display county-level information, and **Scatter Plot 1** to display the exact location of death. Change the name of **Scatter Plot 1 Geographic ID** to **Individual**, **Region Plot 2 Geographic ID** to **County**, and **Region Plot 1 Geographic ID** to **State**.

Region plots also have required **Color** roles. Change the name of **Region Plot 2 Color** to **Color (County)** and **Region Plot 1 Color** to **Color (State)**.

You can also add additional roles for the scatter plot. Add a **Data tip** role called **Data Tip** that uses any classification and allows multiple data assignments and add a **Color** role called **Color (Individual)** that uses category data items and is not required. (See Figure 7.16.)

Figure 7.16: Configuring Roles

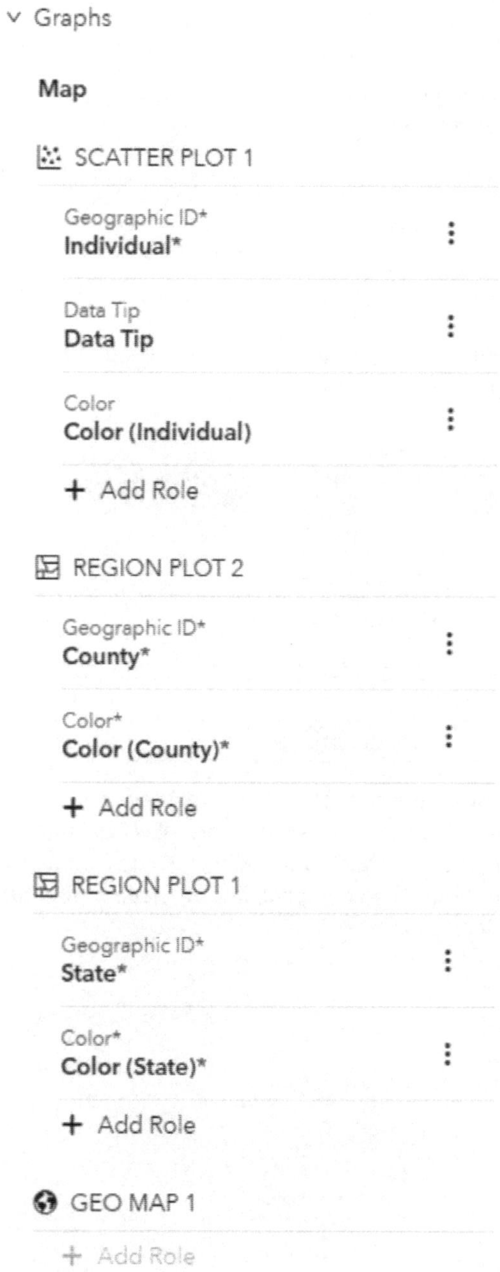

∨ Graphs

Map

⚃ SCATTER PLOT 1

Geographic ID*
Individual*   ⋮

Data Tip
Data Tip   ⋮

Color
Color (Individual)   ⋮

+ Add Role

▦ REGION PLOT 2

Geographic ID*
County*   ⋮

Color*
Color (County)*   ⋮

+ Add Role

▦ REGION PLOT 1

Geographic ID*
State*   ⋮

Color*
Color (State)*   ⋮

+ Add Role

🌐 GEO MAP 1

+ Add Role

Step 4: Adjust Appearance

Next modify the appearance for **Scatter Plot 1** by changing **Marker style** to **X-bold**. The exact location of death appears in the map as a bolded X.

Step 5: Save and Use

After the graph template has been saved and imported into SAS Visual Analytics, use it to display the death locations. Assign data items (from the **ACCIDENTAL_DRUG_DEATHS** table) to roles for the custom graph. (See Table 7.1.)

Exact locations of deaths are represented as a bolded X, and the color indicates the county of death. Counties are displayed as yellow regions, and the state is displayed as a blue region. To simplify the chart, in the Options pane, clear **Map background**.

Then add a filter action between the list control and the custom geo map to display deaths in the following counties: Fairfield, Middlesex, and Tolland. (See Figure 7.17.)

Table 7.1: Data Item Assignments for the Custom Map

Role	Data Item
State (Region 2)	DeathState
Color (State) (Region 2)	Number of Deaths
County (Region 1)	DeathCounty
Color (County) (Region 1)	Number of Opioid Deaths
Individual (Coordinate)	ID
Color (Individual) (Coordinate)	DeathCounty

Note: For **DeathState**, **DeathCounty**, and **ID** to be assigned to the custom map, they need to be classified as geography data items. **DeathState** uses predefined geographic roles (US State Names), **DeathCounty** uses a geographic data provider (County-State-US), and **ID** uses latitude and longitude in data. For more information about how the geographic data provider is created, see Appendix A: Loading Geographic Polygon Data to CAS.

Figure 7.17: Viewing Deaths in Selected Counties

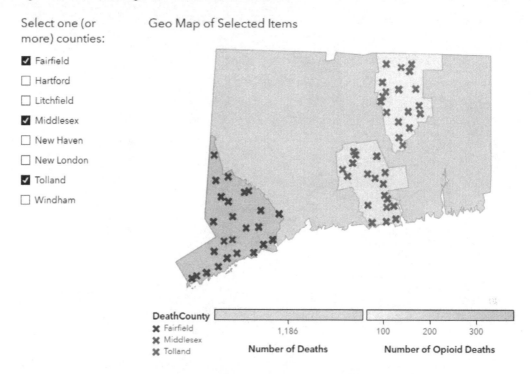

Note: You can hide and show the various layers in the geo map by clicking the **Hide or show layers** icon in the object toolbar and selecting the layers to hide. In Figure 7.18, notice that the **State** layer is hidden.

Figure 7.18: Hiding the State Layer

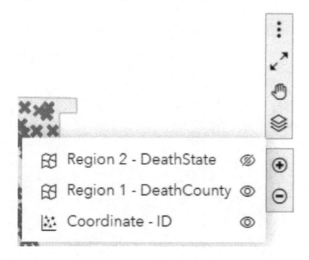

Chapter 8: Using Data-Driven Content to Create Custom Graphs

Introduction

SAS Visual Analytics provides a wide array of objects that can be used when creating a report: tables, graphs, geo maps, controls, analytics, containers, and content. In addition, report designers can create their own custom graph templates using SAS Graph Builder to extend the list of available objects. (See Chapter 7.)

Sometimes, however, these objects might not meet your visualization needs. For example, you might want to use a chart in your report (like a circle packing plot, an organizational chart, a calendar, a leaflet map, or a radar chart) that isn't one of the predefined objects in SAS Visual Analytics. Alternatively, you might want to show data in a unique way (like display a series of book covers or product images). The Data-driven content object (found in the Content group in the Objects pane) extends the capabilities of SAS Visual Analytics by enabling you to display your data using third-party visualizations.

Note: The Data-driven content object is available only in SAS Visual Analytics on SAS Viya, version 8.2 and later.

Note: For the examples in this chapter, the code and the reports have already been created.

Requirements

Third-party visualizations can be authored in any JavaScript charting framework, like D3.js, Google Charts, or CanvasJS. If you want to create your own visualizations, you'll need some knowledge of the Document Object Model (DOM). You'll also need to understand how HTML pages are structured, know a little JavaScript, and understand at least one of those frameworks. The examples in this chapter use D3, an open-source JavaScript library, but some additional examples can be found at the SAS GitHub repository: https://github.com/sassoftware/sas-visualanalytics-thirdpartyvisualizations. For some examples of the types of visualizations that can be created with D3, see the D3 Gallery: https://github.com/d3/d3/wiki/Gallery. If you know nothing about how websites are structured, JavaScript, or D3, don't panic! See Appendix B: Working with Data-Driven Content for a high-level overview of these topics, as well as more detailed explanations of the code used in this chapter.

In addition, to use your visualizations in SAS Visual Analytics, the code must be externally hosted; that is, it must be available on the web. You can host the code on a website or in a GitHub repository. The benefit of using a GitHub repository is that it's easy to set up and extremely easy to use.

Benefits

The ability to create third-party visualizations (and integrate them with SAS Visual Analytics) enables you to create any chart that you need to showcase your data. This is especially useful for creating charts that don't already exist in SAS Visual Analytics, like a radar plot, a calendar, a circle packing chart, or even a three-dimensional image of an assembly line to point out where bottlenecks occur.

The beauty is that, once these third-party visualizations are created, they work like any other object in SAS Visual Analytics. CAS processes and sends the data to SAS Visual Analytics, and the third-party visualization can interact with filters, ranks, and actions in the same manner as other objects in your report.

Even if you have no JavaScript experience, it's easy to start using third-party visualizations in SAS Visual Analytics. The SAS GitHub repository has many examples that you can use today; no coding is required.

Third-party visualizations, when used in SAS Visual Analytics, also take on all the advantages of SAS security. Even though the code of the visualization itself is open and available to many, the data used in your report is rendered only inside of SAS Visual Analytics, which means that it's accessible only to those users who have the appropriate privileges.

In this chapter, you start by using existing visualizations from the SAS GitHub repository, view the JavaScript code to determine the number and type of columns needed, and see how to make small changes to modify the look of the visualization in your report.

Next you use the Goodreads book-rating data (from Chapter 3) to create a visualization that shows a grid of cover images. First, you create the visualization to display sample data on a web page. Then you see how to use data from SAS Visual Analytics to populate the visualization. Finally, to fully integrate the visualization in SAS Visual Analytics, you see how to use the visualization as the target of a filter action, how to highlight selected values in the visualization (when a linked selection action is added), and how to use the visualization as the source of an action. These examples can be found at my GitHub repository: https://github.com/idig007/Visual-Analytics-Examples/tree/main/samples.

Example: Using a Circle Packing Plot

For this example, you want to display product information in a circle packing plot. Specifically, you would like to look at the sale amounts for various product levels: brand, line, and make. This type of visualization, however, doesn't exist as a report object in SAS Visual Analytics. You can use the Data-driven content object to point to a sample visualization in the SAS GitHub repository.

Before using the Data-driven content object, it's a good idea to get a broad understanding of the third-party visualization. Many third-party visualizations can be viewed with sample data using the Web content object in SAS Visual Analytics.

To display the third-party visualization using the Web content object:

❶ From the Objects pane, drag the **Web content** object (in the Content group) to the canvas. (See Figure 8.1.)
❷ In the Options pane, enter the URL to reference the circle packing chart from the SAS GitHub repository.

Note: To reference the examples in the SAS GitHub repository, use the following URL: https://sassoftware.github.io/sas-visualanalytics-thirdpartyvisualizations/samples/*<name-of-chart>*.html

This gives you a good idea of what the visualization will look like and the type of data that can be used with the visualization. For example, the circlePacking plot (https://github.com/sassoftware/sas-visualanalytics-thirdpartyvisualizations/blob/master/samples/d3_circlePacking.html) is a treemap that uses circles instead of rectangles. Notice that the sample data shows three levels of data: US (the largest circle), regions (the middle circles), and states (the smallest circles). A tooltip also appears that displays the levels and the value of the measure (for example, US.Northeast. New York $1,800). (See Figure 8.2.)

Figure 8.1: Displaying the Circle Packing Plot Using the Web Content Object

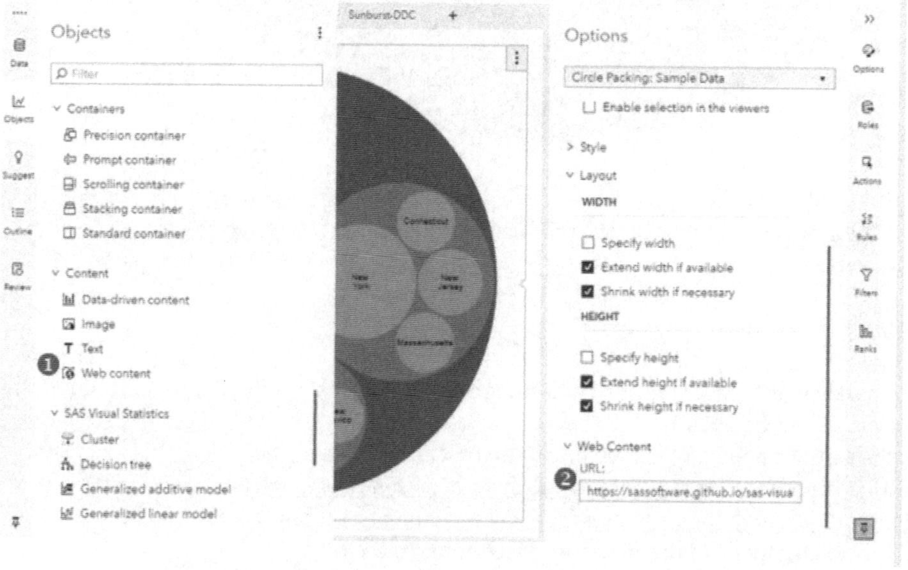

Figure 8.2: Viewing Sample Data for the Circle Packing Plot

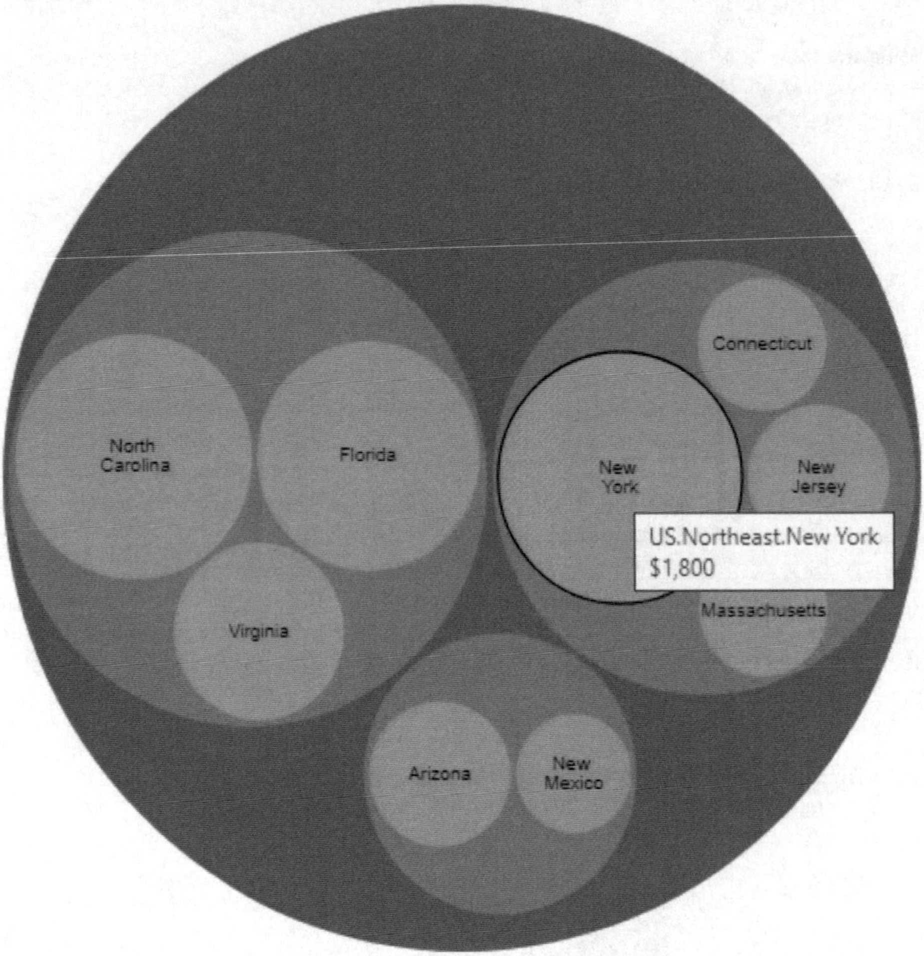

Next use the Data-driven content object to display the third-party visualization using data from SAS Visual Analytics.

To use data-driven content:

❶ From the Objects tab, drag the **Data-driven content** object (in the Content group) to the canvas. (See Figure 8.3.)
❷ In the Options pane, enter the URL to reference the circle packing chart from the SAS GitHub repository: https://sassoftware.github.io/sas-visualanalytics-thirdpartyvisualizations/samples/d3_circlePacking.html.
❸ In the Roles pane, add the necessary data items to the object.

Figure 8.3: Using the Data-Driven Content Object

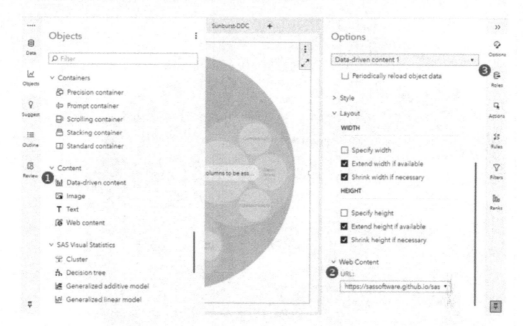

The type, number, and order of data items required differ for each visualization. Many visualizations display a message that lists these requirements. For example, the circle packing plot expects three strings (starting with the broadest level and ending with the most specific) and a numeric value. (See Figure 8.4.)

For the product data, **Product Brand** is the highest level (with 2 distinct values), followed by **Product Line** (with 8 distinct values), and **Product Make** (with 71 distinct values). **Product Sale** is assigned as the measure. The circle packing plot displays four levels of circles: total (which includes sales from all brands), product brand, product line, and product style. (See Figure 8.5.)

Figure 8.4: Required Data Items for Circle Packing Plot

This Circle-Packing chart expects columns to be assigned in this order:
1. Level 1 (string)
2. Level 2 (string)
3. Level 3 (string)
4. Value (numeric)

Figure 8.5: Viewing Product Data in Circle Packing Plot

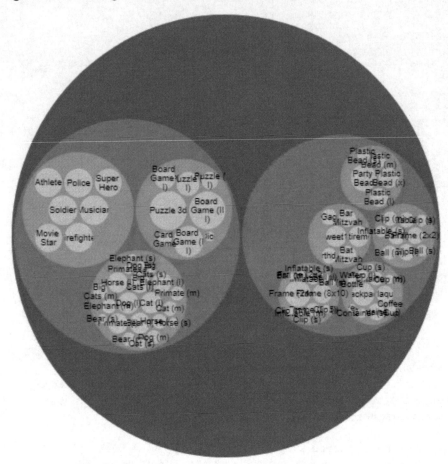

Example: Using and Modifying a Sunburst Plot

For this example, you want to display product information in a sunburst plot. Specifically, you would like to look at the sale amounts for various product levels: brand, line, and make. This type of visualization also doesn't exist as a report object in SAS Visual Analytics, but the SAS GitHub repository does have a sample visualization that creates a sunburst plot.

Before using the sunburst plot, you want to view it with sample data just like you did with the circle packing plot. This visualization, however, contains code that will not display the sample data if it's called from within an iFrame (like the Web content object or the Data-driven content object in SAS Visual Analytics). However, you can view this plot on a web page: https://sassoftware. github.io/sas-visualanalytics-thirdpartyvisualizations/samples/D3Thursday/10_Sunburst.html.

Figure 8.6: Viewing Sample Data for the Sunburst Plot

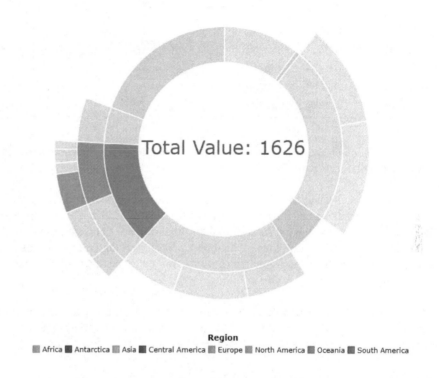

This plot displays hierarchical data using a series of rings. Each level of the hierarchy is represented by a circle in which the broadest level is displayed in the center ring and the more detailed information is displayed in the outer rings. (See Figure 8.6.)

Notice that the sample data shows three levels: continent, country, and state. Placing your cursor on one of the rings shows additional details in a ribbon in the upper left corner of the visualization. The ribbon displays each of the levels, the (unformatted) value of the measure, and the percentage of data that slice represents for that level (for example, North America – United States – North Carolina 59 (3.63%)). A key value label appears in the middle of the chart that displays the string **Total**, the name of the measure (**Value**), and the (unformatted) value of the measure.

This visualization requires a measure and a category but can take up to five additional categories. (See Figure 8.7.)

Using the product data, assign the following data items (in the specified order): **Product Sale**, **Product Brand**, **Product Line**, and **Product Make**. Notice that the order of the data items

Figure 8.7: Required Data Items for Sunburst Plot

D3 Sunburst Chart expects columns to be assigned in this order:
1. Measure (number)
2. Category (string)
3. Category (string) [optional]
4. Category (string) [optional]
5. Category (string) [optional]
6. Category (string) [optional]
7. Category (string) [optional]

assigned must match the order specified by the sunburst plot (one measure, one category, and up to five optional categories).

The sunburst plot displays three rings (product brand, product line, and product style) where each ring is divided to show the portion of sales from each distinct value in that level. (See Figure 8.8.) Notice, that the product sale values, however, are not formatted even though in SAS Visual Analytics this data item uses a Dollar (DOLLAR12.) format. This is because numeric data is passed to the third party visualization as unformatted data. Any formatting needs to be specified in the code for the third party visualization.

In this instance, the **Product Sale** value is displayed in two locations: at the end of the ribbon (which shows sales for the selected level) and in the center of the chart (which shows total sales for all levels). To change this, you can use the JavaScript number formatter.

To modify the visualization, do the following:

Copy the sample visualization from the SAS GitHub repository to your personal repository or website. My copy (with changes) can be found here: https://github.com/idig007/Visual-Analytics-Examples/blob/main/samples/SunburstFormatted.html

Using JavaScript, define a new variable formatter to format a number using dollar signs and commas. (See Program 8.1.)

Program 8.1: Defining a Variable: Formatter

```
// Format data using dollars
var formatter= new Intl.NumberFormat('en-US', {
  style: 'currency',
  currency: 'USD',
});
```

Use the formatter to display the total value in the center of the chart. (See Program 8.2.)

Figure 8.8: Viewing Product Data in a Sunburst Plot

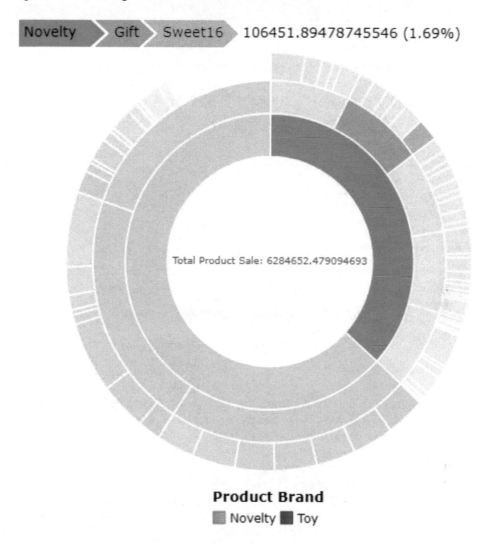

Product Brand

■ Novelty ■ Toy

Program 8.2: Using the Formatter to Display the Total

```
KEY_VALUE_TEXT.enter()
  .append("text")
  .classed("key-value-text", true)
  .text("Total " + METADATA.value.label + ": " +
      formatter.format(ROOT.value))
        //Change to use formatter.format
  .merge(KEY_VALUE_TEXT)
  .style("font-size", "1em")
```

```
    .style("font-size", function() {
      return (2 * INNER_RADIUS - 2 * KEY_VALUE_TEXT_PAD) /
            this.getComputedTextLength() + "em";
    });
```

Use the formatter to display the value at the end of the ribbon. (See Program 8.3.)

Program 8.3: Using the Formatter to Display the Ribbon Value

```
  G_TRAIL_AREA.select(".trail-end-text")
    .transition()
    .delay(function() {
      return heightChanged && !entered ?
            HEIGHT_CHANGE_DELAY : 0;
    })
    .duration(TRANS_TIME/2)
    .tween("text", function() {
      const that = d3.select(this);
      const oldVal = TRAIL_END.value /
            OLD_ROOT.descendants()[0].value;
      const newVal = TRAIL_END.value / ROOT.value;
      const i = d3.interpolateNumber(oldVal, newVal);
      return function(t) {
        that.text(formatter.format(TRAIL_END.value) + " ("
                + FORMAT_PERCENT(i(t)) + ")");
                //Change to use formatter.format
    };
  });
```

As you can see, knowing what to search for (the string 'Total' for the key value label and the **FORMAT_PERCENT** variable (which is used to add the percent sign in the percentage value at the end of the ribbon) and knowing a little bit of JavaScript can help you modify an existing visualization to enhance the appearance.

After replacing the URL for the Data-driven content object with the link to the formatted code (https://github.com/idig007/Visual-Analytics-Examples/blob/main/samples/SunburstFormatted. html), the **Product Sale** values now have dollar signs and commas and are a bit easier to read. (See Figure 8.9.)

Note: As an alternative, you can use the d3.js third-party helper function (https://github.com/ sassoftware/sas-visualanalytics-thirdpartyvisualizations/blob/master/thirdPartyHelpers/d3.js) to use the column metadata from SAS Visual Analytics to configure D3 formats.

Example: Creating a Visualization

For the remaining examples, the report displays information about book ratings from Goodreads (www.goodreads.com). The data source contains a column **Title** that includes the 10,000 most

Figure 8.9: Viewing Formatted Product Sale

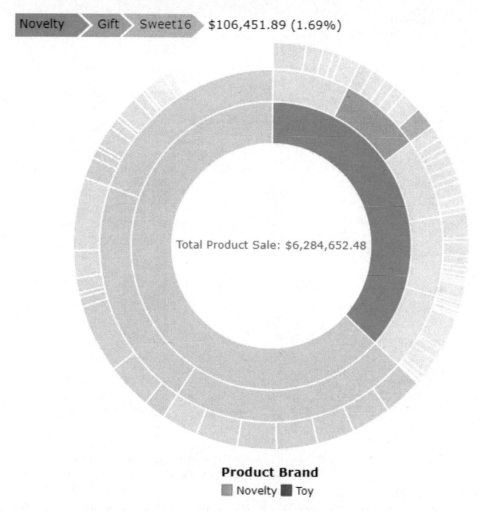

Product Brand

popular books (based on the number of ratings) on Goodreads and a column **image_url** that includes a URL to an image of the book cover. A page prompt enables the viewer to filter for a range of ratings. Three key value objects show the number of books, the most frequent author, and the highest average rating, respectively. A list table shows details about the book, including the title, the year of publication, the average rating, and a list of authors. (See Figure 8.10.)

You want to use the Data-driven content object to display the cover images for the books in the list table (using the **image_url** column). In addition, you want the data-driven content to be the target and source of an action. This same process could be used to display any images in your report (like country or state flags or images of products).

Figure 8.10: Viewing Book Details

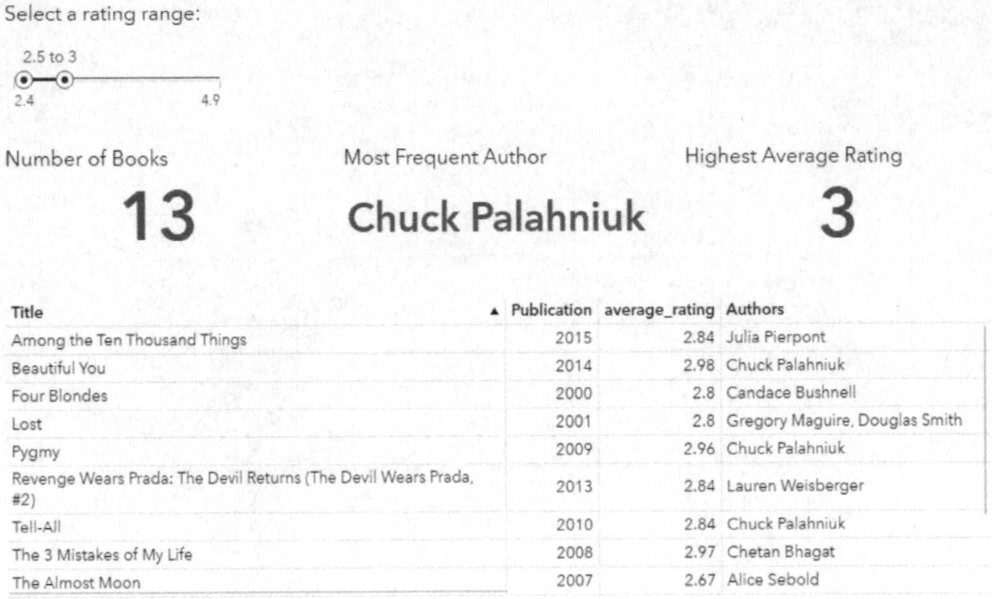

Select a rating range:

2.5 to 3

2.4   4.9

Number of Books	Most Frequent Author	Highest Average Rating
13	**Chuck Palahniuk**	**3**

Title	▲ Publication	average_rating	Authors
Among the Ten Thousand Things	2015	2.84	Julia Pierpont
Beautiful You	2014	2.98	Chuck Palahniuk
Four Blondes	2000	2.8	Candace Bushnell
Lost	2001	2.8	Gregory Maguire, Douglas Smith
Pygmy	2009	2.96	Chuck Palahniuk
Revenge Wears Prada: The Devil Returns (The Devil Wears Prada, #2)	2013	2.84	Lauren Weisberger
Tell-All	2010	2.84	Chuck Palahniuk
The 3 Mistakes of My Life	2008	2.97	Chetan Bhagat
The Almost Moon	2007	2.67	Alice Sebold

Displaying Sample Data

To start, create the visualization using sample data and view it on a web page. Once you get the code and the structure of the visualization set up, you can then incorporate it into SAS Visual Analytics. (See https://github.com/idig007/Visual-Analytics-Examples/blob/main/samples/Creating.html to view the code for this example.)

In this case, the sample data consists of the five rows from the Goodreads data, specifically the **image_url**, **id**, and **title** columns. A variable (**SAMPLE_MESSAGE**) has been created to hold the sample data. Notice that **SAMPLE_MESSAGE** is an array that consists of five objects (one for each book) where *key* represents the data item name and *value* represents the data value. (See Program 8.4.)

Program 8.4: Creating SAMPLE_MESSAGE

```
// Sample data
const SAMPLE_MESSAGE = [
     {image_url:
     'https://images.gr-assets.com/books/1447303603m/2767052.jpg',
      id: 1,
      title: "The Hunger Games (The Hunger Games, #1)"},
     {image_url:
     'https://images.gr-assets.com/books/1474154022m/3.jpg',
      id: 2,
      title:
      "Harry Potter and the Sorcerer's Stone (Harry Potter, #1)"},
```

```
      {image_url:
      'https://images.gr-assets.com/books/1361039443m/41865.jpg',
       id: 3,
       title: "Twilight (Twilight, #1)"},
      {image_url:
      'https://images.gr-assets.com/books/1361975680m/2657.jpg',
       id: 4,
       title: "To Kill a Mockingbird"},
      {image_url:
      'https://images.gr-assets.com/books/1490528560m/4671.jpg',
       id: 5,
       title: "The Great Gatsby"}
   ];
```

A dynamic variable (**DATA**) has been created to (eventually) hold the data from SAS Visual Analytics, and some selection variables have been created for building the visualization in the DOM: **GRID** for the background grid, **BOOK** for each book, and **IMAGE** for the book cover image. (See Program 8.5.)

Program 8.5: Creating Dynamic and D3 Variables

```
// Dynamic data variables
let DATA; // Data to be parsed from VA data message

// D3 variables
let GRID; // Grid for book images
let BOOK; // Book data-join
let IMAGE; // Book image
```

For this example, because no data is coming from SAS Visual Analytics, **DATA** is assigned the value of **SAMPLE_MESSAGE**, the sample data. (See Program 8.6.)

Program 8.6: Displaying Sample Data

```
// No data from VA, so display sample data
DATA=SAMPLE_MESSAGE;
```

A function (drawElements) draws the visualization. Within the function, a grid background is created (**GRID**) that creates a div element under the body element in the DOM. (See Program 8.7.)

Program 8.7: Creating the Grid

```
//Creates a grid
GRID=d3.select('body')
      .append('div')
       .attr('id','grid')
       .attr('class','grid');
```

The div element displays a grid (as defined by CSS styles) with as many columns as needed to fill the size of the visualization and as many rows as needed to display all the data. (See Program 8.8 and Figure 8.11.)

Figure 8.11: Viewing the Grid

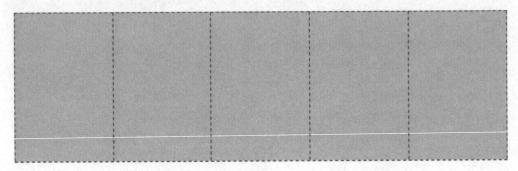

Program 8.8: Displaying the Grid (CSS Styles)

```
.grid{
  display: grid;
  grid-template-columns: repeat(auto-fill, minmax(98px, 1fr));
  grid-auto-rows: auto;
}
```

Then, for the grid, an element (g) is added to the DOM for each row of data, or each book. (See Program 8.9.) In the case of the sample data, five g elements are added.

Program 8.9: Adding a g Element for Each Book

```
//Adds g for each book
BOOK=GRID.selectAll('g')
        .data(DATA, function(d) {
           return d.id
         })
        .enter()
        .append('g')
          .attr('id','book');
```

Then, for each book, an SVG element is added to the DOM to display the image (as defined by CSS styles) using the value of the **image_url** column in the sample data. In addition, a tooltip for each book displays the title of the book. (See Program 8.10.)

Program 8.10: Displaying Image and Tooltip

```
//Adds image to each g
IMAGE=BOOK.append('svg')
          .append('svg:image')
            .classed('book-image', true)
            .attr('xlink:href', function(d) {
               return d.image_url;
             })
          .append('title')
```

```
        .text(function(d) {
            return d.title;
        });
```

The book image will take up the entire width of the SVG element, as defined by CSS styles. (See Program 8.11.)

Program 8.11: Defining Book Image Styles

```
/* Define book-image styles */
.book-image{
  width: 100%;
}
```

Viewing the visualization on a web page (or using the Web content object in SAS Visual Analytics) shows images of the five book covers and a tooltip that displays the name of the book. (See Figure 8.12.)

Displaying JSON-Formatted Data

You eventually want this visualization to display data being passed from SAS Visual Analytics instead of displaying sample data. (See https://github.com/idig007/Visual-Analytics-Examples/ blob/main/samples/Creating_JSON.html to view the code for this example.) SAS Visual Analytics passes data to the data-driven content as a JSON object. Therefore, the code needs a slight modification to match how data is passed to the object from SAS Visual Analytics.

First, you need to reconstruct the **SAMPLE_MESSAGE** variable as a JSON object. Luckily, the SAS GitHub repository contains a visualization (jsonDataViewer.html) that can be used to display your data as a JSON object. To view your data as a JSON object, do the following:

1. Add a Data-driven content object to the report.
2. In the Options pane, specify the URL for the jsonDataViewer sample visualization: https://sassoftware.github.io/sas-visualanalytics-thirdpartyvisualizations/samples/ jsonDataViewer.html

Figure 8.12: Viewing Book Cover Images and Tooltip

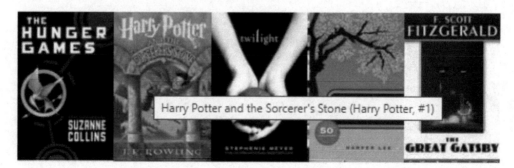

3. In the Roles pane, add the data items (in the order in which they appear in the **SAMPLE_MESSAGE** object). This shows you the data message SAS Visual Analytics is sending to the third-party visualization.

4. Replace the **SAMPLE_MESSAGE** variable in your code with the data message shown in the jsonDataViewer. (See Program 8.12.)

Program 8.12: Creating SAMPLE_MESSAGE as a JSON Object

```
// Sample data
const SAMPLE_MESSAGE = {
  version: "1",
  resultName: "sample",
  rowCount: 5,
  availableRowCount: 5,
  data: [
    ['https://images.gr-assets.com/books/1447303603m/2767052.jpg',
     1,
     "The Hunger Games (The Hunger Games, #1)"],
    ['https://images.gr-assets.com/books/1474154022m/3.jpg',
     2,
     "Harry Potter and the Sorcerer's Stone (Harry Potter, #1)"],
    ['https://images.gr-assets.com/books/1361039443m/41865.jpg',
     3,
     "Twilight (Twilight, #1)"],
    ['https://images.gr-assets.com/books/1361975680m/2657.jpg',
     4,
     "To Kill a Mockingbird"],
    ['https://images.gr-assets.com/books/1490528560m/4671.jpg',
     5,
     "The Great Gatsby"]
  ],
  columns: [
    {
      name: "image_url",
      label: "image_url",
      type: "string"
    },
    {
      name: "id",
      label: "id",
      type: "string"
    },
    {
      name:'title',
      label: 'title',
      type: 'string'
    }
  ]
};
```

Now that the data is coming into the visualization in a different format, you need to add some code to restructure the data from a two-dimensional array (the JSON object) to the array of objects used to render the visualization. (See Program 8.13.) Arrays in JavaScript are 0-based indexed, so column 0 represents the first column (**image_url**) and column 2 represents the third column (**title**). In addition, SAS Visual Analytics sends an additional column to handle brushing (or linked selection actions). In this case, column 3 is 0 if a row is not selected through brushing and 1 if the row is selected through brushing. For information about how to incorporate brushing into your data-driven content, see Example: Highlighting Selected Values in the Visualization in this chapter.

Program 8.13: Restructuring Data

```
// Restructure data from 2d array to array of objects
DATA = [];
for (let i = 0; i < SAMPLE_MESSAGE.data.length; i++) {
  DATA.push({
    image_url: SAMPLE_MESSAGE.data[i][0],
    id: SAMPLE_MESSAGE.data[i][1],
    title: SAMPLE_MESSAGE.data[i][2],
    brushed: SAMPLE_MESSAGE.data[i][3],
    index: i
  });
}
```

This visualization shows the same results as the previous example: images of the five sample book covers and a tooltip that displays the name of the book.

Example: Incorporating a Visualization into SAS Visual Analytics

For this example, you want to use the Data-driven content object to display data coming from SAS Visual Analytics instead of the sample data. (See https://github.com/idig007/Visual-Analytics-Examples/blob/main/samples/Incorporating.html to view the code for this example.)

Before incorporating the visualization into SAS Visual Analytics, it's important to understand how SAS Visual Analytics and the Data-driven content object interact: (See Figure 8.13.)

- **Data messages**: SAS Visual Analytics sends messages with the data (assigned in the Roles pane) and metadata about that data to the Data-driven content object in JSON format. This message contains an additional column that indicates whether a row of data is selected when the data-driven content is the target of a linked selection action.
- **Instructional messages**: The Data-driven content object sends messages with instructions to SAS Visual Analytics. These messages typically contain details about the type, number, and order of data items required for the visualization.

Figure 8.13: Understanding Messages Passed between SAS Visual Analytics and the Data-Driven Content

SAS Visual Analytics   **Data-driven content**

- **Selection messages**: The Data-driven content object sends messages to SAS Visual Analytics about selections made in the third-party visualization. This enables the third-party visualization to be used as the source of an action. Selection messages are covered in a later example. (See Example: Using a Visualization as the Source of an Action.)

To enable the visualization to send and receive the appropriate messages from SAS Visual Analytics, two utilities from the SAS GitHub repository need to be used: messagingUtil.js and contentUtil.js.

Using Utilities

messagingUtil.js contains the functions needed to send messages to SAS Visual Analytics and receive messages from SAS Visual Analytics. For this example, the following functions are used:

- setOnDataReceivedCallback- sets a callback function to handle data messages from SAS Visual Analytics.
- postInstructionalMessage- sends an instructional message to SAS Visual Analytics that describes the required roles, their assignment order, and the types of data items required for the visualization.

contentUtil.js contains functions needed to validate the data received from SAS Visual Analytics. For this example, the following function is used:

- validateRoles- checks whether the data received from SAS Visual Analytics contains the required columns of the appropriate type and in the appropriate order.

For more information about these utilities and the functions available, see Appendix B: Working with Data-Driven Content.

To use the functions in these utilities, add the following code to the head element of the web page: (See Program 8.14.)

Program 8.14: Importing Utilities

```html
<!-- Import utilities  -->
<script type="text/javascript" src="../util/messagingUtil.js"></script>
<script type="text/javascript" src="../util/contentUtil.js"></script>
```

Note: For this example, I copied the utilities to my GitHub repository, so if the SAS utilities are updated, they won't break the sample code used in this chapter.

Creating Dynamic Variables

Two additional dynamic variables have been added to hold the data message from SAS Visual Analytics (**VA_MESSAGE**) and the result name of the object (**VA_RESULT_NAME**), which is required to send messages back to SAS Visual Analytics. (See Program 8.15.) The result name of the object is the unique string that represents the Data-driven content object in the report.

Program 8.15: Creating Variables for SAS Visual Analytics

```javascript
// Dynamic data variables
let VA_MESSAGE; // Data message from VA
let VA_RESULT_NAME; // Result name required to send messages to VA
```

Setting Up Callback Functions

Two callback functions are set up: one to attach an event to the data message from SAS Visual Analytics (using the setOnDataReceivedCallback function from messagingUtil.js) and one to display the visualization with sample data if it's being viewed outside of SAS Visual Analytics or if there is no data attached. (See Program 8.16.)

Program 8.16: Setting Up Callback Functions

```javascript
// Attach event for data message from VA
va.messagingUtil.setOnDataReceivedCallback(onDataReceived);

// If not being rendered in iFrame (outside of VA), render with
// sample data
if (!inIframe()) {
  onDataReceived(SAMPLE_MESSAGE);
}
```

The first callback function calls a function, onDataRecieved, which is used to render the third-party visualization using data received from SAS Visual Analytics.

The second callback function calls a function, inIframe, which is used to determine whether the third-party visualization is rendered inside an iFrame. If not, then it's likely being viewed outside of SAS Visual Analytics and should use the sample data to render the visualization. This is helpful for debugging purposes. (See Appendix B: Working with Data-Driven Content or the sample code to view the details of this function.)

Initializing and Validating Data

The onDataReceived function takes one argument, messageFromVA, which represents the data message received from SAS Visual Analytics. When the data is received, this data is assigned to **VA_MESSAGE** and the result name for the data-driven content is assigned to **VA_RESULT_NAME**.

Next, using the data received from SAS Visual Analytics, the code checks to see whether the assigned columns are of the appropriate type (in this case, three strings: one for **image_url**, one for **id**, and one for **title**). Remember, an additional column is being passed from SAS Visual Analytics that contains information about brushing; that column should be a number.

If the data is not valid (or if there is no data), an instructional message is sent from the Data-driven content object to SAS Visual Analytics to display details about the required columns: the name, the type, and the order.

Two additional snippets are included: the code to restructure the data (as seen in the previous example) and the code to draw/update the visualization. (See Program 8.17.)

Program 8.17: Viewing the onDataReceived Function

```
function onDataReceived(messageFromVA) {

    // Initialize data variables
    VA_MESSAGE = messageFromVA;
    VA_RESULT_NAME = messageFromVA.resultName;

    // Validate data roles
    if (
        // If roles are invalid or no data, post instructional msg
        !va.contentUtil.validateRoles(
            messageFromVA,
            ["string", "string", "string"],
            ["number"]
        )
    ) {
        va.messagingUtil.postInstructionalMessage(
            VA_RESULT_NAME,
            "D3 Book Images expects columns to be assigned in this order:\n" +
            " 1. Image URL (string)\n" +
            " 2. ID (string)\n" +
            " 3. Title (string)"
        );
        return;
    }
```

```
// Code to restructure data
// Code to draw/update the visualization

}
```

Drawing/Updating the Visualization

The code to draw/update the visualization uses an IF statement to check whether the div element is empty. (This means that the visualization has not been previously drawn.) If it's empty, then the drawElements function executes. This is the same function used in the previous example. If it's not empty, then that means the visualization has previously been drawn but new data is being passed from SAS Visual Analytics. In that case, the updateElements function executes. (See Program 8.18.) This function is discussed in more detail in the next example.

Program 8.18: Drawing/Updating the Visualization

```
// Initialize chart if first draw, otherwise process data and
// update elements accordingly
if (d3.select('div').empty()) {
  drawElements();
 } else {
  updateElements();
 }
}
```

Viewing in SAS Visual Analytics

Adding a Data-driven content object to SAS Visual Analytics and specifying the URL displays an instructional message that describes the required data. (See Figure 8.14.)

In this case, the following actions take place:

1. The code checks whether the visualization is being displayed in an iFrame. It is, so sample data is not being displayed.
2. SAS Visual Analytics sends the visualization a data message that contains no data.

Figure 8.14: Viewing the Instructional Message (Required Roles)

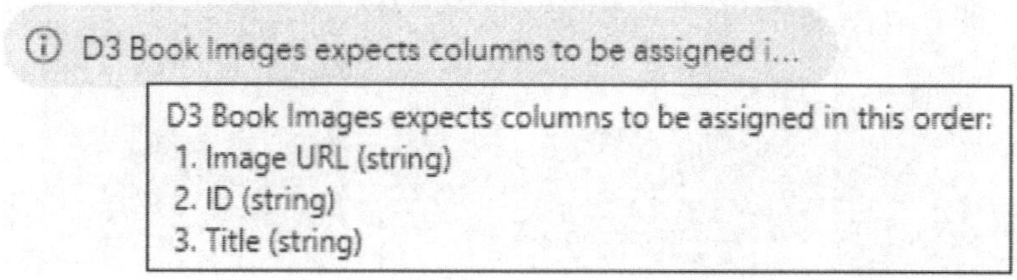

ⓘ D3 Book Images expects columns to be assigned i...

D3 Book Images expects columns to be assigned in this order:
1. Image URL (string)
2. ID (string)
3. Title (string)

3. Because no data is being passed, the roles are not validated.
4. The visualization sends an instructional message to SAS Visual Analytics with details about the required roles.
5. Processing stops.

Adding the required data (in the specified order) to the Roles pane displays all book cover images in a grid. (See Figure 8.15.)

1. SAS Visual Analytics sends the visualization a data message (as a JSON object).
2. The code concludes that the data items are valid, so it restructures the data set.
3. The code checks the div element and finds it to be empty, so the drawElements function executes, creates a grid, adds a g element for each book, adds the image of each book cover to the visualization, and adds a tooltip that displays the title of the book.

Notice that the data contains more books than can fit on the current view of the screen, so a scroll bar is automatically added to scroll through the images. (The layout and the scroll bar were all added courtesy of the CSS code that creates the grid.)

Note: This example cannot be viewed in the Web content object because that object is rendered in an iFrame. In the next example, you see how to display sample data if the visualization is rendered in an iFrame, but no data is being passed to the visualization.

Figure 8.15: Viewing Book Images in a Grid

Example: Using a Visualization as the Target of an Action

Suppose the data sent to the third-party visualization is updated. This data update can come from an applied filter (such as a data filter, a basic or advanced filter, or a filter action), page or report prompts, or a rank. Because the previous code did not specify any actions for the updateElements function, the visualization doesn't change. In most cases, you want your third-party visualization to be dynamic and participate in actions. In this example, you see how to modify the code so that the visualization updates when the data dynamically updates in the report. (See https://github.com/idig007/Visual-Analytics-Examples/blob/main/samples/Target.html to view the code for this example.)

Using Sample Data when No Data Is Available

In the previous example, the code checked to see whether the visualization was being displayed in an iFrame (outside of SAS Visual Analytics). If the visualization wasn't in an iFrame, the code used sample data to display the visualization. By updating the logic, you can also use sample data if no data is being supplied from SAS Visual Analytics. (See Program 8.19.) This enables the visualization to be viewed using the Web content object (which uses an iFrame but doesn't pass data).

Program 8.19: Using Sample Data when No Data Is Available

```
// If not being rendered in iFrame (outside of VA) or if there is
// no data, render with sample data
if (!inIframe() || !DATA) {
  onDataReceived(SAMPLE_MESSAGE);
}
```

Updating the Visualization

The updateElements function redraws the visualization on a data change. Specifically, it selects all g elements in the visualization (remember, these elements were created for each book image) and either updates those elements (if the data changed), adds more elements (if more data is being displayed, like when a filter is removed), or removes elements (if less data is being displayed, like when a filter is applied).

The .enter() method identifies any elements that need to be added to the DOM when the data being passed from SAS Visual Analytics is longer than the current number of elements being displayed in the visualization. This function is usually followed by the .append() method, which adds elements to the DOM.

The .exit() method, on the other hand, identifies any elements that need to be removed from the DOM when the data being passed from SAS Visual Analytics is shorter than the current number of elements being displayed in the visualization. This function is usually followed by the .remove() method, which removes elements from the DOM. (See Program 8.20.)

Program 8.20: Updating Elements on a Data Change

```
// Redraw data-dependent elements on data change
function updateElements() {

   // Change in data (no enter or exit images)
   BOOK=d3.select('#grid')
          .selectAll('g')
          .data(DATA, function(d) {
              return d.id;
              });

   // Enter/Update images
   BOOK.enter()
       .append('g')
       .append('svg')
       .append("svg:image")
         .classed('book-image', true)
         .attr('xlink:href', function(d) {
           return d.image_url;
           })
       .append('title')
         .text(function(d) {
           return d.title;
           });

   // Exit images
   BOOK.exit()
       .remove();
}
```

Notice that the image is given a class of 'book-image' so that it uses the CSS properties to display that element.

Viewing in SAS Visual Analytics

Now that sample data is displayed when the visualization is viewed outside of an iFrame or if no data is being passed to the visualization, it can be viewed in a Web content object. In this case, the following actions occur:

1. The code checks if the visualization is being displayed in an iFrame or if no data is being passed to the visualization. No data is being passed, so sample data is used.

2. The sample data is determined to be valid, so the data is restructured.
3. Because no data is being passed, the roles are not validated.
4. The code checks the div element and finds it to be empty, so the drawElements function executes, creates a grid, adds a g element for each book, adds the image of each book cover to the visualization, and adds a tooltip that displays the title of the book.

In addition, sample data is also displayed when no data is assigned to the Data-driven content object. (See Figure 8.16.)

When the data-driven content is added to the report, filtering for a range of ratings using the page prompt (books with an average rating of 3.1) updates the visualization and shows the covers for the three books with an average rating of 3.1. (See Figure 8.17.) The following actions occur:

1. SAS Visual Analytics sends the visualization a data message (as a JSON object).
2. The code concludes that the data items are valid, so it restructures the data set.
3. The code checks the div element and finds it not to be empty. Because sample data is being displayed when no data is passed, the sample data creates the div element in the visualization.
4. The updateElements function executes, updates the g elements with the available data, and checks to see whether the number of g elements in the visualization (five from the sample data) matches the number of rows being passed to the visualization (three).
5. Because there are fewer rows being passed from SAS Visual Analytics than the number of g elements available, the .exit() method removes additional g elements from the visualization. Three g elements remain after the filter is applied.

Figure 8.16: Viewing Sample Data when No Data Is Assigned

Figure 8.17: Viewing Images for Books with an Average Rating of 3.1

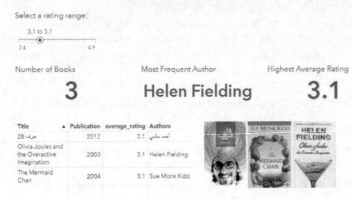

Adding a filter action from the list table to the data-driven content enables you to select a book in the list table (**The Mermaid Chair**) to show the cover for only that book in the visualization (the .exit() method in action!). The following actions occur:

1. SAS Visual Analytics sends the visualization a new data message (as a JSON object).
2. The code concludes that the data items are valid, so it restructures the data set.
3. The code checks the div element and finds that it's not empty because the visualization has previously been rendered.
4. The updateElements function executes, updates the g elements with the available data, and checks to see whether the number of g elements in the visualization (three) matches the number of rows being passed to the visualization (one).
5. Because there are fewer rows being passed from SAS Visual Analytics than the number of g elements available, the .exit() method removes additional g elements from the visualization. One g element remains after the filter is applied.

Deselecting a book in the list table shows covers for all books with a 3.1 average rating (the .enter() method in action!). The following actions occur:

1. SAS Visual Analytics sends the visualization a new data message (as a JSON object).
2. The code concludes that the data items are valid, so it restructures the data set.
3. The code checks the div element and finds that it's not empty because the visualization has previously been rendered.
4. The updateElements function executes, updates the g elements with the available data, and checks to see whether the number of g elements in the visualization (one) matches the number of rows being passed to the visualization (three).
5. Because there are more rows being passed from SAS Visual Analytics than the number of g elements available, the .enter() method adds additional g elements to the visualization. The visualization now contains three g elements.

Example: Highlighting Selected Values in the Visualization

The previous example explored how to use the visualization as the target of a filter action, but what if you want the visualization to be the target of a linked selection action? That is, you want to highlight the selected book in the list of books instead of filtering the visualization. This is where the additional column passed in the data message from SAS Visual Analytics can be used. Remember, in Example: Creating a Visualization, an additional column (**brushed**) was defined from the JSON object passed from SAS Visual Analytics to the third-party visualization.

In this example, you use **brushed**, along with CSS styles and additional logic, to highlight a selected book in the visualization. (See https://github.com/idig007/Visual-Analytics-Examples/blob/main/samples/Highlighting.html to view the code for this example.)

Updating CSS Styles

When a book is selected in the list table, you want the selected book to stand out in some way. You can use CSS styles to define what a selected book will look like in the visualization. In this case, a solid red line (of 5 pixels wide) is added around the border of the image. (See Program 8.21.)

Program 8.21: Defining Styles for Brushing

```
/* Define styles for brushing */
.brushed{
  border: 5px solid red;
}
```

Applying CSS Styles

In addition to specifying the appearance of the selected book, you also need to specify when that action will occur. Specifically, you want a cover image to be highlighted when the book is selected in the list table (that is, **brushed** has a value of 1, or true).

You can use the .classed() method to set the class of the g element in the DOM when **brushed** is true. This needs to be done within both the drawElements function (when the visualization is initially created, see Program 8.22) and the updateElements function (when the data is updated and when new data is added to the visualization, see Program 8.23).

Note: The code displayed below shows only the changes made to the drawElements function. To see all the code for the drawElements function, see Appendix B: Working with Data-Driven Content or the code sample in the GitHub repository.

Program 8.22: Using the .classed() Method: drawElements

```
//Adds g for each book
BOOK=GRID.selectAll('g')
        .data(DATA, function(d) {
          return d.id
        })
        .enter()
        .append('g')
          .classed('brushed', function(d) {
            return d.brushed;
          });
```

In the updateElements function, you also need to remove the brushed class for any exiting elements. (See Program 8.23.)

Program 8.23: Using the .classed() Method: updateElements

```
// Change in data (no enter or exit images)
BOOK=d3.select('#grid')
        .selectAll('g')
        .data(DATA, function(d) {
          return d.id;
        })
          .classed('brushed', function(d) {
            return d.brushed;
          });


// Enter/Update images
BOOK.enter()
    .append('g')
        .classed('brushed', function(d) {
          return d.brushed;
        })
    .append('svg')
    .append("svg:image")
      .classed('book-image', true)
      .attr('xlink:href', function(d) {
        return d.image_url;
      })
    .append('title')
      .text(function(d) {
        return d.title;
      });

// Exit images
BOOK.exit()
        .classed('brushed', false)
    .remove();
}
```

Viewing in SAS Visual Analytics

Changing the filter action from the list table to the data-driven content to a linked selection action enables you to select a book in the list table (*Olivia Joules and the Overactive Imagination*) and highlight the book cover in the visualization. (See Figure 8.18.) The following actions occur:

1. SAS Visual Analytics sends the visualization a new data message (as a JSON object). This data message sets **brushed** to 1 for the selected book (*Olivia Joules and the Overactive Imagination*) and to 0 for all other books.
2. The code concludes that the data items are valid, so it restructures the data set.
3. The code checks the div element and finds that it's not empty because the visualization has previously been rendered.
4. The updateElements function executes and updates the g elements with the available data.
5. Any rows that have a 1 for **brushed** are given a class of 'brushed'.
6. CSS styles are applied to any elements with a class of 'brushed', and those elements are highlighted with a red border.

Deselecting a book in the list table removes the highlighting in the visualization, as follows:

1. SAS Visual Analytics sends the visualization a new data message (as a JSON object). This data message sets **brushed** to 0 for all books (because no book is selected).
2. The code concludes that the data items are valid, so it restructures the data set.
3. The code checks the div element and finds that it's not empty because the visualization has previously been rendered.
4. The updateElements function executes and updates the g elements with the available data.

Figure 8.18: Highlighting a Book Cover Image

Select a rating range:

3.1 to 3.1

2.4   4.9

Number of Books	Most Frequent Author	Highest Average Rating
3	**Helen Fielding**	**3.1**

Title	Publication ▲	average_rating	Authors
حرف 28	2012	3.1	أحمد حلمي
Olivia Joules and the Overactive Imagination	2003	3.1	Helen Fielding
The Mermaid Chair	2004	3.1	Sue Monk Kidd

5. All rows are found to have a 0 for **brushed**, so no items are given a class of 'brushed' and all books are displayed in the default manner.

Example: Using a Visualization as the Source of an Action

For the final example, you update the visualization so that it can be used as the source of an action. You'll be able to select a book cover in the visualization and see details only for the selected book in the list table (a filter action) or see the selected book highlighted in the list table (a linked selection action).

To do this, you add CSS styles and two functions: one to deselect all elements when the body element of the visualization is clicked and one to select elements when an image is clicked in the visualization. (See https://github.com/idig007/Visual-Analytics-Examples/blob/main/samples/Source.html to view the code for this example.)

Updating CSS Styles

When a book is selected in the visualization, you want the book to be highlighted in some way. You can use CSS styles to define what that highlight action will look like. In this case, a solid blue line (of 5 pixels wide) is added around the border of the image. (See Program 8.24.)

Program 8.24: Defining Styles for Selecting an Image

```
/* Define styles for selecting an image */
.selectable.selected {
  border: 5px solid blue;
}
```

Deselecting All Elements

As users begin to select elements in the visualization, you want them to be able to clear their selections (by deselecting all book images). For this example, when the user clicks anywhere in the div element, all previously selected book images are deselected. The .on() method specifies what happens when the user clicks in the div area: The deselectAllElements function executes. (See Program 8.25.)

Program 8.25: Deselecting All Elements

```
//Creates a grid
GRID=d3.select('body')
      .append('div')
```

```
.attr('id','grid')
.attr('class','grid')
.on('click', deselectAllElements);
```

The deselectAllElements function changes the class of all elements in the visualization with a class of "selectable" and "brushed" to false, so it deselects all brushed or highlighted elements. (See Program 8.26.) Then it sends a message back to SAS Visual Analytics that no elements are selected (so the target of the action is updated to either show all data when using a filter action or to highlight no data when using a linked selection action).

Program 8.26: deselectAllElements Function

```
// Deselect all on body click
function deselectAllElements() {
  // Deselect all elements
  d3.selectAll(".selectable").classed("brushed", false);

  // Post message to VA that no elements are selected
  va.messagingUtil.postSelectionMessage(VA_RESULT_NAME, []);
}
```

Applying CSS Styles to Selected Elements

To enable users to select an element in the visualization, you need to change the class of elements that will be selectable. In this case, all g elements in the visualization will be selectable. (That is, the user can click on them, and they will be highlighted in blue.) In addition, on a click, the selectElement function executes. (See Program 8.27 and Program 8.28.)

Note: The code displayed below shows only the changes made to the drawElements function. To see all the code for the drawElements function, see Appendix B: Working with Data-Driven Content or the code sample in the GitHub repository.

Program 8.27: Applying CSS Styles to Selected Elements (drawElements)

```
//Adds g for each book
BOOK=GRID.selectAll('g')
        .data(DATA, function(d) {
            return d.id
        })
        .enter()
        .append('g')
          .attr('id','book')
          .classed('selectable', true)
          .classed('brushed', function(d) {
              return d.brushed;
          })
          .on('click', selectElement);
```

Note: The code displayed below shows only the changes made to the updateElements function. To see all the code for the updateElements function, see Appendix B: Working with Data-Driven Content or the code sample in the GitHub repository.

Program 8.28: Applying CSS Styles to Selected Elements (updateElements)

```
// Change in data (no enter or exit images)
BOOK=d3.select('#grid')
       .selectAll('g')
       .data(DATA, function(d) {
          return d.id;
       })
       .classed('selectable', true)
       .classed('brushed', function(d) {
          return d.brushed;
       })
       .on('click', selectElement);

// Enter/Update images
BOOK.enter()
    .append('g')
       .classed('selectable', true)
       .classed('brushed', function(d) {
          return d.brushed;
       })
       .on('click', selectElement)
    .append('svg')
    .append("svg:image")
       .classed('book-image', true)
       .attr('xlink:href', function(d) {
          return d.image_url;
       })
    .append('title')
       .text(function(d) {
          return d.title;
       });
```

The selectElement function uses the event.stopPropagation() function to prevent a selection in the g element from propagating to other elements in the DOM (like the div, which would trigger the deselectAllElements function).

The IF statement checks to see whether the Ctrl key on the keyboard is held down on the click (for multi-selections). If it is held down, the existing array is preserved. (That is, all existing elements with a class of "brushed" do not change.) If it is not held down, then the existing array is wiped clean and only the selected element is passed to the array (given a class of "brushed").

Finally, an array of all selected elements is created, along with the indexes of the selected elements, and sent back to SAS Visual Analytics so that the action can complete. (See Program 8.29.)

Program 8.29: selectElement Function

```
// Handle selection on element
function selectElement() {
  // Prevent event from falling through to underlying elements
  event.stopPropagation();

  // If control is held toggle selected on click preserving array,
  // otherwise select only clicked element
  if (event.ctrlKey) {
    // Toggle selection on clicked element
    d3.select(this)
        .classed("brushed", !d3.select(this).classed("brushed"));
  } else {
    // Deselect all elements
    d3.selectAll(".selectable")
        .classed("brushed", false);

    // Select clicked element
    d3.select(this)
        .classed("brushed", true);
  }

  // Build array of selected elements
  const selections = [];
  d3.selectAll(".selectable")
    .each(function(d) {
      if (d3.select(this).classed("brushed")) {
        selections.push({ row: d.index });
      }
    });

  // Post message to VA
  va.messagingUtil.postSelectionMessage(VA_RESULT_NAME,
      selections);
}
```

Viewing in SAS Visual Analytics

Changing the linked selection action from the data-driven content to the list table to a filter action enables you to select a book cover in the visualization (*The Mermaid Chair*) and filter the list table. (See Figure 8.19.) The following actions occur:

1. SAS Visual Analytics sends the visualization a new data message (as a JSON object).
2. The code concludes that the data items are valid, so it restructures the data set.
3. The code checks the div element and finds that it's not empty because the visualization has previously been rendered.
4. The updateElements function executes, updates the g elements with the available data, and gives all elements a class of "selectable".
5. On the click action, the selectElement function executes and sets the class of the selected element to "brushed".

6. CSS styles are applied to any elements with a class of "brushed" and "selectable", and those elements are highlighted with a blue border.
7. All elements that have a class of "selectable" and "brushed" are added to an array called **selections**.
Note: If the user holds down the Ctrl key and selects other covers in the visualization, the **selections** array is updated to add the newly selected elements.
8. The visualization sends a message that contains the list of selected elements and their indexes back to SAS Visual Analytics.
9. SAS Visual Analytics updates the data in the list table to display only the selected rows.

Additional Considerations

The examples explored in this chapter use URL links in a data source to display images with a third-party visualization. This is a relatively simple example because the images don't require any axes to display the data and the grid handles the layout when a resize event occurs (that is, when the window or the Data-driven content object itself is resized). In many cases, you'll need to extend your code to create axes and account for resize events.

Handling Axes

When your data needs to be displayed with a series of axes (like for a bar chart, a line chart, or a steam graph), you need to extend the code to do the following when the chart is initialized:

- Calculate the scale (or bounds) for each axis using the data values passed to the visualization.
- Create an axis element that uses the scale to show increments of data values.
- Add elements to the DOM to represent each set of axes.

In addition, every time that the data changes, you need to repeat those steps to ensure that no data falls out of bounds and is not viewable within the chart. For more details about how this is done, see https://github.com/sassoftware/sas-visualanalytics-thirdpartyvisualizations/blob/master/samples/D3Thursday/3_Dynamic_Bar.html on the SAS GibHub page.

Managing Resize Events

You'll also want to add code that listens for a resize event and redraws the elements of the chart when that resize occurs. The setupResizeListener function (in the contentUtil.js utility) sets a callback function (in our example, drawElements) to handle window resizing events. This means that anytime the window is resized, the visualization is redrawn to fit within the new size. This is one of the reasons the CSS styles for the object are set to span the entire width (100%) and height (100%) of the available space. The chart should always be displayed so that it fits entirely within the size of the window.

Figure 8.19: Filtering the List of Books

Select a rating range:

3.1 to 3.1

2.4   4.9

Number of Books	Most Frequent Author	Highest Average Rating
3	**Helen Fielding**	**3.1**

Title	▲ Publication	average_rating	Autho
The Mermaid Chair	2004	3.1	Sue M

Saving URL Mappings

Once you've created your own third-party visualizations, you probably want others in your organization to use them. Administrators can save URL mappings for third-party visualizations so that the URLs can easily be selected in the Options pane. To save a URL mapping, do the following:

❶ Click the **More** icon for the report and select **Edit administration settings**. (See Figure 8.20.)
❷ Select **Data Driven Content** in the left pane of the Administration Settings window.
❸ Click **New**.
❹ Specify a nickname for your third-party visualization.
❺ Enter the URL for the third-party visualization.

This will save you (and your colleagues) from hunting down the URL for all the awesome visualizations that you'll be creating!

Figure 8.20: Saving URL Mappings

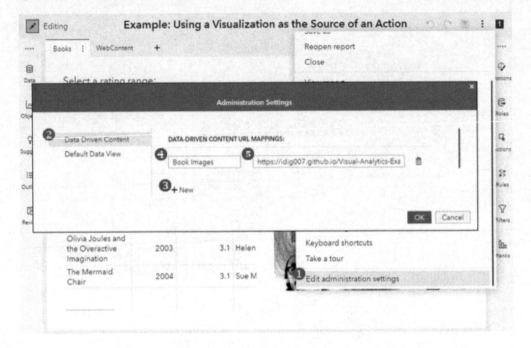

Chapter 9: Working with Jobs in SAS Visual Analytics

Introduction

SAS Visual Analytics is extremely versatile. Not only can you perform data manipulation and transformation from within the application, but you can also enhance your reports and extend the functionality of SAS Visual Analytics with SAS Viya jobs. A SAS Viya job is a SAS program combined with a job definition. This means that anything you can code in SAS, you can add to your report. With SAS code you can transform data, perform complex calculations, generate charts, and add data to, update data in, or delete data from tables.

Note: In SAS Visual Analytics 7.5 on SAS®9, stored processes can be created to extend your reports using SAS code and provide equivalent functionality as SAS Viya jobs. SAS Viya 3.5 introduced preliminary support for promoting stored processes to jobs in SAS Viya. For more information about promoting stored processes to SAS Viya, see "Jobs: Stored processes in Viya" by Gerry Nelson in SAS Blogs.

SAS Viya jobs can be created using either the Job Execution Web Application (which can be accessed through the following URL: http://your-server-name/SASJobExecution) or, starting with SAS Viya 3.5, through SAS Studio, which is the preferred application for programming in SAS Viya. Once jobs are created, they are executed on the SAS Compute Server through the SAS Launcher Server. For this chapter, SAS Studio is used exclusively to create, execute, and test jobs. Jobs can be executed through a web page (outside of SAS Studio) and from within a SAS Visual Analytics report.

Note: You can write SAS code that can execute in CAS, but you need to use CAS-enabled PROC and DATA steps in your code or write your own CASL (or CAS language) code.

To create a job, follow four simple steps:

1. Create the SAS program.
2. Create the job definition.
3. Create the job form.
4. Execute and test.

Note: Before creating jobs, it might be helpful to have some SAS coding experience, some experience with HTML (to create HTML forms), and some experience with SAS prompting (to create job prompts).

Step 1: Create the SAS Program

Before working with jobs, it's a good idea to start with a working SAS program that accomplishes the tasks that you want the job to perform. For example, if you want a job to display some type of output in SAS Visual Analytics, it's easier to start with simple SAS code that creates the output. The code should use hardcoded values (instead of parameters) and be free of errors.

Step 2: Create the Job Definition

Next, create a job definition in SAS Studio. The job definition contains the SAS code to execute when the job is called. Jobs created in SAS Studio automatically start with the **%JESBEGIN** macro and end with the **%JESEND** macro, and they produce HTML output by default.

The job definition can also contain default parameters and user-defined parameters that can be populated when the job is called.

By default, two parameters are available in the job definition: **_contextName** and **_action**. **_contextName** specifies the compute service context name, and **_action** specifies the actions that the job takes when executed. The **_action** parameter supports the following values: (See Table 9.1.)

Step 3: Create the Job Form

Next you can associate a job form with the job definition. Two types of forms are available: HTML form or task prompt. Both forms enable the user to specify values for parameters that need to be passed to the SAS code. The HTML form is created using HTML code, and the task prompt is

Table 9.1: Values for the _action Parameter

Value	Description
background	Executes the job in the background.
execute	Executes the job.
form	Displays an HTML input form stored in the folder structure before job execution.
Json	Returns a list of unexpired jobs or sample jobs in JSON format.
lastjob	Displays output from a previous job execution if it has not yet expired.
prompts	Displays a prompt form stored in the folder structure before job execution.
schedule	Indicates that a job is to be scheduled using SAS Environment Manager.
wait	Displays a wait screen with information text while the job is executing.

Figure 9.1: Associating an Existing Form with a Job

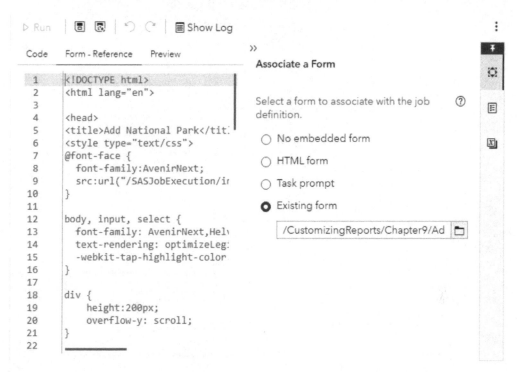

created using the common task model (CTM). The benefit of using a task prompt is that you can use values from a table to populate the choices presented to the user. For the HTML form, you would need to hardcode the values. In addition, the task prompt can be used to create cascading prompts, in which a selection in one prompt updates values in the next prompt.

Job forms can be embedded in the job definition or exist as separate files (which would be useful if you want to use the same form for many job definitions). When job forms are in separate files, the job looks for forms stored in the same folder that have the same name as the job definition. If your form has a different name (or is stored in a different location), you can use the Associate a form pane in the job definition to point to the existing form (see Figure 9.1) or use the **_form** parameter when executing the job.

Finally, to ensure that the forms are displayed when the job is called, the **_action** parameter should have a value of **form** (for an HTML form) or **prompts** (for a task prompt).

Step 4: Execute and Test

To execute a job, you need the job submit URL. This can be found at the bottom of the Properties pane in the job definition. (See Figure 9.2.)

Figure 9.2: Locating the Job Submit URL

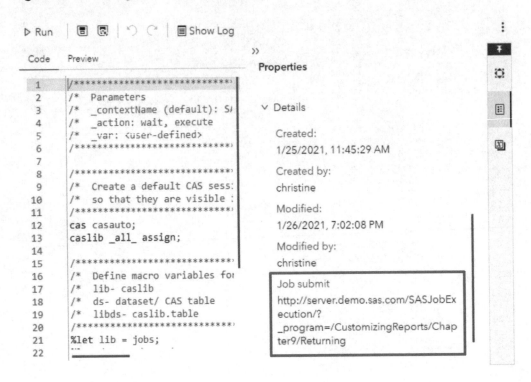

To test the job, do one of the following:

- Run the job definition in SAS Studio. This works only if parameter values are not required for the job to execute.
- Execute the job using direct URL access. By entering the job submit URL in your web browser (followed by a list of name/value pairs for the required parameters in the form *&parameter-name=parameter-value*), you can verify that the job can be executed outside of SAS Studio.
  Note: Jobs with defined job forms can be executed by simply entering the job submit URL in the web browser. The job form is displayed, and the user can specify values for any required parameters.
- Execute the job in SAS Visual Analytics. Jobs can be referenced via embedded links in a Text object, using the Web content object, using the Data-driven content object, or by adding a URL link to an object.
  Note: Starting in SAS Visual Analytics 2020.1.5 (April 2021), a new Job content object is available. This object enables you to display the output from SAS Viya jobs like the Web content object.

Example: Returning SAS Results

For this example, you want to display SAS output in a report. Specifically, you would like to run the UNIVARIATE procedure on data items used in forecasting. This enables users to see moments, basic statistical measures, tests for location, quantiles, extreme observations, and missing values for the selected measure, which can help with building forecasts and models.

The report currently contains a forecast of order totals with various cost measures added as possible underlying factors: order distribution cost, order marketing cost, order product cost, and order sales cost. Currently, only order marketing cost has been identified as a contributing factor. (See Figure 9.3.)

You create a hyperlink (in a Text object) to call the job and display the descriptive information for the selected measure.

Step 1: Create the SAS Program

The SAS program executes PROC UNIVARIATE on a CAS table (**jobs.orders43k**). This program accepts one parameter (**_var**) that references the selected variable used in PROC UNIVARIATE. This value is eventually passed to the job on execution. Notice that, in the SAS program, the **_var** parameter is hardcoded to **orderproductcost**. This ensures that the program runs.

Because the program references a CAS table, the program must create a default CAS session and create SAS librefs for existing caslibs. This makes caslibs visible in the SAS Studio Libraries tree and makes them available for the program. (See Program 9.1.)

Figure 9.3: Forecasting Order Totals

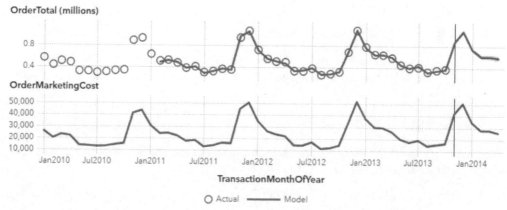

v About this forecast

- 95% forecast confidence.
- The forecast for OrderTotal has the following contributing factor(s): OrderMarketingCost

Program 9.1: Displaying PROC UNIVARIATE Results

```
/*********************************************************************/
/*  Create a default CAS session and create SAS librefs for        */
/*  existing caslibs so that they are visible in the SAS Studio     */
/*  Libraries tree.                                                 */
/*********************************************************************/

cas casauto;
caslib _all_ assign;


/*********************************************************************/
/*  Define macro variables for:                                     */
/*  lib- caslib                                                     */
/*  ds- dataset/ CAS table                                          */
/*  libds- caslib.table                                             */
/*********************************************************************/

%let lib = jobs;
%let ds = orders43k;
%let libds = &lib..&ds.;

%let _var=orderproductcost;


/*********************************************************************/
/*  Execute PROC UNIVARIATE with selected variable                 */
/*********************************************************************/

proc univariate data=&libds.;
     var &_var.;
run;
```

Note: Macro variables are used for the caslib, the data set, and the table reference so that they can be easily modified for an environment with different caslibs and table names.

Step 2: Create the Job Definition

Next create a job definition using the SAS program. To create a job definition in SAS Studio, select **New → Job → Definition**. (See Figure 9.4.)

Figure 9.4: Creating a Job Definition

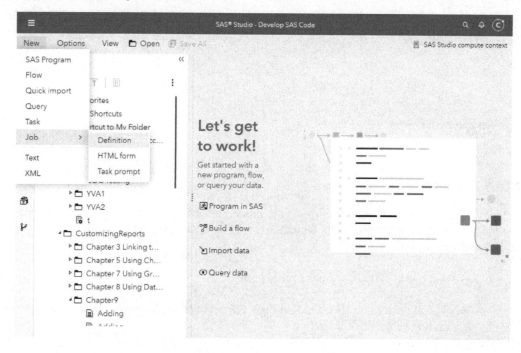

Enter the code (minus the %LET statement for **_var**) on the Code tab and specify parameters for the job in the Parameters pane.

The following parameters should be listed, with the specified type and default values: (See Table 9.2.)

The **_action** parameter instructs the job to display a "Please wait" message while executing. (See Figure 9.5.)

The **_var** parameter is the value that the user specifies for the PROC UNIVARIATE step.

Step 3: Create the Job Form

For this example, a job form is not needed.

Table 9.2: Parameters for Returning SAS Results

Name	Field type	Default value	Required
_contextName	Character	SAS Studio compute context	No
_action	Character	wait,execute	No
_var	Character	<none>	Yes

Figure 9.5: Message Displayed while Job Executes

Please wait...

Step 4: Execute and Test

Before adding the job to the SAS Visual Analytics report, test it in the web browser by specifying the Job submit URL and appending **&_var=OrderTotal**. The PROC UNIVARIATE output for **OrderTotal** is displayed.

Finally, add a text object with a hyperlink to the report:

❶ From the Objects pane, drag the **Text** object (from the Content group) to the right of the **Forecasting** object. (See Figure 9.6.)

Figure 9.6: Adding a Text Object with a Hyperlink

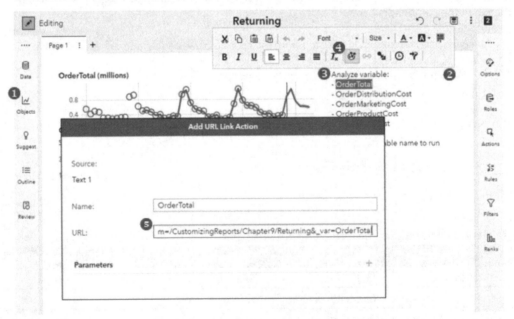

❷ Double-click in the Text object to add text.
❸ Enter text that contains a list of variables and instructions for accessing SAS output.
❹ Highlight each variable name and click **Add URL link** on the font formatting toolbar.
❺ In the **URL** field, specify the job submit URL and append **&_var=** for the specified variable. Repeat for each variable.

The viewer can now click one of the hyperlinks in the text object to see the results of the job on a separate browser tab.

Example: Returning SAS Results Using an HTML Form

In the previous example, the SAS output was displayed on a separate tab in the browser. For this example, you want to display SAS output within the report. You create an HTML form so that the viewer can select a variable, submit the job, and see the output all displayed within the report.

The report currently contains a forecast of order totals with various cost measures added as possible underlying factors: order distribution cost, order marketing cost, order product cost, and order sales cost. Currently, only the order marketing cost has been identified as a contributing factor.

You use a Web content object to call the job and display the descriptive information for the selected measure in the report.

Step 1: Create the SAS Program

This example uses the same SAS program from the previous example.

Step 2: Create the Job Definition

The code for the job definition is the same as before with one minor addition added before the PROC UNIVARIATE step. (See Program 9.2.)

Program 9.2: Adding a Footnote with a Link

```
footnote '<a href= "/SASJobExecution/?_program=/CustomizingReports/Chapter9/
Returning_HTML"> Click here to pick a different variable</a>';
```

This generates a link below the output that enables viewers to reload the form so that they can resubmit the form multiple times.

Then update the **_action** parameter in the Parameters pane to have the default values of **form,wait,execute**. This instructs the job to display a form. After the form is submitted, the job displays a "Please wait" message while the job executes.

Figure 9.7: Creating an Embedded HTML Form

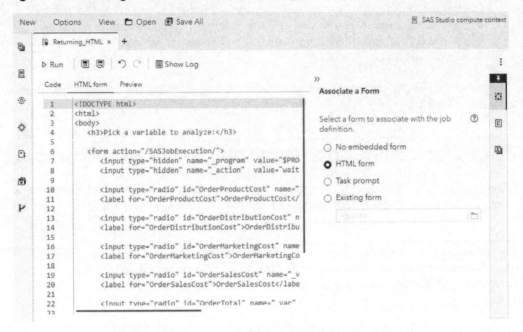

Step 3: Create the Job Form

For this example, you want to create an embedded HTML form. On the Properties tab, select **HTML form**, and an HTML form tab appears in the job definition. (See Figure 9.7.) This is where you enter the HTML code to generate the form.

On the HTML form tab, enter HTML code to create the form. (See Program 9.3.)

Program 9.3: Creating the HTML Form

```
<!DOCTYPE html>
<html>
<body>
    <h3>Pick a variable to analyze:</h3>

    <form action="/SASJobExecution/">
        <input type="hidden" name="_program" value="$PROGRAM$">
        <input type="hidden" name="_action"  value="wait,execute">

        <input type="radio" id="OrderProductCost" name="_var"
            value="OrderProductCost">
        <label for="OrderProductCost">OrderProductCost</label><br>

        <input type="radio" id="OrderDistributionCost" name="_var"
```

```
                value="OrderDistributionCost">
        <label for="OrderDistributionCost">OrderDistributionCost
            </label><br>

        <input type="radio" id="OrderMarketingCost" name="_var"
            value="OrderMarketingCost">
        <label for="OrderMarketingCost">OrderMarketingCost
            </label><br>

        <input type="radio" id="OrderSalesCost" name="_var"
            value="OrderSalesCost">
        <label for="OrderSalesCost">OrderSalesCost</label><br>

        <input type="radio" id="OrderTotal" name="_var"
            value="OrderTotal">
        <label for="OrderTotal">OrderTotal</label><br><br>

        <input type="submit" value="Analyze Variable">
    </form>
</body>
</html>
```

This code creates a form with radio buttons for each measure: **OrderProductCost**, **OrderDistributionCost**, **OrderMarketingCost**, **OrderSalesCost**, and **OrderTotal**.

For the **action** attribute of the form tab, you must specify **/SASJobExecution/**. This indicates that the form data is submitted to the SAS Job Execution Web Application for processing. In addition, you can specify **_tab** for the **target** attribute (of the form tab) if you want the output to appear in a new tab within the application. In this case, you want the output to be displayed directly in the Web content object in SAS Visual Analytics, so this attribute is omitted.

The first input tag specifies that a non-visual object named **_program** has a value of **$PROGRAM$**. When the HTML input form is displayed, the path and name of the job are substituted for this value. This is also how you specify macro variable values in the HTML input form.

The second input tag specifies **wait,execute** for the **_action** parameter, which overrides the default value specified for the job. It displays a "Please wait" message as it executes the job.

The next five input tags specify the type of selector used (**radio**), the ID for each input, the parameter that's populated when that option is selected (**_var**), and a label for each radio button.

The last input tag displays a button with the value **Analyze Variable**. When the viewer selects a value and clicks that button, the value is passed to the job using the specified parameter (**_var**).

Figure 9.8: Redirecting to the HTML Form

Extreme Observations			
Lowest		Highest	
Value	Obs	Value	Obs
0.0825552	14901	35.4785	40087
0.0851985	15113	35.5381	40044
0.1039164	39042	36.2255	39259
0.1068318	14654	37.0633	39867
0.1300603	37648	37.4927	38975

Click here to pick a different variable

Step 4: Execute and Test

Before adding the job to the SAS Visual Analytics report, test it in the web browser by specifying the Job submit URL. The HTML form is displayed. Select a variable and click **Analyze Variable** to see the PROC UNIVARIATE results. At the bottom of the output, a link appears that redirects the user back to the HTML form. (See Figure 9.8.)

Now add a Web content object to call the job in the report.

➊ From the Objects pane, drag the **Web content** object (from the Content group) to the right of the **Forecasting** object. (See Figure 9.9.)
➋ In the Options pane, enter the Job submit URL in the **URL** field.

The viewer can now select a variable to see the PROC UNIVARIATE results within the report.

Figure 9.9: Using a Web Content Object to Call a Job

Example: Adding Data to a Table

The next three examples enable the viewer to modify the CAS table by adding data to, updating data in, and deleting data from the table. The report currently contains a geo map that shows national park locations in the United States. (See Figure 9.10.) The table contains the name of the national park, the state (or states), the acreage, and location information (latitude and longitude values).

For this example, not all national parks are displayed. Specifically, four new national parks have been added since 2018 (Gateway Arch, Indiana Dunes, White Sands, and New River Gorge) and the table doesn't include national parks in outlying territories (American Samoa and the Virgin Islands).

You need to create a job that enables the viewer to add additional national parks to the table so that they appear on the map. You use a Web content object to call the job.

Step 1: Create the SAS Program

The SAS program creates a new CAS table in the **casuser** caslib that contains the information about the missing park: **ParkName**, **State**, **Acres**, **Latitude**, and **Longitude** (assigned through macro variables). The **casuser** caslib is your own private, global caslib that you can use to store personal data sources. For the next few examples, this caslib is used to store transitional data

Figure 9.10: Viewing US National Park Locations

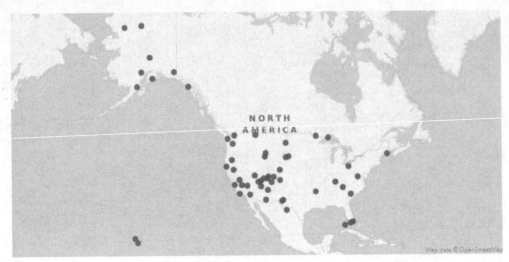

(that is, the data that the job will modify). In this case, the **casuser** caslib stores the new table that contains just the information for the missing park.

Then the information from the CAS table used in the report (**JOBS.NATIONAL_PARKS**) is appended to the missing park information.

Note: For the append action to work, the type and length of the columns in the *casuser* caslib must match the type and length of the columns in the CAS table used in the report. Notice that in the code, both **ParkName** and **State** are specified as varchar data items.

Finally, the CASUTIL procedure is used to drop the CAS table used in the report, promote the new table (stored in your **casuser** caslib), and save a permanent copy of the new table with the missing park information. (See Program 9.4.)

Program 9.4: Adding Data to a CAS Table

```
/*******************************************************************/
/*  Create a default CAS session and create SAS librefs for       */
/*  existing caslibs so that they are visible in the SAS Studio    */
/*  Libraries tree.                                                */

/*******************************************************************/

cas casauto;
caslib _all_ assign;
```

```
/******************************************************************/
/*  Define macro variables for:                               */
/*  lib- caslib                                               */
/*  ds- dataset/ CAS table                                    */
/*  libds- caslib.table                                       */
/******************************************************************/
%let lib = jobs;
%let ds = NATIONAL_PARKS;
%let libds = &lib..&ds.;

%let _name=Gateway Arch;
%let _state=mo;
%let _acres=193;
%let _lat=38.63;
%let _lon=-90.19;


/******************************************************************/
/*  Add new data to casuser.parks table                       */
/******************************************************************/
data casuser.&ds.;
        length ParkName varchar(46) State varchar(10) Acres Latitude
            Longitude 8.;
        ParkName="&_name.";
        State="&_state.";
        Acres=&_acres.;
        Latitude=&_lat.;

        Longitude=&_lon.;
run;


/******************************************************************/
/*  Append data from CAS to table with new data               */
/******************************************************************/
data casuser.&ds. (append=yes);
        set &libds.;
run;


/******************************************************************/
/*  Drop existing CAS table and add table with new data       */
/******************************************************************/
```

```
proc casutil;
      droptable incaslib="&lib." casdata="&ds.";
      promote incaslib="casuser" outcaslib="&lib." casdata="&ds.";
      save casdata="&ds." incaslib="&lib." outcaslib="&lib." replace;
run;
```

This program uses five parameters: **_name**, **_state**, **_acres**, **_lat**, and **_lon** (one for each data item in the **NATIONAL_PARKS** table). In this program, the values for those parameters are hardcoded with details about Gateway Arch. Eventually, the values for the missing parks are passed to the job on execution.

After this program is executed, Gateway Arch is added to the **NATIONAL_PARKS** table. To see the new park in the SAS Visual Analytics report, you need to reopen the report.

Note: An option can be set to periodically reload data when the report is viewed. This updates the data used for the report without the viewer needing to reopen the report. This option is discussed and set a bit later.

Step 2: Create the Job Definition

Next create the job definition. The code is the same as the SAS program minus the hardcoded values for the five input parameters (**_name**, **_state**, **_acres**, **_lat**, **_lon**) plus some additional code to display a success message and reload the form once the park has been added to the table.

To enable the reload, two new parameters (**url** and **reload_url**) have been created in the job. (See Program 9.5.)

Program 9.5: Creating New Parameters

```
%let url= %nrstr(/SASJobExecution/?_program=/CustomizingReports/Chapter9/
Adding);
%let reload_url="&url.";
```

The **url** macro variable uses the %nrstr function to mask special characters in the job submit URL from the macro processor. Notice that the link used is the relative job submit URL (found in the Properties pane for the job). Here, a relative URL is used, so this same job definition will work even if it's run on an environment with a different host. The **reload_url** macro variable surrounds the value with quotation marks.

Then, after the updated table is promoted, a DATA _NULL_ step is used in conjunction with the FILE _WEBOUT statement and HTML code to display a success message and reload the form. The **setTimeout** method reloads the URL after 2500 ms, or 2.5 seconds. (See Program 9.6.)

Program 9.6: Displaying Success Message and Reloading Form

```
/******************************************************************/
/*  Display success message and reload form                      */
/******************************************************************/

data _null_;

file _webout;
put '
<!DOCTYPE html>
<html lang="en">

<head>
<title>Add New Park</title>
<style type="text/css">
@font-face {
  font-family:AvenirNext;
  src:url("/SASJobExecution/images/AvenirNextforSAS.woff") format("woff");
}

body, input, select {
  font-family: AvenirNext,Helvetica,Arial,sans-serif;
  text-rendering: optimizeLegibility;
  -webkit-tap-highlight-color: rgba(0,0,0,0);
}

.pointer {
  cursor: pointer;
}

u {
      font-size: 15pt;
}
</style>
</head>

<body role="main">


<h1><center>';
put '
Successful!
</h1>
<h3><center>
Park named <u>
';
put "&_name.</u> has been added to the table";
put '
</h3>
```

```
<h5><center>
User entry form will automatically reload
</h5>


</body>
';
put '

<script>
    setTimeout(function(){
        window.location.href =
 ';
 put "%bquote(&reload_url)";
 put ';
    }, 2500);
</script>

</html>

';
run;
```

The job definition should also contain the following parameters: (See Table 9.3.)

The **_output_type** parameter is necessary for the success message to be displayed and for the reload to occur.

Step 3: Create the Job Form

For this example, you want to create an external HTML form. To create an external HTML form, select **New → Job → HTML form** in SAS Studio. (See Figure 9.11.)

Table 9.3: Parameters for Adding Data to a Table

Name	Field type	Default value	Required
_contextName	Character	SAS Studio compute context	No
_action	Character	form,wait,execute	No
_name	Character	<none>	Yes
_state	Character	<none>	Yes
_acres	Character	<none>	Yes
_lat	Character	<none>	Yes
_lon	Character	<none>	Yes
_output_type	Character	html	No

Figure 9.11: Creating an HTML Form

The form will contain the HTML code needed to generate the form displayed when the job is executed. This form presents text boxes for the viewer to enter the park name and the state, and number boxes for the viewer to enter the acres, latitude, and longitude. Notice that the latitude and longitude values have defined minimums and maximums so that a viewer cannot accidentally enter an invalid value. (See Program 9.7.)

Program 9.7: Creating the HTML Form for Adding Data

```
<!DOCTYPE html>
<html lang="en">

<head>
<title>Add National Park</title>
<style type="text/css">
@font-face {
  font-family:AvenirNext;
  src:url("/SASJobExecution/images/AvenirNextforSAS.woff") format("woff");
}

body, input, select {
  font-family: AvenirNext,Helvetica,Arial,sans-serif;
  text-rendering: optimizeLegibility;
  -webkit-tap-highlight-color: rgba(0,0,0,0);
}

div {
      height:200px;
      overflow-y: scroll;
}
```

```
.pointer {
  cursor: pointer;
  margin: 5px;
  font-size: 16px;
  padding: 10px 20px;
  background-color: #F7F7F7;
}

h1{
       font-size: 20pt;
       margin-bottom: 0px;
}

select {
       font-size: 16px;
}

</style>
</head>

<body role="main">
<center>

<h1>Add New Park</h1>

<form id="entry_form" action="/SASJobExecution/">
<input type="hidden" name="_program"      value="$PROGRAM$"/>
<input type="hidden" name="_action"       value="wait,execute"/>

<br/>
<table>
<tr>
       <td>Park Name: </td>
       <td>
       <input type="text" name="_name" required>
       </td>
</tr>
<tr>
       <td>State: </td>
       <td>
       <input type="text" name="_state" required>
       </td>
</tr>
<tr>
       <td>Acres: </td>
       <td>
       <input type="number" name="_acres" min="0" required>
       </td>
</tr>
<tr>
       <td>Latitude: </td>
```

```
      <td>
      <input type="number" name="_lat" min="-90" max="90" step="0.01"
required>
      </td>
</tr>
<tr>
      <td>Longitude: </td>
      <td>
      <input type="number" name="_lon" min="-180" max="180" step="0.01"
required>
      </td>
</tr>
</table>

<br/>

<button type="submit" class="pointer">Submit</button>

</form>

</center>
</body>

</html>
```

Remember, forms that have the same name and that are stored in the same location as the job definition are automatically displayed if the **_action** parameter for the job has a default value of **form**.

Step 4: Execute and Test

Before adding this job to the report, set the option to periodically reload data at the report level. To do this:

    ❶ In the Options pane, select the report. (See Figure 9.12.)
    ❷ In the General section, select **Periodically reload report data**.
    ❸ Specify **5 Seconds** as the time interval for reloads.

Note: This option can also be set at the page level or the object level. This option applies only when viewing the report. To see the reload happen, make sure that you are viewing the report before you add a new park.

Then add a **Web content** object (to the Add New Park page) that references the job. The HTML form is displayed and the details for the new park can be entered. (See Figure 9.13.)

Clicking **Submit** executes the job. As the job executes, a "Please wait" message is displayed. Upon completion, a success message appears (See Figure 9.14.), and the form automatically reloads.

Figure 9.12: Periodically Reloading Data

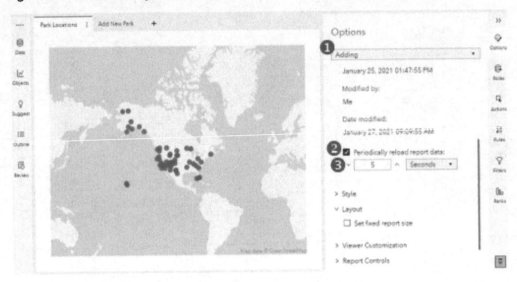

Figure 9.13: Adding a New Park

Add New Park

Park Name: | Indiana Dunes

State: | in

Acres: | 15349

Latitude: | 41.65

Longitude: | -87.05

Submit

Figure 9.14: Viewing the Success Message

Successful!

Park named <u>Indiana Dunes</u> has been added to the table

User entry form will automatically reload

The report automatically reloads the new data, and the park is displayed in the geo map.

Add the following parks to the CAS table using the job form: (See Table 9.4.)

Note: Some of these details are incorrect (the acreage of White Sands and the latitude of New River Gorge). These mistakes are fixed in the next example.

Example: Updating Data in a Table

In the previous example, you added details for six additional national parks. However, some of the data entered was incorrect (the acreage of White Sands and the latitude of New River Gorge). In fact, New River Gorge is currently displayed in Florida in the map instead of West Virginia. (See Figure 9.15.)

You can use a job to update this information. Specifically, you create a job that is called when double-clicking a park in the map. This job will show the current details for that park and enable you to modify details, submit them, and update the table. This is done using a URL link action from the geo map that calls the job.

Step 1: Create the SAS Program

The SAS program reads data from the CAS table used in the report (**JOBS.NATIONAL_PARKS**) and updates the data for the selected park using new values for each parameter, if entered. (See

Table 9.4: Details for Additional National Parks

ParkName	State	Acres	Latitude	Longitude
Indiana Dunes	in	15349	41.65	-87.05
White Sands	nm	1463	32.78	-106.17
New River Gorge	wv	7021	28.07	-81.08
American Samoa	as	8257	14.25	-170.68
Virgin Islands	vg	15053	18.33	-64.73

Figure 9.15: Viewing Incorrect Placement for New River Gorge

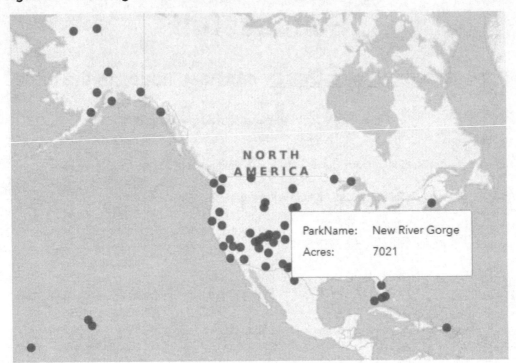

Program 9.8.) If new values are not entered for each parameter, then the existing information is retained. This updated data is saved in a new CAS table in the **casuser** caslib.

Then PROC CASUTIL is used to drop the CAS table used in the report, promote the updated table (stored in your **casuser** caslib), and save a permanent copy of the new table (with the updated park information).

Program 9.8: Updating Data in a CAS Table

```
/*****************************************************************/
/*  Create a default CAS session and create SAS librefs for     */
/*  existing caslibs so that they are visible in the SAS Studio  */
/*  Libraries tree.                                              */
/*****************************************************************/

cas casauto;
caslib _all_ assign;
```

```
/******************************************************************/
/*  Define macro variables for:                              */
/*  lib- caslib                                              */
/*  ds- dataset/ CAS table                                  */
/*  libds- caslib.table                                     */
/******************************************************************/
%let lib = jobs;
%let ds = NATIONAL_PARKS;
%let libds = &lib..&ds.;

%let _name=White Sands;
%let _state=nm;
%let _acres=146344;
%let _lat=32.78;
%let _lon=-106.17;

%let _name_o=White Sands;
%let _state_o=nm;
%let _acres_o=1463;
%let _lat_o=32.78;
%let _lon_o=-106.17;


/******************************************************************/
/*  Update data in casuser.parks table                       */
/******************************************************************/
data casuser.&ds.;
        set &libds.;
        if ParkName="&_name_o." and State="&_state_o." and Acres=&_acres_o.
           and Latitude=&_lat_o. and Longitude=&_lon_o. then do;

                if "&_name." = '' then ParkName = "&_name_o.";
                else ParkName = "&_name.";

                if "&_state."= '' then State="&_state_o.";
                else State="&_state.";

                if "&_acres." = "" then Acres="&_acres_o.";
                else Acres="&_acres.";

                if "&_lat." = "" then Latitude="&_lat_o.";
                else Latitude="&_lat.";

                if "&_lon." = "" then Longitude="&_lon_o.";
                else Longitude="&_lon.";
        end;
run;
```

```
/***************************************************************/
/*  Drop existing CAS table and add table with new data        */
/***************************************************************/
proc casutil;
       droptable incaslib="&lib." casdata="&ds.";
       promote incaslib="casuser" outcaslib="&lib." casdata="&ds.";
       save casdata="&ds." incaslib="&lib." outcaslib="&lib." replace;
run;
```

This program uses ten parameters: five to hold original values of each data item (those ending with **_o**) and five to hold new values for each data item. In this program, the values for those parameters are hardcoded with details about White Sands, including the correct acreage information. Eventually, the values for the updated parks are passed to the job on execution.

Note: The IF conditions check the values of the macro variables with new values. If a value is missing, the code sets the value of the data item to the original value. Otherwise, the code sets the value of the data item to the new value. Remember, macro variables are stored as strings, so the conditions check whether the resolved value of the macro variable (*"&_macro-var"*) is missing (*""*).

After this program is executed, White Sands is updated in the **NATIONAL_PARKS** table.

Step 2: Create the Job Definition

Next create the job definition. The code is the same as the SAS program minus the hardcoded values for the 10 input parameters, plus some additional code to display a success message once the park information has been updated. (See Program 9.9.)

After the table is updated, a DATA _NULL_ step is used in conjunction with the FILE _WEBOUT statement and HTML code to display a success message.

Program 9.9: Displaying a Success Message

```
/***************************************************************/
/*  Display success message                                    */
/***************************************************************/

data _null_;

file _webout;
put '
<!DOCTYPE html>
<html lang="en">

<head>
<title>Update Park Information</title>
```

```
<style type="text/css">
@font-face {
  font-family:AvenirNext;
  src:url("/SASJobExecution/images/AvenirNextforSAS.woff") format("woff");
}

body, input, select {
  font-family: AvenirNext,Helvetica,Arial,sans-serif;
  text-rendering: optimizeLegibility;
  -webkit-tap-highlight-color: rgba(0,0,0,0);
}

.pointer {
  cursor: pointer;
}

u {
      font-size: 15pt;
}
</style>
</head>

<body role="main">


<h1><center>';
put '
Successful!
</h1>
<h3><center>
';
put "The park information has been updated";
put '
</h3>

<h5><center>
Close this window to view updated results in the dashboard
</h5>


</body>

</html>

';
run;
```

The job definition should also contain the following parameters: (See Table 9.5.)

Remember, the **_output_type** parameter is necessary for the success message to be displayed after the job executes.

Table 9.5: Parameters for Updating Data in a Table

Name	Field type	Default value	Required
_contextName	Character	SAS Studio compute context	No
_action	Character	form,wait,execute	No
_output_type	Character	html	No
_name	Character	<none>	Yes
_state	Character	<none>	Yes
_acres	Character	<none>	Yes
_lat	Character	<none>	Yes
_lon	Character	<none>	Yes
_name_o	Character	<none>	Yes
_state_o	Character	<none>	Yes
_acres_o	Character	<none>	Yes
_lat_o	Character	<none>	Yes
_lon_o	Character	<none>	Yes

Before saving the job, click **Show Log** on the toolbar of the job definition to see the log displayed after the job executes. (See Figure 9.16.) This option is helpful for displaying detailed error messages when the job doesn't execute successfully.

Step 3: Create the Job Form

For this example, you want to create an external HTML form. The form will contain the HTML code needed to generate the form displayed when the job is executed. This form presents text boxes that display the current values for each data item along with a **Change** button next to each value. A user can click the **Change** button to enable the text box and enter new information. (Note that this is accomplished with the JavaScript at the end of the form definition.) Notice that all the original value parameters are used to create the form but are hidden (so that the viewer cannot see them). Because those values are used in the job definition, they need to be available to the form. (See Program 9.10.)

Figure 9.16: Displaying the Log

Program 9.10: Creating the HTML Form for Updating Data

```
<!DOCTYPE html>
<html lang="en">

<head>
<title>Change Park Information</title>
<style type="text/css">
@font-face {
  font-family:AvenirNext;
  src:url("/SASJobExecution/images/AvenirNextforSAS.woff") format("woff");
}

body, input, select {
  font-family: AvenirNext,Helvetica,Arial,sans-serif;
  text-rendering: optimizeLegibility;
  -webkit-tap-highlight-color: rgba(0,0,0,0);
}

div {
      height:200px;
      overflow-y: scroll;
}

.pointer {
  cursor: pointer;
  margin: 5px;
  font-size: 16px;
  padding: 10px 20px;
  background-color: #F7F7F7;
}

h1{
      font-size: 20pt;
      margin-bottom: 0px;
}

select {
      font-size: 16px;
}

input {
      font-size: 16px;
}

.textinput{
      width:120px;
}

table {
      border-spacing: 7px 2px;
}
```

```
</style>
</head>

<body role="main">
<center>

<h1>Edit Park Record: "$_name$"

</h1>

<form id="entry_form" action="/SASJobExecution/" target="_self">
<input type="hidden" name="_program" value="$PROGRAM$">
<input type="hidden" name="_action" value="wait,execute">
<input type="hidden" name="_name_o" value="$_name$">
<input type="hidden" name="_state_o" value="$_state$">
<input type="hidden" name="_acres_o" value="$_acres$">
<input type="hidden" name="_lat_o" value="$_lat$">
<input type="hidden" name="_lon_o" value="$_lon$">

<br/>
<table>
<tr>
      <td>Park Name: </td>
      <td>
      <input type="text" class="textinput" name="_name" id="_name" disabled
value="$_name$">
      </td>
      <td><button type="button" id="button_name">Change</button></td>
</tr>
<tr>
      <td>State: </td>
      <td>
      <input type="text" class="textinput" name="_state" id="_state"
disabled value="$_state$">
      </td>
      <td><button type="button" id="button_state">Change</button></td>
</tr>
<tr>
      <td>Acres: </td>
      <td>
      <input type="number" name="_acres" id="_acres" min="0" disabled
value="$_acres$">
      </td>
      <td><button type="button" id="button_acres">Change</button></td>
</tr>
<tr>
      <td>Latitude: </td>
      <td>
      <input type="number" name="_lat" id="_lat" min="-90" max="90"
step="0.01" disabled value="$_lat$">
      </td>
```

```
      <td><button type="button" id="button_lat">Change</button></td>
</tr>
<tr>

      <td>Longitude: </td>
      <td>
      <input type="number" name="_lon" id="_lon" min="-120" max="120"
step="0.01" disabled value="$_lon$">
      </td>
      <td><button type="button" id="button_lon">Change</button></td>
</tr>
</table>

<br/>

<button type="submit" class="pointer">Submit</button>

</form>

</center>
</body>

<script type="text/javascript">

function changebutton(button,id) {
    document.getElementById(id).removeAttribute("disabled");
    document.getElementById(button).setAttribute("disabled", "disabled");
}

document.getElementById("button_name").onclick = function() {
    changebutton("button_name","_name");
};
document.getElementById("button_state").onclick = function() {
    changebutton("button_state","_state");
};
document.getElementById("button_acres").onclick = function() {
    changebutton("button_acres","_acres");
};
document.getElementById("button_lat").onclick = function() {
    changebutton("button_lat","_lat");
};
document.getElementById("button_lon").onclick = function() {
    changebutton("button_lon","_lon");
};

</script>

</html>
```

Remember, forms that have the same name and that are stored in the same location as the job definition are automatically displayed on job execution if the **_action** parameter for the job has a default value of **form**.

Step 4: Execute and Test

Before adding this job to the report, be sure to set the **Periodically reload report data** option at the report level.

Then add a URL link to the geo map that references the job. To pass the values for each park to the job, the geo map must have those data items assigned to at least one of the roles. The geo map currently uses **ParkName** as the geography data item and displays **Acres** in the data tip. The remaining data items can be added to the **Hidden** role: **State**, **Latitude**, and **Longitude**.

Then add the URL link:

❶ In the Actions pane, expand **URL Links**. (See Figure 9.17.)
❷ Click **New URL Link**.
❸ Specify a name for the URL link action.
❹ Enter the job submit URL in the **URL** field.

Figure 9.17: Adding a URL Link that Calls a Job

❺ Add parameters for each data item included in the table, mapped to the appropriate parameters from the job.

In addition, add a title to the geo map to describe the actions needed to update the park information.

Double-clicking the bubble for **New River Gorge** displays the HTML form on a new tab. (See Figure 9.18.)

Click **Change** next to **Latitude** and enter the correct value (**38.07**), and then click **Submit** to execute the job and update the table. A success message is displayed and informs the viewer to close the window to see the updated information. Below the success message, the full SAS log appears because **Show Log** was selected in the job definition.

The report automatically reloads the new data and the park is updated in the geo map.

Example: Deleting Data from a Table

In the previous examples, you added details for six additional national parks and updated details for two that were entered incorrectly. The geo map currently displays all the national parks in the United States, plus two parks in outlying territories (American Samoa and Virgin Islands). You want to enable the viewer to delete data for the outlying territories.

Figure 9.18: Editing Park Information

Edit Park Record: "New River Gorge"

Park Name:	New River Gorge	Change
State:	wv	Change
Acres:	7021	Change
Latitude:	28.07	Change
Longitude:	-81.08	Change

Submit

You can use a job to delete records from the table. Specifically, you create a job that will be called from a Web content object in the second page of the report (**Delete Park**). The job will use a task prompt that enables you to select one of the national parks for deletion.

Note: You need to carefully consider whether you want viewers to be able to delete records from the CAS table. Any viewer who can access the report will be able to delete records from the table.

Step 1: Create the SAS Program

The SAS program reads data from the CAS table used in the report (**JOBS.NATIONAL_PARKS**) and removes the record for the selected park. (See Program 9.11.) This updated data is saved in a new CAS table in the **casuser** caslib.

Then PROC CASUTIL is used to drop the CAS table used in the report, promote the updated table (stored in your **casuser** caslib), and save a permanent copy of the new table (with the updated park information).

Program 9.11: Deleting Data from a CAS Table

```
/******************************************************************/
/*   Create a default CAS session and create SAS librefs for      */
/*   existing caslibs so that they are visible in the SAS Studio   */
/*   Libraries tree.                                              */
/******************************************************************/

cas casauto;
caslib _all_ assign;


/******************************************************************/
/*   Define macro variables for:                                  */
/*   lib- caslib                                                  */
/*   ds- dataset/ CAS table                                       */
/*   libds- caslib.table                                          */
/******************************************************************/
%let lib = jobs;
%let ds = NATIONAL_PARKS;
%let libds = &lib..&ds.;


%let _name=American Samoa;
%let _state=as;
%let _acres=8257;
%let _lat=14.25;
%let _lon=-170.68;
```

```
/*****************************************************************/
/*  Delete data in casuser.parks table                         */
/*****************************************************************/
data casuser.&ds.;
      set &libds.;
      where ParkName ne "&_name." and State ne "&_state." and
          Acres ne &_acres. and Latitude ne &_lat. and
          Longitude ne &_lon.;
run;


/*****************************************************************/
/*  Drop existing CAS table and add table with new data        */
/*****************************************************************/
proc casutil;
      droptable incaslib="&lib." casdata="&ds.";
      promote incaslib="casuser" outcaslib="&lib." casdata="&ds.";
      save casdata="&ds." incaslib="&lib." outcaslib="&lib." replace;
run;
```

This program uses five parameters, one for each data item in the **NATIONAL_PARKS** table. In this program, the values for those parameters are hardcoded with details about American Samoa. Eventually, the values for the deleted parks are passed to the job on execution.

After this program is executed, American Samoa is removed from the **NATIONAL_PARKS** table.

Step 2: Create the Job Definition

Next create the job definition. The code is the same as the SAS program minus the hardcoded values for the input parameters plus some additional code to display a success message once the park information has been deleted.

After the table is updated, a DATA _NULL_ step is used in conjunction with the FILE _WEBOUT statement and HTML code to display a success message. This code is similar to the code used to display the success message for the previous example.

The job definition should also contain the following parameters: (See Table 9.6.)

Table 9.6: Parameters for Deleting Data from a Table

Name	Field type	Default value	Required
_contextName	Character	SAS Studio compute context	No
_action	Character	prompts,wait,execute	No
_output_type	Character	html	No

Figure 9.19: Creating an Embedded Task Prompt

Because this job will use a task prompt, the **_action** parameter needs to be updated to **prompts,wait,execute** so that the task prompt is displayed when the job is called. Also remember, the **_output_type** parameter is necessary for the success message to display after the job executes. This job definition does not need a parameter for **ParkName**. This is because the task prompt passes the selected park value directly to the job definition using the name of the data item (not a parameter).

Step 3: Create the Job Form

For this example, you want to create an embedded task prompt. On the Properties tab, select **Task prompt**, and a Task prompt tab appears in the job definition. This is where you enter the XML code needed to generate the prompt. (See Figure 9.19.)

On the Task prompt tab, enter code to create the task prompt. (See Program 9.12.)

Program 9.12: Creating the Task Prompt

```
<?xml version="1.0" encoding="utf-8"?>
<Task schemaVersion="7.2">
  <Registration>
    <Name>Dynamic Prompts Using PARKS Data</Name>
    <Description></Description>
    <Version>5.2</Version>
  </Registration>
  <Metadata>
    <DataSources>
      <DataSource name="dataset" defaultValue="jobs.national_parks"
          where="false" required="true" readOnly="true">
```

```
      <Filters>
        <Filter name="filterPark">
          <Column column="ParkName" sortBy="label"
            sortDirection="ascending"/>
        </Filter>
      </Filters>
    </DataSource>
  </DataSources>

  <Options>
    <Option name="_program" inputType="inputtext" active="true"
        value="$PROGRAM$"/>
    <Option name="_action"  inputType="inputtext" active="true"
        value="wait"/>

    <Option name="blankline" inputType="string"/>

    <Option name="header" inputType="markdown">
      &lt;h1&gt;SAS&amp;#174; Job Execution&lt;/h1&gt;</Option>

    <Option name="name" inputType="markdown">&lt;b&gt;Dynamic
      Prompts Using PARKS Data&lt;/b&gt;</Option>
    <Option name="desc" inputType="string" readOnly="true">
      This sample uses data in the JOBS.NATIONAL_PARKS data set
      to source dynamic prompts.
    </Option>

    <Option name="hr" inputType="markdown">&lt;hr&gt;</Option>

    <Option name="dataset_label" inputType="string">Data set:
      </Option>

    <Option name="ParkName" inputType="combobox"
        filter="filterPark" required="true">Select a park
        name:</Option>

    <Option name="_debug_label" inputType="string">Show SAS Log:
      </Option>
    <Option name="_debug" inputType="combobox"
        defaultValue="_debug_1"></Option>
    <Option inputType="string" name="_debug_1"
        returnValue="">No</Option>
    <Option inputType="string" name="_debug_2"
        returnValue="log">Yes</Option>
</Options>
</Metadata>
<UI>
  <OptionItem option="header"/>
  <OptionItem option="name"/>
  <OptionItem option="desc"/>
```

```
    <OptionItem option="hr"/>

    <OptionItem option="dataset_label"/>
    <DataItem data="dataset"/>
    <OptionItem option="blankline"/>

    <OptionChoice option="ParkName"/>
    <OptionItem option="blankline"/>

    <HorizontalLayout>
      <OptionItem option="_debug_label"/>
      <OptionChoice option="_debug">
        <OptionItem option="_debug_1"/>
        <OptionItem option="_debug_2"/>
      </OptionChoice>
    </HorizontalLayout>
  </UI>
  <CodeTemplate/>
</Task>
```

Note: The common task model (CTM) defines the template for the prompt. In the CTM file, you define how the prompt appears to the user.

The prompt is defined by several elements:

- Task element – This element defines the schemaVersion associated with the prompt (7.2) and contains three children: Registration, Metadata, and UI.
  - Registration element – This element identifies the type of prompt: the name (**Dynamic Prompts using PARKS data**), the description, and the version (5.2).
  - Metadata element – This element specifies the input table required to run the task (if any). In this example, the **ParkName** column from the **JOBS.NATIONAL_PARKS** table is used to run the task. Specifically, a user selects a park name (from the list of available parks) to be deleted. Within the Metadata element, any role assignments are specified in the Roles element and any options are specified in the Options element.
    - Roles element – This element specifies details about the variables that are required for the task: the type, the minimum or maximum number of variables required for each role, and a label or description that appears in the prompt. This example does not contain a Roles element.
    - Options element – This element specifies how the options will be displayed in the prompt. Notice for this example that the element references the **_program** parameter (which calls the job definition) and the **_action** parameter (which specifies the action to perform). It also specifies a string input type for the data set value (which displays informational text to the user but cannot be modified) and a combobox input type for **ParkName** (which displays a drop-down list of all parks available in the **JOBS.NATIONAL_PARKS** table). In addition, a combobox input type is specified for the **Show SAS Log** option.
  - UI element – This element describes how to present the prompt to the user. Only linear layouts are supported. For this example, the layout is constructed as follows:

> header (SAS Job Execution)
> name (Dynamic Prompts Using NATIONAL_PARKS data)
> description (This sample uses data in the JOBS.NATIONAL_PARKS data set to source dynamic prompts.)
> hr (an HTML tag that displays a thematic break between paragraph-level elements)
> dataset_label (Data set:)
> dataset (jobs.national_parks, which is required and not modifiable)
> blankline (a line break)
> ParkName (the combobox used to select a park and is required)
> blankline (a line break)
> _debug_label (Show SAS Log:) followed by the combo box to select an option (displayed in a horizontal layout)

- OptionDependencies element – This element is used to define dependencies between prompts (for example, to create cascading prompts where a selection in one prompt filters the list of choices available in another prompt). In this case, no dependencies are defined.

This code creates a task prompt as described by the UI element.

Step 4: Execute and Test

Before adding this job to the report, make sure to set the **Periodically reload report data** option at the report level.

Then add a Web content object (to the Delete Park page) that references the job. The task prompt is displayed, and the park to delete can be selected. (See Figure 9.20.)

Clicking **Submit** in the upper left corner of the task prompt executes the job. A new tab is displayed with the "Please wait" message. When execution completes, a success message appears, and the SAS log is displayed below the message if specified.

The report automatically reloads, and the park is deleted from the geo map.

Note: Some requirements must be met for tasks prompts to work in SAS Viya and SAS Visual Analytics:

- A global caslib must be created in SAS Viya for the CAS table. In this example, the **Jobs** caslib was created using SAS Data Explorer.
- All authenticated users must have at least *Read* access to the global caslib.
- A new library needs to be created in SAS Studio that points to the global caslib. For the new library, the **Make data sources available to all users** option must be set. (See Figure 9.21.) This option ensures that the task prompt can query the CAS table to display a list of parks.

Figure 9.20: Deleting a Park

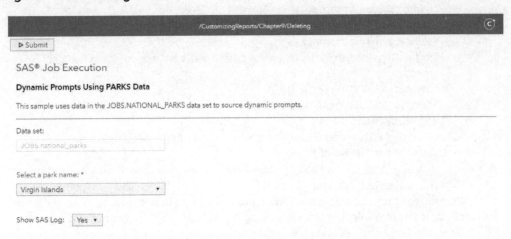

- Your data set must not contain any column names that include spaces or special characters. If it does, you can use SAS Data Studio to rename the columns. Any data sets that contain columns with spaces or special characters cannot be queried from the task prompt.
- A configuration change is needed in SAS Environment Manager to allow pop-ups to be displayed from a Web content object in SAS Visual Analytics. In the Configuration section of Environment Manager, view the list of definitions and search for **sas.visualanalytics**. Edit **iFrame Sandbox Attribute Value** to include **allow-popups**. (See Figure 9.22.)

Figure 9.21: Creating a Library in SAS Studio

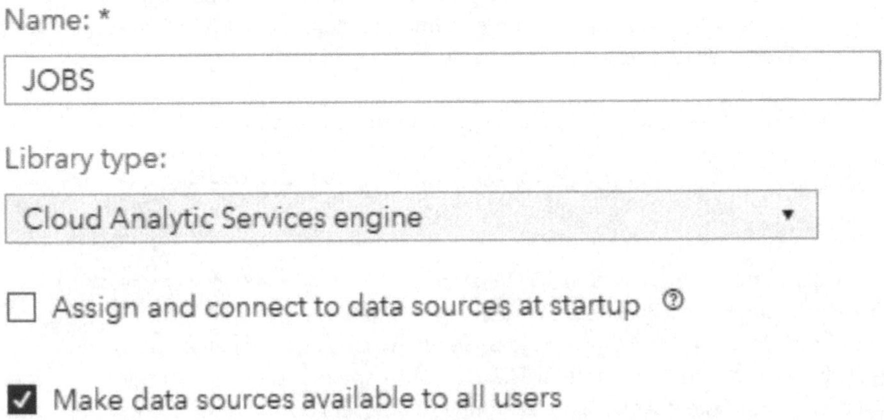

Name: *

JOBS

Library type:

Cloud Analytic Services engine ▾

☐ Assign and connect to data sources at startup ⑦

☑ Make data sources available to all users

Figure 9.22: Allowing Pop-Ups in SAS Visual Analytics

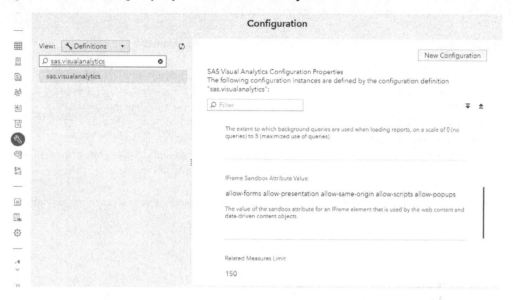

Note: You need administrative privileges to make a configuration change. If you cannot make this change, you can add a Text object with a hyperlink to the report that calls the job.

Additional Considerations

For the previous three examples, if you have multiple users that will be adding to, updating, or deleting records from the same data set, you might be worried about what will happen if two users are trying to access the data at the same time. In CAS, multiple append and update processes execute in serial, never running concurrently. The CAS session that accesses the global table first is able to append or update the data, and other processes must wait in a queue until the table is available. Therefore, it's important to not hold on to the CAS table longer than is necessary. In these examples, the data was appended and updated using a personal table (stored in the **casuser** caslib), and the CAS table in the report was dropped, updated, and saved to disk at the last possible second. See Appendix C: Additional Resources for more details about this process.

SAS Viya jobs, by themselves, open the realm of possibilities when integrated into your SAS Visual Analytics reports. Just imagine what could be possible when calling jobs using the Data-driven content object (the focus of the previous chapter). If you want to include some interaction with the data in the report, then use a job to take the data passed from SAS Visual Analytics, process the data in some way, and use that data to render the visualization. This can further extend the capabilities of your report. In general, if you don't want your job to interact with selections made in your report (like filters or actions), then use the Web content object to display the job. If you do want to use selected data in the job, then the Data-driven content object is the way to go.

Just remember that data is passed from SAS Visual Analytics to the data-driven content as a JSON object, so your code might need to restructure the data for processing.

Here are some examples of calling a job in a Data-driven content object:

- Creating a questionnaire that records answers in a CAS table. After answering each question, the percentage of users who responded in the same manner are displayed.
- Displaying details about a selected customer or item by querying information in another database.
- Approving or disapproving data before it's used in a report.
- Creating a table from a subset of an existing table, aggregating the table, and loading it to CAS so that it can be explored just like any other in-memory table.

See the "Additional Examples" section in Appendix C: Additional Resources for more examples.

Chapter 10: Sharing Reports

Introduction

Once you've created interactive reports using the techniques learned in this book, it's time to share those reports with others. Users can view your reports in SAS Visual Analytics, using the SAS Visual Analytics app, or from a website with help from the SAS Visual Analytics SDK. When viewing reports using one of these interfaces, all interactivity and customizations are available. These options make it easy for users to connect to SAS Visual Analytics in a way that is convenient for them using any device that they have handy.

Viewing Reports in SAS Visual Analytics

After you've finished creating your SAS Visual Analytics reports, you'll want to view them to ensure all your interactions, links, and filters work as expected and to verify that the report is displayed in the way that you intended. You can easily view and interact with reports in SAS Visual Analytics by clicking the **View report** icon in the upper left corner of the report. (See Figure 10.1.)

When you view the report, the left and right panes are hidden. However, you can access some functionality in the right pane by clicking the **Show side pane** icon in the upper right corner of the report. (See Figure 10.2.) This enables you to view details about the data used, the display rules assigned, the filters added, and the ranks applied, as well as view and add comments to objects in the report. Depending on the **Viewer customization** level set for the report, viewers might also be able to make changes to the report.

Starting with SAS Visual Analytics 8.4, the report designer can set the **Viewer customization** level for the report to control the changes that the viewer can make to the report. **Viewer customization** is set at the report level and applies to all users who can access the report. Three levels of customization are available:

1. **Simple edits**: This option enables viewers to make minor changes to the report (like how the data is sorted in objects or to show or hide legends and data values in an object). These changes *do not change* the report designer's original intent for the report but make it easier for the viewers to interact with the report in a way that suits them.

Figure 10.1: Viewing a Report in SAS Visual Analytics

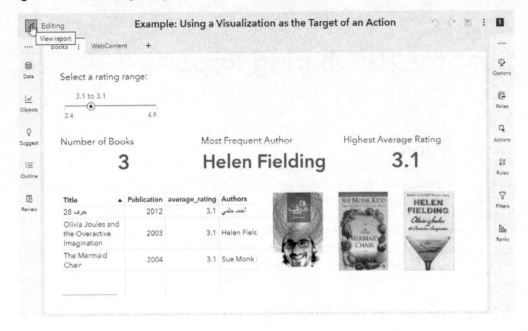

Figure 10.2: Showing the Side Pane

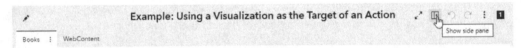

2. **Comprehensive edits** (default): This option enables viewers to make changes to object types used in the report. For example, the viewer can change a bar chart to a box plot or another type of object. These changes *might change* the report designer's original intent for the report.
3. **Data edits**: This option enables viewers to make significant changes to the objects and data used in the report. For example, the viewer can change data assignments, filters, and ranks that are used in the report. These changes *can vastly change* the report designer's original intent for the report.

Note: These levels of customization are additive. When **Viewer customization** is set to **Comprehensive edits**, users can also change the sort order and show or hide legends and data values in an object. When **Viewer customization** is set to **Data edits**, viewers can make those same changes as well as change the type of the object.

As a viewer modifies a report, the viewer state is remembered. This means that the next time the viewer opens the same report, all the previous selections, actions, and modifications made by that viewer are in place. To return to the original report state, in the upper right corner of the report, click the **More** icon and select **Restore default report state**. (See Figure 10.3.)

Note: Users who are authorized to edit reports in the deployment and those who have permissions to edit the current report can see the **Edit report** option. Users who don't have those permissions are only able to view the report, not edit it. However, if a user makes changes to the report while viewing it, that person can always save a copy of the report and share it with others.

In addition to interacting and customizing the report, viewers can also maximize objects to view details, interact with geo maps by adding location pins and radius-based selections, export data and images, and print the report, pages in the report, or objects.

To view a report in SAS Visual Analytics, the user either needs credentials to sign in to SAS Viya or guest access must be enabled for the installation. Guest access uses a shared account to enable users to view reports in SAS Viya without needing credentials to sign in. Because a shared account is used to access SAS Viya, the report state is not remembered and guests cannot save a copy of any changes that they make to the report. However, the **Viewer customization** level still applies to guests. This means that guests can make all the changes other viewers can make to the report, but they aren't able to save the changes or see them applied the next time that they view the report.

Note: Guest access can also be used to access reports with the SAS Visual Analytics Apps and the SAS Visual Analytics SDK.

Figure 10.3: Restoring the Default Report State

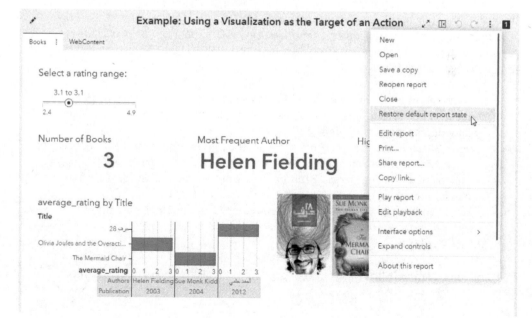

SAS Visual Analytics Apps

Users can also view and interact with reports on a mobile device using the SAS Visual Analytics Apps (formerly called SAS Mobile BI). The SAS Visual Analytics Apps are available for free from the Apple App Store (for iPhones and iPads), Google Play (for Android devices), and the Microsoft Store (for PCs and tablets running Windows 10).

Administrators control how mobile devices using the SAS Visual Analytics Apps can access reports and data on the SAS Visual Analytics server. For example, administrators can create an allowlist or denylist to specify which devices can access the system, require a passcode for the app, set a time-out property for the app, specify whether a network connection to the server is required to view reports, and limit the functionality of the app (for adding and viewing reports, sharing links, adding and viewing comments, and using Favorites or Recent views and alerts).

You can also create a custom app for your organization and use the SAS SDK (Software Development Kits) to include SAS Visual Analytics content. This enables you to create an app using your corporate theme and logo and preload and embed SAS Visual Analytics content into the app. The SAS SDK is free and is available for iOS and Android devices. For more information about the SAS SDK (including documentation and downloads), see https://support.sas.com/en/software/sdk-support.html.

SAS Visual Analytics SDK

The SAS Visual Analytics SDK enables you to embed SAS Visual Analytics content into your own websites and applications. Using the SAS Visual Analytics SDK requires some setup on the SAS Viya server, so typically an administrator would perform these tasks. Once this setup is performed, however, you can embed a report, a page from a report, or objects in the report on your own web page or application. To create the custom HTML tags to embed the entire report in your web page, do the following:

❶ At the report level, click the **More** icon and select **Copy link**. (See Figure 10.4.)
❷ In the Options group, select **Guest access** (if applicable), **Interactive report**, and **Embeddable web component**.
   Note: Guest access enables users to bypass the sign-in window and automatically use guest credentials, which enables public users to view SAS Visual Analytics content embedded on the web page. If guest access is not enabled, then users are asked to sign in before they can view the SAS Visual Analytics content.
   Note: The **Embeddable web component** option is required to create the custom HTML tags needed to embed SAS Visual Analytics content on your web page.
❸ Click **Copy Link**.

Then add the custom HTML tag to your web page to embed SAS Visual Analytics content.

Figure 10.4: Creating Custom HTML Tags

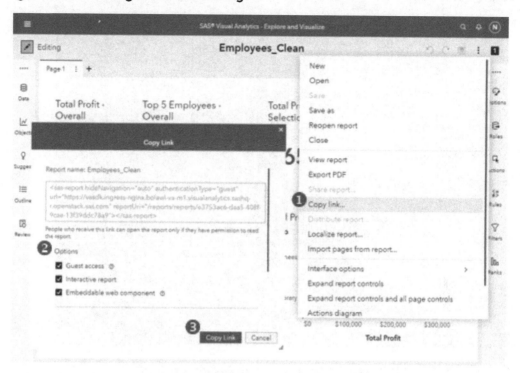

You can also copy the link for a page of your report (by clicking the **Page menu** icon and selecting **Copy link**) or for an object in your report (by clicking the **Object menu** icon for the object and selecting **Copy link**).

See the SAS COVID-19 Public Dashboard for an example of using the SAS Visual Analytics SDK (https://tbub.sas.com/COVID19/). The Summary page displays objects from the SAS Visual Analytics report, like the data update text and key value objects that show the total confirmed cases and total deaths. (See Figure 10.5.)

The Full Report page displays the entire SAS Visual Analytics report, which contains multiple pages and interactivity. (See Figure 10.6.)

For more details about using the SAS Visual Analytics SDK, see "SAS Visual Analytics SDK: Embed SAS Visual Analytics Insights in Your Web Pages and Web Apps" by Brad Morris and Robby Powell (https://www.sas.com/content/dam/SAS/support/en/sas-global-forum-proceedings/2020/4309-2020.pdf).

Figure 10.5: SAS COVID-19 Public Dashboard: Summary

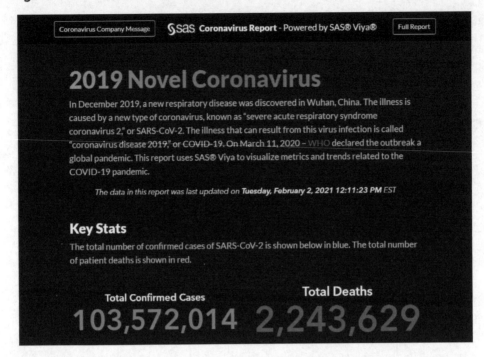

Figure 10.6: SAS COVID-19 Public Dashboard: Full Report

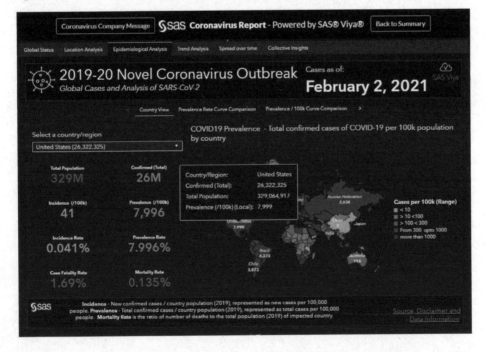

Appendix A: Loading Geographic Polygon Data to CAS

Out of the box, SAS Visual Analytics can display geographic maps with colored regions for countries and their first-level subdivisions (like US states). If you want to display regions for other geographic levels (like counties, postal codes, school districts, or sales regions), you must define a custom polygon provider that contains information about the boundaries for these levels (polygon data). To define a custom polygon provider, do the following:

1. **Obtain polygon data**: This data can be stored in a SAS data set or an Esri shapefile. The Esri shapefiles (the .shp, .shx, .dbf, and .prj files) must be loaded to the server machine.
2. **Create or identify sequence variable**: The sequence variable is used to ensure that the polygon segments are read in the correct order. If your polygon data does not contain a sequence variable, you can use the **_n_** automatic variable in a SAS DATA step or the Unique Identifier transform in SAS Data Studio to create a sequence variable. For Esri shapefiles, the **__seq__** variable is created automatically when the **%SHPIMPRT** autocall macro is executed.
3. **Convert the shapefile into a SAS data set**: For Esri shapefiles, the **%SHPIMPRT** autocall macro converts the shapefile into a SAS data set and loads the data into CAS.
4. **Subset polygon data to decrease the level of detail (optional)**: SAS Visual Analytics, by default, can only retrieve up to 250,000 vertices at a time. Reducing the level of detail can improve performance and might enable a greater number of map regions to be displayed at one time. If you have access to SAS/GRAPH, then you can use the GREDUCE procedure to create a **DENSITY** variable that enables you to reduce the density of your polygon data. Sometimes this variable is already present.
5. **Load the SAS data set to CAS**: SAS data sets can be loaded to CAS like any other data (for example, by using self-service import, by defining a caslib that points to the location of the SAS data set on the server machine, or by using the PROC CASUTIL LOAD statement in SAS code). Esri shapefiles are loaded to CAS when the **%SHPIMPRT** autocall macro executes.
6. **Define a custom polygon provider**: The custom polygon provider can be created in SAS Visual Analytics and accesses data stored in CAS or an Esri feature service.
7. **Create a geographic data item**: If the custom polygon provider contains polygon information, then a geo region map can be created from the geographic data item.
8. **Test custom polygons**: Create a geo map in SAS Visual Analytics to test the custom polygons. Remember, only 250,000 vertices can be displayed at a time, by default. You might need to filter the data to ensure that the custom polygons work as expected.

Users who follow these steps must have the following:

- **Access to polygon data**
- **Access to a SAS programming interface, like SAS Studio**: This is required for executing the autocall macros that help you inspect and load Esri shapefiles to CAS.
- **Access to the server machine, the CAS Controller**: The autocall macros access data loaded to the server machine. The user who executes the macros needs to have Read and Execute access to the directory where the polygon data is stored.
- **Permissions in SAS Viya to define and edit polygon providers**: The */maps/providers* URI controls access to polygon providers.

For Example: Selecting a Region in Chapter 5 and Example: Building a Custom Map with Polygon Layers in Chapter 7, you need to create a geographic polygon provider that contains polygon information at three geographic levels: county, state, and US.

Step 1: Obtain Polygon Data

Esri shapefiles for US counties are available from the United States Census Bureau. These shapefiles are specifically designed for small-scale mapping. After downloading these shapefiles, you need to store them on the server machine (the CAS controller) in a location where you have Read and Execute access (for example, your */home/user-name* directory).

The polygon data for the two other levels (state and US) is available in the **US_STATES** and **WORLD** tables in the **MAPSGFK** predefined library. This library contains map data sets that are licensed through GfK Geomarketing and are provided with SAS/GRAPH software.

Step 2: Create or Identify the Sequence Variable

For the county shapefiles, the **%SHPCNTNT** autocall macro displays the contents of the shapefile so that you can familiarize yourself with the structure of the data and determine which variable should be used as the ID variable. The **%SHPIMPRT** autocall macro automatically creates a sequence variable, **__seq__**. (See Program A.1 and Table A.1.)

Program A.1: Displaying Contents of Shapefiles

```
/********************************************/
/* Display the contents of the shapefiles */
/********************************************/
%shpcntnt(shapefilepath=/home/christine/cb_2017_us_county_500k.shp)
```

Table A.1: Defining Parameters for %SHPCNTNT

Parameter	Description
shapefilepath	Specifies the full path to the shapefile on the server machine with the .shp extension. Do not enclose the file path in quotation marks.

For the **MAPSGFK** data sets, you need to create a sequence variable. You can do this by determining the maximum value of **__seq__** created for the county data, adding 1, and incrementing by 1 (using a SUM statement) for each row in the data set. (See Step 3.)

Step 3: Convert Shapefile into a SAS Data Set

For the county shapefiles, the **%SHPIMPRT** autocall macro converts the shapefile into a SAS data set and loads it to CAS. (See Program A.2 and Table A.2.)

Program A.2: Converting Shapefile into a SAS Data Set

```
/*************************************************************/
/* Convert shapefile into SAS data set and load into CAS */
/*************************************************************/
%shpimprt(shapefilepath=/home/christine/cb_2017_us_county_500k.shp,
          id=geoid,
          outtable=Counties,
          cashost=controller.sas-cas-server-default.edu.svc.cluster.local,
          casport=5570,
          caslib=Public)
```

Note: SAS/GRAPH software is required to reduce the density.

This step is not required for the state and US levels because the data is already stored in a SAS data set.

Table A.2: Defining Parameters for %SHPIMPRT

Parameter	Description
shapefilepath	Specifies the full path to the shapefile on the server machine with the .shp extension. Do not enclose the file path in quotation marks.
id	Specifies a field in the shapefile that identifies the polygons in the map. This variable can be determined by viewing the output from the **%SHPCNTNT** autocall macro.
outtable	Specifies the name of the output table that is loaded into CAS.
cashost	Specifies the machine name of the CAS server. The machine name can be found on the **Servers** page in SAS Environment Manager.
casport	Specifies the port for the CAS server. The port can be found on the **Servers** page in SAS Environment Manager.
caslib	Specifies the library on the CAS server where the output table is loaded. The list of libraries can be found on the **Data** page in SAS Environment Manager.
reduce (optional)	Specifies whether to reduce the density of the polygon data. A value of 1 specifies that the data density is reduced, and a value of 0 (default) specifies that the data density is not reduced.

Step 4: Subset Polygon Data to Decrease the Level of Detail (Optional)

You can use the REDUCE option in the **%SHPIMPRT** autocall macro to reduce the level of detail for the county shapefiles or use the **DENSITY** variable created from the GREDUCE procedure to subset the state and US polygon data. For both types of data, SAS/GRAPH software is required.

Step 5: Load the SAS Data Set into CAS

The **%SHPIMPRT** autocall macro automatically loads the county shapefiles into CAS. However, for this example, you want to create a CAS table that includes county-level, state-level, and US-level polygon information. You can do this using SAS code. (See Program A.3.)

Program A.3: Creating a CAS Table with County-Level, State-Level, and US-Level Polygon Information

```
/******************************************************************/
/*   STEP 1                                                       */
/*   Create a default CAS session and create SAS librefs for existing */
/*   caslibs so that they are visible in the SAS Studio Libraries tree. */
/******************************************************************/
cas;
caslib _all_ assign;

/******************************************************************/
/*   STEP 2                                                       */
/*   Determine max value of __seq__ for states                   */
/******************************************************************/
proc sql;
     select max(__seq__) into :max_county from public.counties;
quit;

%put &=max_county;

/******************************************************************/
/*   STEP 3                                                       */
/*   Modify MAPSGFK.US_STATES to match COUNTIES data set:        */
/*   Create goeid, __seq__, format state names, rename variables  */
/******************************************************************/
data us_states(rename=(long=x lat=y));
     set mapsgfk.us_states;
     if _n_=1 then __seq__=&max_county.;
     length geoid $5.;
     geoid=cats(put(state,z2.),'000');
     __seq__+1;
     name=stnamel(statecode);
     drop x y resolution density id state statecode;
run;
```

```
/*************************************************************************/
/*  STEP 4                                                               */
/*  Load SAS data set from a Base engine library (work.us_states) into   */
/*  the specified caslib ("Public") and save as "States".                */
/*************************************************************************/
proc casutil;
      load data=us_states outcaslib="Public"
      casout="States" promote;
run;


/*************************************************************************/
/*  STEP 5                                                               */
/*  Determine max value of __seq__ for US                                */
/*************************************************************************/
proc sql;
      select max(__seq__) into :max_state from us_states;
quit;

%put &=max_state;


/*************************************************************************/
/*  STEP 6                                                               */
/*  Modify MAPSGFK.WORLD to match COUNTIES data set:                     */
/*  Filter for US, create geoid, __seq__, rename variables               */
/*************************************************************************/
data us(rename=(long=x lat=y idname=name));
      set mapsgfk.world;
      where id='US';
      if _n_=1 then __seq__=&max_state.;
      length geoid $5.;
      geoid='00000';
      __seq__+1;
      drop x y id iso isoalpha2 resolution density cont lake;
run;

/*************************************************************************/
/*  STEP 7                                                               */
/*  Load SAS data set from a Base engine library (work.us) into          */
/*  the specified caslib ("Public") and save as "US".                    */
/*************************************************************************/
proc casutil;
      load data=us outcaslib="Public"
      casout="US" promote;
run;
```

This program does the following:

1. Creates a default CAS session and creates SAS library references for existing caslibs so that they are available in the SAS Studio Libraries tree. This step is needed to load the combined data to CAS.

2. Determines the maximum value of the **__seq__** variable created for the county data. This variable is incremented to create a sequence variable for state-level data in the next step.
3. Modifies the structure of the **US_STATES** data set to match the county data. This step renames variables, creates the **GEOID** variable as the two-digit State FIPS code plus '000', increments the **__seq__** variable for state data, and creates a variable that contains full state names.
4. Loads the SAS data set created in the previous step to CAS.
5. Determines the maximum value of the **__seq__** variable created for state data. This variable is incremented to create a sequence variable for US-level data in the next step.
6. Modifies the structure of and filters the **WORLD** data set to match the county data. This step renames variables, creates the **GEOID** variable as '00000', increments the **__seq__** variable for US data, and filters the table to include only polygon data for the US.
7. Loads the SAS data set created in the previous step to CAS.

Then a plan in SAS Data Studio appends the state-level and US-level data to the county data to create a single CAS table, **COUNTIES_STATES_US**.

Step 6: Define a Custom Polygon Provider

In SAS Visual Analytics, a custom polygon provider (or a geographic data provider) can be defined while you are creating a geography data item:

❶ In the Edit Geography Item window, select **Geographic data provider** for the **Geography data** field. (See Figure A.1.)
❷ Click the menu icon for the **Geographic data provider** field and select **New**.
❸ Specify a name and label for the geographic data provider. The name must be unique and must have a length of 32 characters or less and can contain letters, numbers, underscores, hyphens, spaces, or DBCS characters. The label can be up to 256 characters long.
❹ For the **Type** field, select **CAS Table**. If you have Esri premium services enabled, you can also create a geographic data provider using **Esri feature service** as the type.
❺ Select the CAS server, the library, and the table that contains the polygon information.
❻ Select the ID column for the polygon table. This column identifies each polygon.
❼ Select the sequence column for the polygon table. This column specifies the order in which polygon segments are read to create the regions.
❽ In the Advanced section, select values for **Segment Column**, **Latitude (y) Column**, **Longitude (x) Column**, and **Coordinate Space** for the polygon table. The segment column identifies each segment for each region, the latitude and longitude columns specify the columns that contain latitudes and longitude values, respectively, and the coordinate space column specifies the coordinate space used for the polygon data.

Figure A.1: Defining a Custom Polygon Provider

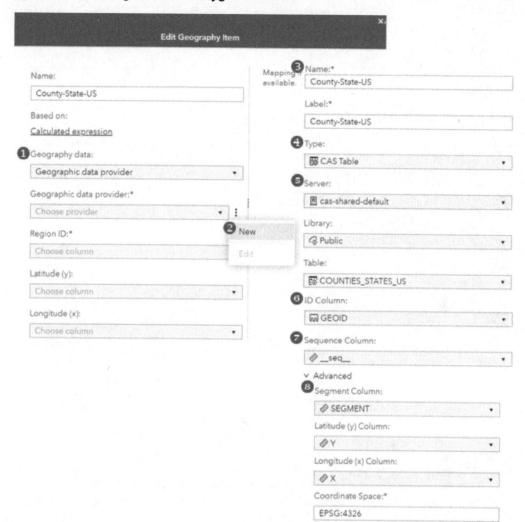

Step 7: Create a Geographic Data Item

In SAS Visual Analytics, the custom polygon provider can be used to create the geography data item:

- ❶ In the Edit Geography Item window, select **Geographic data provider** for the **Geography data** field. (See Figure A.2.)
- ❷ For the **Geographic data provider** field, select the custom polygon provider.

Figure A.2: Creating a Geographic Data Item

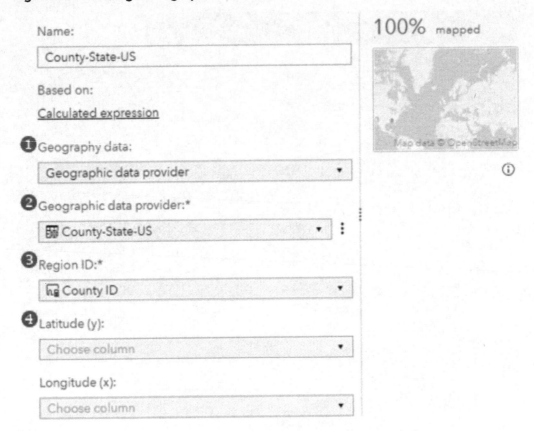

❸ Specify the region ID column in the report data set. The values for the region ID column should match the values of the ID column for the custom polygon provider.

❹ Specify **Latitude (y)** and **Longitude (x)** columns in the report data set. If these columns are not specified, SAS Visual Analytics calculates the centroids of each region automatically.

Step 8: Test Custom Polygons

Finally, verify that the custom polygons work as expected by creating a region geo map in SAS Visual Analytics using the geographic data item.

Appendix B: Working with Data-Driven Content

In Chapter 8, you use D3 to create a third-party visualization that displays book cover images and interacts with data from SAS Visual Analytics. To create your own third-party visualizations, you need to be aware of the Document Object Model (DOM), understand how HTML pages are structured, know a little JavaScript, and have some familiarity with at least one of the JavaScript charting frameworks (like D3.js. Google Charts, or CanvasJS). If you do not meet these requirements, then this appendix is for you! In this appendix, you will see how to create a basic HTML document from the very beginning. Specifically, you create the document used for the third-party visualization in Chapter 8.

HTML

HTML (Hypertext Markup Language) is the standard language for creating web pages. It consists of a series of elements arranged in a hierarchical structure. These elements tell the web browser how to display the content on a web page. When writing HTML code, you add tags to create elements. Some common elements, and elements that are used in the examples in Chapter 8, are as follows:

- **<!DOCTYPE html>**: This element is the document type declaration. It must be the first thing in the HTML document.
- **<html>**: This element surrounds all HTML content in the document.
- **<head>**: This element contains the metadata for the file. It usually contains scripts and other metadata information. For this example, the **<script>** tag is used within **<head>** to embed external script files (like JavaScript or the SAS Visual Analytics utility scripts).
- **<body>**: This element contains all the visible contents of an HTML document. There can be only one **<body>** element in the HTML document.
- **<div>**: This element defines a division within the HTML document. It's often used for grouping related elements. For this example, the **<div>** element creates the grid that will be used to display all book cover images.
- **<g>**: This element is used to group SVG shapes together. It's often used with D3 as a way of grouping all the components of a chart (like the chart area, the axes, and the legend). For this example, this element is used to group the SVG element in the grid with the appropriate image file.
- **<svg>**: This element is a container for SVG graphics (like boxes, circles, paths, texts, and images).

Attributes

HTML elements can be assigned attributes to define the element's behavior. Some elements require specific attributes, and other elements have optional attributes. All elements can be assigned the **class** and **id** attributes to easily identify elements later in the code. In general, **id** attributes should be applied if only one element of that type exists in the DOM (for our example, **<div>**). Otherwise, **class** attributes should be applied.

Scripts

To use D3 (and many of the SAS Visual Analytics utilities), you need to use the **<script>** tag in the **<head>** element to embed the scripts in your code. In Program B.1, the **<script>** tag is importing D3.js so that D3 can be used later in the code.

Program B.1: Importing D3.js

```
<!-- Import D3.js -->
<script type="text/javascript"
src="https://d3js.org/d3.v6.min.js"></script>
```

Program B.2 imports the SAS Visual Analytics utilities, which are used to send and receive the appropriate messages from SAS Visual Analytics. More details about the functions available in these import utilities can be found in the SAS Visual Analytics Utilities section later in this appendix.

Program B.2: Importing the SAS Visual Analytics Utilities

```
<!-- Import utilities -->
<script type="text/javascript" src="../util/messagingUtil.js"></script>
<script type="text/javascript" src="../util/contentUtil.js"></script>
```

The DOM

The DOM (Document Object Model) is an object-based representation of the HTML document. Basically, it describes the logical structure of HTML so that elements within the code can be easily accessed and manipulated using various programs, like JavaScript. It structures the HTML elements as a series of nodes with parent-child relationships.

In Program B.3, the code creates an HTML document that produces elements in the DOM. (See Figure B.1.) You can also add elements dynamically using JavaScript, which is explored later.

Program B.3: Creating Elements in the DOM

```
<!DOCTYPE html>
<html>
<head>
  <script type="text/javascript"
src="https://d3js.org/d3.v6.min.js"></script>
```

```
</head>
<body>
  <style type="text/css">
   /* Insert CSS code here */
</style>
<script>
    /* Insert JavaScript code here */
</script>
</body>
</html>
```

To view these elements in Google Chrome and Microsoft Edge, right-click the web page and select **Inspect**. For Internet Explorer and Firefox, right-click the web page and select **Inspect element**.

As you begin to create elements using JavaScript, this view enables you to see created elements and can be very helpful for debugging.

CSS

CSS (Cascading Style Sheets) is a language used to describe the look of the HTML document. The HTML contains the instructions for building the structure of the file, and CSS provides the decoration. With CSS, you apply properties to selectors. The selectors typically reference the type of an HTML element or the class of an HTML element.

Styling Elements

For example, the CSS code in Program B.4 defines how the **html**, **body**, and **svg** elements should be styled. Notice that, if multiple elements will be styled using the same properties, you can specify the styles for these elements simultaneously by using a comma-delimited list of elements.

Figure B.1: Viewing Elements in the DOM

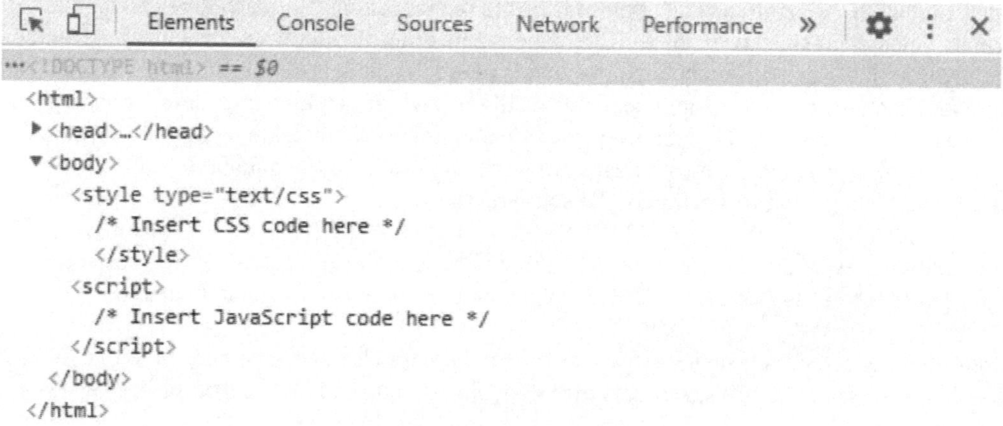

Program B.4: Styling the html, body, and svg Elements

```
html, body, svg {
    margin: 0px;
    width: 100%;
    height: 100%;
}
```

Here the **html**, **body**, and **svg** elements are set to have no margin and fill the entire space available (100% of the width and 100% of the height). Normally, for third-party visualizations used in SAS Visual Analytics, you would also set the **overflow** property to **hidden**. This ensures that parts of the visualization aren't clipped and rendered outside of the box. For this example, however, the number of book images can be quite high, so we want a scroll bar to be added automatically if all the images won't display in the specified area. (This is the default.)

Styling Classes

The CSS code in Program B.5 defines styles for the **grid** class. This class is added to the **<div>** element using JavaScript a bit later. Notice that classes of elements are referenced by adding a period (.) before the class value.

Program B.5: Styling the grid Class

```
.grid{
    display: grid;
    grid-template-columns: repeat(auto-fill, minmax(98px, 1fr));
    grid-auto-rows: auto;
}
```

The **display: grid** property turns the element into a grid container that contains multiple rows and columns. All direct children of the grid (in this example, children of the **<div>** element will be **<g>** elements, one for each row in the data source) become grid items.

The **grid-template-columns** property specifies the number and widths of the columns in the grid. In this case, the **repeat()** function specifies to repeat columns as many times as needed, where you can specify how many times to repeat. The **auto-fill** option specifies that the number of columns for each row should be as many as is needed to fit in the available space. If there is ample space, there can be a lot of columns. As the screen gets smaller, the number of columns falls as well. The **minmax()** function specifies a minimum width for columns so that they don't get too narrow. In this case, most images are 98 by 148 pixels, so the minimum width will be 98px, but it can go up to 1 fraction of the space on the grid.

The **grid-auto-rows** property specifies a size for the rows in the grid container. The **auto** option specifies that the size of each row is determined by the size of the largest item in a row.

Some additional CSS code defines styles for the **book-image** class, which is applied to the image itself. (See Program B.6.) This code sets the width of each image to fill 100% of the available space.

Program B.6: Styling the book-image Class

```
.book-image{
  width: 100%;
}
```

When you incorporate your visualization into SAS Visual Analytics and start adding interactivity through actions, you'll also need to specify styles for selected items: those that are selected through brushing (images highlighted in the visualization when something is selected in another object in SAS Visual Analytics) and those that are selected within the visualization itself.

The CSS code in Program B.7 specifies that elements that have the **brushed** class (these are images highlighted through brushing) have a solid red border of 5 pixels wide.

Program B.7: Styling the brushed Class

```
.brushed{
  border: 5px solid red;
}
```

Program B.8 specifies that elements that have both the **selectable** and **brushed** classes (these are images that are selected by the user in the visualization) have a solid blue border of 5 pixels wide.

Program B.8: Styling the selectable and brushed Class

```
.selectable.brushed {
  border: 5px solid blue;
}
```

More information about how to apply these styles is covered in two examples from Chapter 8. Example: Highlighting Selected Values in the Visualization covers the **brushed** class and Example: Using a Visualization as the Source of an Action covers the **selectable** class.

JavaScript

HTML defines how the document should be structured, CSS handles the formatting and color, and JavaScript defines the interactivity. JavaScript is an object-oriented computer programming language that is often used to display dynamic content (like interactive maps and animated graphics) and react to common events (like mouse clicks, movements, and keyboard input).

console.log

One of the most important things to know in JavaScript (and one function that helps with debugging) is console.log(). This method prints a message to the user, which appears on the Console tab of the web development tools in your browser. (See Figure B.2.)

Figure B.2: Using console.log for Debugging

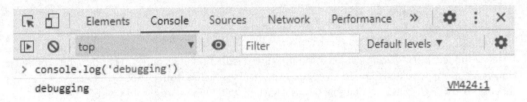

Variables

Variables can be created to store a piece of data, specifically data that will be used in another place in the program. To define variables in JavaScript whose values will not change, use a **const** statement. In Program B.9, the **const** statement is used to define a constant object, **SAMPLE_ MESSAGE**. This constant is defined as an array of objects. Specifically, each object defines a row of a sample data set where each row contains values for **image_url**, **id**, and **title**. (See Figure B.3.)

Program B.9: Defining SAMPLE_MESSAGE

```
const SAMPLE_MESSAGE = [
    {image_url: 'https://images.gr-assets.com/books/1447303603m/2767052.
jpg',
     id: 1,
     title: "The Hunger Games (The Hunger Games, #1)"},
    {image_url: 'https://images.gr-assets.com/books/1474154022m/3.jpg',
     id: 2,
     title: "Harry Potter and the Sorcerer's Stone (Harry Potter, #1)"},
    {image_url: 'https://images.gr-assets.com/books/1361039443m/41865.jpg',
     id: 3,
     title: "Twilight (Twilight, #1)"},
    {image_url: 'https://images.gr-assets.com/books/1361975680m/2657.jpg',
     id: 4,
     title: "To Kill a Mockingbird"},
```

Figure B.3: Viewing SAMPLE_MESSAGE

```
> SAMPLE_MESSAGE
⟨· ▼(5) [{…}, {…}, {…}, {…}, {…}] 🔢
    ▼0:
       id: 1
       image_url: "https://images.gr-assets.com/books/1447303603m/2767052.jpg"
       title: "The Hunger Games (The Hunger Games, #1)"
     ▶__proto__: Object
   ▶1: {image_url: "https://images.gr-assets.com/books/1474154022m/3.jpg", i…
   ▶2: {image_url: "https://images.gr-assets.com/books/1361039443m/41865.jpg…
   ▶3: {image_url: "https://images.gr-assets.com/books/1361975680m/2657.jpg"…
   ▶4: {image_url: "https://images.gr-assets.com/books/1490528560m/4671.jpg"…
     length: 5
```

```
    {image_url: 'https://images.gr-assets.com/books/1490528560m/4671.jpg',
     id: 5,
     title: "The Great Gatsby"}
  ];
```

To define a variable in JavaScript whose value will change, use a **let** statement. In Program B.10, the **let** keyword is used to create variables that will be given values dynamically in the code.

Note: The **var** statement can also be used to define variables whose values will change.

Program B.10: Defining Dynamic Variables

```
// Dynamic data variables
let VA_MESSAGE; // Data message from VA
let VA_RESULT_NAME; // Result name required to send messages back to VA
let DATA; // Data to be parsed from VA data message

// Selection and d3 variables
let GRID; // Grid for book images
let BOOK; // Book data-join
let IMAGE; // Book image
```

Program B.11 takes data passed from SAS Visual Analytics and assigns it to variables created earlier in the code.

Program B.11: Assigning Values to Dynamic Variables

```
VA_MESSAGE = messageFromVA;
VA_RESULT_NAME = messageFromVA.resultName;
```

The if Statement

An **if** statement can be used to execute code only when certain conditions are met. For example, Program B.12 calls the drawElements() function if the **<div>** element is empty (doesn't have a value). If **<div>** does have a value (that is, the elements have been previously drawn), then it calls the updateElements() function.

Note: These functions are discussed in more detail in the D3 section.

Program B.12: Using an if Statement

```
if (d3.select('div').empty()) {
  drawElements();
} else {
  updateElements();
}
```

If statements can also evaluate multiple conditions before executing code. In Program B.13, the onDataReceived() function executes if the code is not being rendered in an iFrame (! represents the logical condition not) or if the **DATA** variable does not have data assigned (|| represents the logical condition or).

Program B.13: Evaluating Multiple Conditions

```
if (!inIframe() || !DATA) {
   onDataReceived(SAMPLE_MESSAGE);
}
```

The inIframe() function returns true if the window in which the page is displayed is not the same as the topmost browser window; that is, the page is viewed in an iFrame. (!== is the comparison operator for not equal to.)

Functions

Functions are defined in JavaScript by specifying the **function** keyword followed by the name of the function, any parameters needed for the function in parentheses, and the function code within braces. In Program B.14, the function uses a **try…catch** statement to specify a block of statements to try and specifies a response (**true**) when an exception is thrown. Note that this specifies a response of **true** if the page is viewed within an iFrame.

Program B.14: Using a try…catch Statement in a Function

```
function inIframe() {
  try {
     return window.self !== window.top;
  } catch (e) {
     return true;
  }
}
```

The for Loop

A **for** loop specifies that code within the loop should execute a specific number of times. The number of times is defined by the three numbers displayed in parentheses: the initialization, the stopping condition, and the iteration statement. In Program B.15, the loop should begin with **i=0**, end when **i** is less than the length of the data key of the **VA_MESSAGE** variable, and iterate **i** by 1 each time. (i++ is an increment operator in JavaScript that is identical to the statement i = i +1.)

In Program B.15, the **VA_MESSAGE** variable is a JSON object (more about this later) that contains a data key whose value is an array of arrays. The **i < VA_MESSAGE.data.length** code is determining the length of this array (for example, 5). The code within the outermost braces will iterate five times (when i=0, i=1, i=2, i=3, i=4). At each iteration, an object is being added to the **DATA** variable that contains five keys: **image_url**, **id**, **title**, **brushed**, and **index**. This code is taking data from a JSON object and restructuring it to create an array of objects (**DATA**).

Program B.15: Restructuring Data Using a for Loop

```
for (let i = 0; i < VA_MESSAGE.data.length; i++) {
  DATA.push({
     image_url: VA_MESSAGE.data[i][0],
     id: VA_MESSAGE.data[i][1],
```

```
   title: VA_MESSAGE.data[i][2],
   brushed: VA_MESSAGE.data[i][3],
   index: i
});
```

The **brushed** column is an additional column automatically sent from SAS Visual Analytics. It has a value of 1 if that row is selected in another object in SAS Visual Analytics that is the source of an action on the visualization, and 0 otherwise. This column can be used when the third-party object is the target of an action.

Referencing Utilities

To call the functions available in the SAS Visual Analytics utilities, use . notation. Program B.16 calls the validateRoles() function from the contentUtil script to check to see whether the data being passed from SAS Visual Analytics does not match what is expected for this object (three strings: **image_url**, **id**, and **title**, and one number: **brushed**). If it doesn't match, then the postInstructionalMessage() function from the messagingUtil script is called to post details about what roles are required for the visualization.

Program B.16: Calling Functions from SAS Visual Analytics Utilities

```
if (
  !va.contentUtil.validateRoles(
    messageFromVA,
    ["string", "string",'string'],
    ["number"]
  )
) {
  va.messagingUtil.postInstructionalMessage(
    VA_RESULT_NAME,
    "D3 Book Images expects columns to be assigned in this order:\n" +
      " 1. Image URL (string)\n" +
      " 2. ID (string)\n" +
      " 3. Title (string)"
  );
  return;
}
```

JSON

JSON (JavaScript Object Notation) is a data format used for storing, organizing, and transmitting data as JavaScript objects. When data is passed from SAS Visual Analytics to the third-party visualization, it's passed as a JSON object. For this reason, Program B.17 is modified so that the **SAMPLE_MESSAGE** variable matches the data that will be sent from SAS Visual Analytics. Notice that this object contains keys that specify the version, **resultName** (which is used later in the code to ensure that the actions are executed on the Data-driven content object), the row count, the available row count, the data (which is an array that consists of an array for each row in the data), and definitions for columns.

Program B.17: Creating SAMPLE_MESSAGE as a JSON Object

```
const SAMPLE_MESSAGE = {
  version: "1",
  resultName: "sample",
  rowCount: 5,
  availableRowCount: 5,
  data: [
    [
    'https://images.gr-assets.com/books/1447303603m/2767052.jpg',
     1,
    "The Hunger Games (The Hunger Games, #1)"],
    [
     'https://images.gr-assets.com/books/1474154022m/3.jpg',
     2,
     "Harry Potter and the Sorcerer's Stone (Harry Potter, #1)"],
    [
     'https://images.gr-assets.com/books/1361039443m/41865.jpg',
     3,
     "Twilight (Twilight, #1)"],
    [
     'https://images.gr-assets.com/books/1361975680m/2657.jpg',
     4,
     "To Kill a Mockingbird"],
    [
     'https://images.gr-assets.com/books/1490528560m/4671.jpg',
     5,
     "The Great Gatsby"]
  ],
  columns: [
    {
      name: "image_url",
      label: "image_url",
      type: "string"
    },
    {
      name: "id",
      label: "id",
      type: "string"
    },
    {
      name:'title',
      label: 'title',
      type: 'string'
    }
  ]
};
```

The SAS GitHub repository contains a visualization (jsonDataViewer.html) that can be used to display your data as a JSON object, so you don't have to be an expert on how JSON objects are structured.

D3 and SVG

D3 (Data-Driven Documents) is a JavaScript library that enables you to create dynamic, interactive data visualizations in a web browser. Although D3 is not the only JavaScript charting framework that can be used to create third-party visualizations for SAS Visual Analytics, it is one of the more popular ones and is used to create many of the visualizations found on the SAS GitHub repository.

D3 can be used to generate and manipulate visuals as SVG (Scalable Vector Graphics), which makes it easier and faster to draw many of the visuals needed to create third-party visualizations.

D3 works with selections, which enable you to transform the DOM using data, set attributes and styles, and add interactivity to your visualizations.

Creating the Grid

In Program B.18, the **<body>** element is selected and a **<div>** element is added underneath. The **<div>** element is given an id and a class of **grid**. Remember, CSS styles defined the **grid** class to be a grid, so this statement creates the grid. (See Figure B.4.)

Program B.18: Creating the Grid

```
GRID=d3.select('body')
        .append('div')
          .attr('id','grid')
          .attr('class','grid')
          .on('click', deselectAllElements);
```

In Program B.18, the .on method attaches a click event to the deselectAllElements() function. This function deselects all elements that have been selected in the visualization if the user clicks anywhere in the **<div>** element. (See Program B.19.) Then it sends a message to SAS Visual Analytics using the postSelectionMessage() function, from the messagingUtil script, that passes back a null list of values (as no values are selected).

Figure B.4: Viewing the Grid

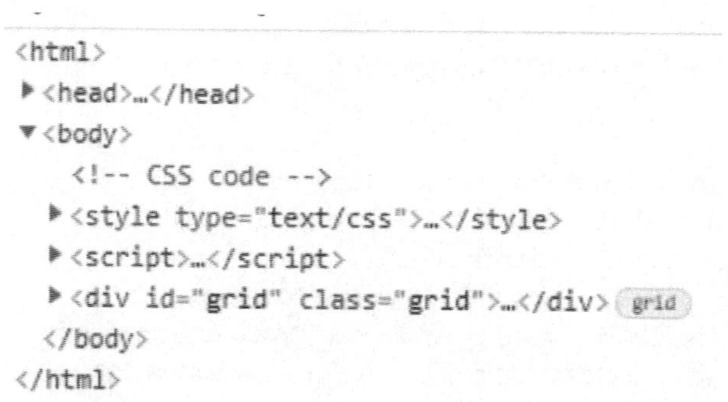

```
<html>
▶ <head>…</head>
▼ <body>
    <!-- CSS code -->
  ▶ <style type="text/css">…</style>
  ▶ <script>…</script>
  ▶ <div id="grid" class="grid">…</div>  grid
  </body>
</html>
```

Program B.19: Deselecting All Elements

```
function deselectAllElements() {
  // Deselect all elements
  d3.selectAll(".selectable").classed("brushed", false);

  // Post message to VA that no elements are selected
  va.messagingUtil.postSelectionMessage(VA_RESULT_NAME, []);
}
```

Creating Elements for Each Row

In Program B.20, a **<g>** element is added as a child to the **<div>** element for every row in the data source. In this case, one **<g>** is added for each book.

The .data() method attaches data to DOM elements. Every method called after the .data() method executes once for each row of data. The .enter() method adds (appends) a **<g>** element for every row in the data source.

The .classed() method is used to set the class of the element. In this case each **<g>** element is given a class of **selectable** (meaning that the user can select the element) and it's given a class of **brushed** if the row has a 1 for the **brushed** column. Remember, the **brushed** column is the additional column passed from SAS Visual Analytics that indicates whether a row is selected or not selected.

Program B.20: Creating g Elements

```
BOOK=GRID.selectAll('g')
            .data(DATA, function(d) {
              return d.id
            })
            .enter()
            .append('g')
              .classed('selectable', true)
              .classed('brushed', function(d) {
                return d.brushed;
              })
              .on('click', selectElement);
```

Figure B.5 shows how the DOM looks after the **<g>** elements have been added for the sample data (which contains five rows).

In Program B.20, the .on method attaches a click event to the selectElement() function. This function creates an array of any elements that are selected in the third-party visualization and sends that information back to SAS Visual Analytics using the postSelectionMessage() function from the messagingUtil script. (See Program B.21.) In addition, it checks to see whether the Ctrl key is used. In SAS Visual Analytics, the Ctrl key is used to multi-select values in an object. If the user is holding down the Ctrl key and selects multiple books in the visualization, then all the books selected are added to the array. If the Ctrl key is not used, then the **brushed** class is

Figure B.5: Viewing the g Elements

```
<html>
▶ <head>...</head>
▼ <body>
    <!-- CSS code -->
  ▶ <style type="text/css">...</style>
  ▶ <script>...</script>
  ▼ <div id="grid" class="grid"> grid
    ▶ <g class="selectable">...</g>
    ▶ <g class="selectable">...</g>
    ▶ <g class="selectable">...</g>
    ▶ <g class="selectable">...</g>
    ▶ <g class="selectable">...</g>
    </div>
  </body>
</html>
```

removed from all previously selected books, and only information about the selected book is passed to SAS Visual Analytics.

Program B.21: Selecting Elements
```
function selectElement() {
    // Prevent event from falling through to underlying elements
    event.stopPropagation();

    // If control is held toggle selected on click preserving array,
otherwise select only clicked element
    if (event.ctrlKey) {
      // Toggle selection on clicked element
      d3.select(this).classed("brushed", !d3.select(this).
classed("brushed"));
    } else {
      // Deselect all elements
      d3.selectAll(".selectable").classed("brushed", false);

      // Select clicked element
      d3.select(this).classed("brushed", true);
    }

    // Build array of selected elements
    const selections = [];
    d3.selectAll(".selectable").each(function(d) {
      if (d3.select(this).classed("brushed")) {
        selections.push({ row: d.index });
      }
    });
```

```
    // Post message to VA
    va.messagingUtil.postSelectionMessage(VA_RESULT_NAME, selections);
  }
```

Adding the Image

In Program B.22, the **<svg>** and **<svg:image>** elements are added to each **<g>** element. Remember, there is one **<g>** element for each row in the data set. The **<image>** element is given a class of **book-image**. CSS styles specify that each element with a class of **book-image** should take up 100% of the width of that element. This ensures that the book image fills the entire element.

An attribute is also added to the image element that returns **image_url**. The **xlink:href** attribute returns the image from **image_url** and places it in the element.

The *.append('title')* method specifies that a tooltip should be included when a user places the cursor over the image. In this case, the title of the book will appear in the tooltip.

Program B.22: Displaying the Image

```
IMAGE=BOOK.append('svg')
          .append('svg:image')
          .classed('book-image', true)
            .attr('xlink:href', function(d) {
                return d.image_url;
            })
            .append('title')
            .text(function(d) {
              return d.title;
            });
```

Figure B.6 shows how the DOM looks after the **<svg>** and **<image>** elements have been added for the sample data (which contains five rows).

Updating Elements

The previous three examples (GRID, BOOK, and IMAGE) make up the drawElements() function. Remember, this function is called if the **<div>** element is empty.

The updateElements() function, on the other hand, is called when any data updates occur. This function contains code that changes the existing elements in the DOM, adds new elements to the DOM if new data is added, and removes elements from the DOM if data is taken away.

Program B.23 updates the existing elements when new data is being passed from SAS Visual Analytics. Notice that it looks very similar to the code that added elements for each row in the data source.

Figure B.6: Viewing the image Elements

```
<html>
▶ <head>...</head>
▼ <body>
    <!-- CSS code -->
  ▶ <style type="text/css">...</style>
  ▶ <script>...</script>
  ▼ <div id="grid" class="grid"> grid
    ▼ <g class="selectable">
      ▶ <svg>...</svg>
      </g>
    ▼ <g class="selectable">
      ▼ <svg>
        ▶ <image class="book-image" href="https://images.gr-assets.com/books/147
          4154022m/3.jpg">...</image>
        </svg>
      </g>
    ▶ <g class="selectable">...</g>
    ▶ <g class="selectable">...</g>
    ▶ <g class="selectable">...</g>
    </div>
  </body>
</html>
```

Program B.23: Updating Existing Elements

```
BOOK=d3.select('#grid').selectAll('g')
    .data(DATA, function(d) {
      return d.id;
    })
    .classed('selectable', true)
    .classed('brushed', function(d) {
        return d.brushed;
    })
    .on('click', selectElement);
```

In Program B.24, new elements are added to the DOM if the data being passed from SAS Visual Analytics is larger than the current selection (the number of elements that currently exist in the DOM). Remember, the .enter() method adds a **<g>** element to the DOM for each row of data. The rest of the code is very similar to the code that added images to the visualization.

Program B.24: Adding Elements

```
BOOK.enter()
    .append('g')
    .classed('selectable', true)
    .classed('brushed', function(d) {
```

```
      return d.brushed;
   })
   .on('click', selectElement)
   .append('svg')
   .append("svg:image")
        .classed('book-image', true)
        .attr('xlink:href', function(d) {
          return d.image_url;
        })
   .append('title')
     .text(function(d) {
       return d.title;
     });
```

Program B.25 removes elements from the DOM when the data being passed from SAS Visual Analytics is shorter than the current selection (the number of elements that currently exist in the DOM). The .exit() and .remove() methods remove elements from the DOM. In addition, if any removed element has a class of **brushed'** then that class is removed as well.

Program B.25: Removing Elements

```
BOOK.exit()
.classed('brushed', false)
  .remove();
```

SAS Visual Analytics Utilities

The SAS GitHub repository contains utility and third-party helper scripts that might be useful when you create your own third-party visualizations. For more information about the third-party helpers, see the SAS GitHub repository (https://github.com/sassoftware/sas-visualanalytics-thirdpartyvisualizations).

messagingUtil.js

The messagingUtil.js script contains functions that you need in order to send messages to SAS Visual Analytics and receive messages from SAS Visual Analytics.

The following functions are used in this example:

- setOnDataReceivedCallback: This function sets a callback function to handle messages received from SAS Visual Analytics. In Program B.26, the function is used to call the onDataRecieved() function. When data is received from SAS Visual Analytics, the onDataRecieved() function executes.

The onDataReceived() function does the following:

- o Validates the data being passed from SAS Visual Analytics
- o Restructures the JSON object to an array of objects

○ Calls the drawElements() function if the **<div>** element is empty (if it is the first time drawing the visualization)

○ Calls the updateElements() function if the **<div>** element is not empty (if new data is being passed from SAS Visual Analytics and visualization has previously been drawn)

Program B.26: Using the setOnDataReceivedCallback() Function

```
va.messagingUtil.setOnDataReceivedCallback(onDataReceived)
```

- postSelectionMessage: This function sends a message to SAS Visual Analytics that contains selections made in the third-party visualization. SAS Visual Analytics can then use that information to filter or brush other objects in the report. (See Program B.27.) It uses the postMessage() function internally.

Program B.27: Using the postSelectionMessage() Function

```
va.messagingUtil.postSelectionMessage(resultName, selections)
```

- postInstructionalMessage: This function sends an instructional message to SAS Visual Analytics. Typically, this function is used to send details about the required data, types, and order of data needed for the visualization. (See Program B.28.)

Program B.28: Using the postInstructionalMessage() Function

```
va.messagingUtil.postInstructionalMessage(resultName, msg)
```

For more information about the other functions available from the messagingUtil.js script, see the SAS GitHub repository (https://github.com/sassoftware/sas-visualanalytics-thirdpartyvisualizations).

contentUtil.js

The contentUtil.js script contains functions that can be used to validate the data received from SAS Visual Analytics.

The following function is used in this example:

- validateRoles: This function checks whether the data received from SAS Visual Analytics contains the columns (number, type, and sequence) required for the visualization. (See Program B.29.)

Program B.29: Using the validateRoles() Function

```
va.contentUtil.validateRoles(resultData, expectedTypes, optionalTypes)
```

For more information about the other functions available from the contentUtil.js script, see the SAS GitHub repository (https://github.com/sassoftware/sas-visualanalytics-thirdpartyvisualizations).

GitHub Repository

GitHub is a code-hosting platform that makes it easy to collaborate with other users. Repositories on GitHub can be used to store a development project. These repositories can be made public, so other users can see and view your code. To use third-party visualizations in SAS Visual Analytics, your code must be externally hosted (that is, available on the web). A GitHub repository can be used for this purpose.

To create a GitHub repository, you need to create an account with GitHub. (It's free!) Then you need to create a repository. The repository must be public, so SAS Visual Analytics can access code stored there. In addition, you need to set up GitHub pages. (This can be done from the Settings tab in the repository.) Then you can access your code using the following URL: https:// your-user-id.github.io/your-repository-name.

Appendix C: Additional Resources

Chapter 1

SAS Institute Inc. 2021. *Data Visualization: What it is and why it matters*. Cary, NC: SAS Institute Inc. https://www.sas.com/en_us/insights/big-data/data-visualization.html

SAS Institute Inc. 2021. *SAS Visual Analytics*. Cary, NC: SAS Institute Inc. https://www.sas.com/en_us/software/visual-analytics.html

SAS Institute Inc. 2021. *SAS Viya*. Cary, NC: SAS Institute Inc. https://www.sas.com/en_us/software/viya.html

SAS Institute Inc. 2020. *The next release of SAS Viya introduces a new category of analytics for the cloud*. Cary, NC: SAS Institute Inc. https://www.sas.com/en_us/news/press-releases/2020/june/sas-viya-4-sgf20.html

Chapter 2

Ball, Nicole, Richard Bell, and Lynn Matthews.. 2019. "Self-Service Data Preparation in SAS Visual Analytics: A Report Designer's Delight." *SAS Global Forum 2019: Proceedings*. https://www.sas.com/content/dam/SAS/support/en/sas-global-forum-proceedings/2019/3140-2019.pdf

Patsilaras, Teri. 2018. "Key Value Object in SAS Visual Analytics." SAS Blogs. https://blogs.sas.com/content/sgf/2018/06/29/key-value-object-in-sas-visual-analytics/

Patsilaras, Teri. 2017. "Relative Period Report in SAS Visual Analytics." SAS Blogs. https://blogs.sas.com/content/sgf/2017/12/21/relative-period-report-in-sas-visual-analytics/

Patsilaras, Teri. 2020. "SAS Visual Analytics example: moving average." SAS Blogs. https://blogs.sas.com/content/sgf/2020/11/10/va-example-moving-average/

Patsilaras, Teri. 2020. "Using common filters in SAS Visual Analytics." SAS Blogs. https://blogs.sas.com/content/sgf/2020/04/10/common-filters-in-visual-analytics/

SAS Communities Library. Cary, NC: SAS Institute Inc.

- SAS Visual Analytics Advanced Calculations (part 1 of 4): AggregateCells: https://communities.sas.com/t5/SAS-Communities-Library/SAS-Visual-Analytics-Advanced-Calculations-part-1-of-4/ta-p/538509
- SAS Visual Analytics Advanced Calculations (part 2 of 4): AggregateTable: https://communities.sas.com/t5/SAS-Communities-Library/SAS-Visual-Analytics-Advanced-Calculations-part-2-of-4/ta-p/538541
- SAS Visual Analytics Advanced Calculations (part 3 of 4): Data Source Operations: https://communities.sas.com/t5/SAS-Communities-Library/SAS-Visual-Analytics-Advanced-Calculations-part-3-of-4-Data/ta-p/538688

- SAS Visual Analytics Report Example: Percent of Total – For All, For Rows, and For Columns: https://communities.sas.com/t5/SAS-Communities-Library/SAS-Visual-Analytics-Report-Example-Percent-of-Total-For-All-For/ta-p/636030
- SAS Visual Analytics: Use Object Templates for consistency and faster report development: https://communities.sas.com/t5/SAS-Communities-Library/SAS-Visual-Analytics-Use-Object-Templates-for-consistency-and/ta-p/560838
- VA Report Example: Moving 30 Day Rolling Sum: https://communities.sas.com/t5/SAS-Communities-Library/VA-Report-Example-Moving-30-Day-Rolling-Sum/ta-p/597448

SAS Institute Inc. 2021. *SAS Visual Analytics: Working with Report Content*. Cary, NC: SAS Institute Inc. https://documentation.sas.com/doc/en/vacdc/default/vaobj/titlepage.htm

SAS Institute Inc. 2021. *SAS Visual Analytics: Working with Report Data*. Cary, NC: SAS Institute Inc. https://documentation.sas.com/doc/en/vacdc/default/vareportdata/titlepage.htm

Chapter 3

Google Maps Platform. 2020 *Maps URLs Guides*. Menlo Park, California: Google.

SAS Institute Inc. 2020. *SAS Visual Analytics: Designing Reports*. Cary, NC: SAS Institute Inc. https://documentation.sas.com/doc/en/vacdc/default/vareports/titlepage.htm

SAS Institute Inc. 2020. *SAS Visual Analytics: Working with Report Data*. Cary, NC: SAS Institute Inc. https://documentation.sas.com/doc/en/vacdc/default/vareportdata/titlepage.htm

Chapter 4

Patsilaras, Teri. 2017. "Cascading Prompts as Report and Page Prompts in SAS Visual Analytics." SAS Blogs. https://blogs.sas.com/content/sgf/2017/06/01/cascading-prompts-as-report-and-page-prompts-in-sas-visual-analytics/

Patsilaras, Teri. 2018. "The power behind a Hidden Data Role in SAS Visual Analytics." SAS Blogs. https://blogs.sas.com/content/sgf/2018/03/12/power-behind-hidden-data-role/

Patsilaras, Teri. 2018. "Using Dynamic Text in a SAS Visual Analytics Report." SAS Blogs. https://blogs.sas.com/content/sgf/2018/05/31/using-dynamic-text-in-a-sas-visual-analytics-report/

SAS Institute Inc. 2021. *SAS Visual Analytics: Working with Report Data*. Cary, NC: SAS Institute Inc. https://documentation.sas.com/doc/en/vacdc/default/vareportdata/titlepage.htm

SAS Institute Inc. 2021. *SAS Visual Analytics: Working with Report Content*. Cary, NC: SAS Institute Inc. https://documentation.sas.com/doc/en/vacdc/default/vaobj/titlepage.htm

Sztukowski, Stu. 2019. "Mastering Parameters in SAS Visual Analytics." *SAS Global Forum 2019: Proceedings*. https://www.sas.com/content/dam/SAS/support/en/sas-global-forum-proceedings/2019/2986-2019.pdf

Chapter 5

Hicks, Scott. 2019. "Creating custom region maps with SAS Visual Analytics." SAS Blogs. https://blogs.sas.com/content/sgf/2019/03/27/creating-custom-region-maps-with-visual-analytics/

Patsilaras, Teri. 2016. "Use parameters to pick your metric in Visual Analytics Reports." SAS Blogs. https://blogs.sas.com/content/sgf/2016/04/27/use-parameters-to-pick-your-metric-in-visual-analytics-reports/

Patsilaras, Teri. 2015. "Using parameters in SAS Visual Analytics." SAS Blogs. https://blogs.sas.com/content/sgf/2015/01/29/using-parameters-in-sas-visual-analytics/

SAS Communities Library. Cary, NC: SAS Institute Inc.

- Debugging SAS Visual Analytics Report Performance Problems: https://communities.sas.com/t5/SAS-Communities-Library/Debugging-SAS-Visual-Analytics-Report-Performance-Problems/ta-p/472235

SAS Institute Inc. 2021. *SAS Visual Analytics: Reference*. Cary, NC: SAS Institute Inc. https://documentation.sas.com/doc/en/vacdc/default/varef/titlepage.htm

SAS Institute Inc. 2021. *SAS Visual Analytics: Working with Report Content*. Cary, NC: SAS Institute Inc. https://documentation.sas.com/doc/en/vacdc/default/vaobj/titlepage.htm

SAS Institute Inc. 2021. *SAS Visual Analytics: Working with Report Data*. Cary, NC: SAS Institute Inc. https://documentation.sas.com/doc/en/vacdc/default/vareportdata/titlepage.htm

SAS Institute Inc. 2021. *SAS Viya Administration: Data Administration*. Cary, NC: SAS Institute Inc. https://documentation.sas.com/doc/en/sasadmincdc/default/caldatamgmtcas/titlepage.htm

Schulz, Falko. 2018. "Building and visualizing custom polygons in SAS Visual Analytics." SAS Blogs. https://blogs.sas.com/content/sascom/2018/01/30/building-visualizing-custom-polygons-sas-visual-analytics/

Schulz, Falko, and Travis Murphy. 2020. *Insightful Data Visualization with SAS Viya*. Cary, NC: SAS Institute Inc.

Sztukowski, Stu. 2019. "Mastering Parameters in SAS Visual Analytics." *SAS Global Forum 2019: Proceedings*. https://www.sas.com/content/dam/SAS/support/en/sas-global-forum-proceedings/2019/2986-2019.pdf

Chapter 6

Patsilaras, Teri. 2020. "How to prompt for a date range in a SAS Visual Analytics Report- Four Part Series." SAS Blogs. https://blogs.sas.com/content/sgf/2020/07/31/date-range-sas-visual-analytics/

Patsilaras, Teri. 2017. "Using Date Parameters in your SAS Visual Analytics Reports." SAS Blogs. https://blogs.sas.com/content/sgf/2017/11/13/using-date-parameters-in-your-sas-visual-analytics-reports/

SAS Institute Inc. 2021. *SAS Visual Analytics: Designing Reports*. Cary, NC: SAS Institute Inc. https://documentation.sas.com/doc/en/vacdc/default/vareports/titlepage.htm

SAS Institute Inc. 2021. *SAS Visual Analytics: Managing Data*. Cary, NC: SAS Institute Inc. https://documentation.sas.com/doc/en/vacdc/default/datahub/titlepage.htm

SAS Institute Inc. 2021. *SAS Visual Analytics: Working with Report Content*. Cary, NC: SAS Institute Inc. https://documentation.sas.com/doc/en/vacdc/default/vaobj/titlepage.htm

SAS Institute Inc. 2021. *SAS Visual Analytics: Working with Report Data*. Cary, NC: SAS Institute Inc. https://documentation.sas.com/doc/en/vacdc/default/vareportdata/titlepage.htm

Sztukowski, Stu. 2019. "Mastering Parameters in SAS Visual Analytics." *SAS Global Forum 2019: Proceedings*. https://www.sas.com/content/dam/SAS/support/en/sas-global-forum-proceedings/2019/2986-2019.pdf

Chapter 7

Hicks, Scott. 2019. "Creating custom region maps with SAS Visual Analytics." SAS Blogs. https://blogs.sas.com/content/sgf/2019/03/27/creating-custom-region-maps-with-visual-analytics/

Hicks, Scott. 2019. "Essentials of Map Coorindate Systems and Projections in Visual Analytics." SAS Blogs. https://blogs.sas.com/content/sgf/2019/05/21/essentials-of-map-coordinate-systems-and-projections-in-visual-analytics/

Hicks, Scott. 2019. "Fundamentals of SAS Visual Analtyics geo maps." SAS Blogs. https://blogs.sas.com/content/sgf/2019/02/08/fundamentals-of-sas-visual-analytics-geo-maps/

Hicks, Scott. 2019. "Using Custom Coordinates for map creation in SAS Visual Analytics." SAS Blogs. https://blogs.sas.com/content/sgf/2019/02/27/using-custom-coordinates-for-map-creation-in-sas-visual-analytics/

SAS Institute Inc. 2021. *SAS Visual Analytics: SAS Graph Builder: User's Guide*. Cary, NC: SAS Institute Inc. https://documentation.sas.com/doc/en/vacdc/default/grbldrug/titlepage.htm

Schulz, Falko. 2018. "Building and visualizing custom polygons in SAS Visual Analytics." SAS Blogs. https://blogs.sas.com/content/sascom/2018/01/30/building-visualizing-custom-polygons-sas-visual-analytics/

Chapter 7: Additional Examples

SAS Communities Library. Cary, NC: SAS Institute Inc.

- 3 steps to build a trend comparison line plot in SAS Visual Analytics: https://communities.sas.com/t5/SAS-Communities-Library/3-steps-to-build-a-trend-comparison-line-plot-in-SAS-Visual/ta-p/533266
- 3 steps to build a US map tile chart in SAS Visual Analytics: https://communities.sas.com/t5/SAS-Communities-Library/3-steps-to-build-a-US-map-tile-chart-in-SAS-Visual-Analytics/ta-p/539108
- 3 steps to building a monthly temperature comparison chart: https://communities.sas.com/t5/SAS-Communities-Library/3-steps-to-building-a-monthly-temperature-comparison-chart/ta-p/544702
- 3 steps to building a monthly temperature strip plot: https://communities.sas.com/t5/SAS-Communities-Library/3-steps-to-building-a-monthly-temperature-strip-plot/ta-p/600800
- 3 Steps to Building an Air Temperature Circle Graph: https://communities.sas.com/t5/SAS-Communities-Library/3-Steps-to-Building-an-Air-Temperature-Circle-Graph/ta-p/620899
- 3 Steps to Building Waterfall Charts with Interactive Subtotals: https://communities.sas.com/t5/SAS-Communities-Library/3-Steps-to-Building-Waterfall-Charts-with-Interactive-Subtotals/ta-p/737704
- 3 steps to create dynamic reference line labels in SAS Visual Analytics: https://communities.sas.com/t5/SAS-Communities-Library/3-steps-to-create-dynamic-reference-line-labels-in-SAS-Visual/ta-p/509370
- 3 steps to label specific data points in SAS Visual Analytics custom graphs: https://communities.sas.com/t5/SAS-Communities-Library/3-steps-to-label-specific-data-points-in-SAS-Visual-Analytics/ta-p/505057
- Building Control Charts for SAS Visual Analytics on Viya: https://communities.sas.com/t5/SAS-Communities-Library/Building-Control-Charts-for-SAS-Visual-Analytics-on-Viya/ta-p/633643

- Comparing similar metrics using SAS Visual Analytics custom graphs: https://communities.sas.com/t5/SAS-Communities-Library/Comparing-similar-metrics-using-SAS-Visual-Analytics-custom/ta-p/507005
- How to create a butterfly line chart in SAS Visual Analytics: https://communities.sas.com/t5/SAS-Communities-Library/How-to-create-a-butterfly-line-chart-in-SAS-Visual-Analytics/ta-p/489398
- How to Upgrade Your VA Bubble Plots with Data Labels: https://communities.sas.com/t5/SAS-Communities-Library/How-Upgrade-Your-VA-Bubble-Plots-With-Data-Labels/ta-p/660068
- Ranking states by turkey production using SAS Visual Analytics: https://communities.sas.com/t5/SAS-Communities-Library/Ranking-states-by-turkey-production-using-SAS-Visual-Analytics/ta-p/514552
- SAS Graph Builder: Custom Line Chart with Reference line for Visual Analytics reports: https://communities.sas.com/t5/SAS-Communities-Library/SAS-Graph-Builder-Custom-Line-Chart-with-Reference-line-for/ta-p/672130
- Three Steps to Building a Bar Chart Heatmap: https://communities.sas.com/t5/SAS-Communities-Library/Three-Steps-to-Building-a-Bar-Chart-Heatmap/ta-p/643020
- Three steps to building a bubble plot with guidelines in SAS Visual Analytics: https://communities.sas.com/t5/SAS-Communities-Library/Three-steps-to-building-a-bubble-plot-with-guidelines-in-SAS/ta-p/577432
- Three Steps to Building a Calendar Heatmap Matrix: https://communities.sas.com/t5/SAS-Communities-Library/Three-Steps-to-Building-a-Calendar-Heatmap-Matrix/ta-p/520854
- Three Steps to Building a Nested Bar Chart: https://communities.sas.com/t5/SAS-Communities-Library/Three-Steps-to-Building-a-Nested-Bar-Chart/ta-p/682769
- Three Steps to Building an Interactive Tally Sheet: https://communities.sas.com/t5/SAS-Communities-Library/Three-Steps-to-Building-an-Interactive-Tally-Sheet/ta-p/724030
- Three steps to building a square area plot in SAS Visual Analytics: https://communities.sas.com/t5/SAS-Communities-Library/Three-steps-to-building-a-square-area-plot-in-SAS-Visual/ta-p/557966

Chapter 8

D3 Gallery: https://github.com/d3/d3/wiki/Gallery
Murray, Scott. 2017. *Interactive Data Visualization for the Web, 2nd Edition*. O'Reilly Media.
Powell, Robby, and Renato Luppi. 2018. "Create Awesomeness: Use Custom Visualizations to Extend SAS Visual Analytics to Get the Results You Need." *SAS Global Forum 2018: Proceedings:* https://www.sas.com/content/dam/SAS/support/en/sas-global-forum-proceedings/2018/1800-2018.pdf
SAS Communities Library. Cary, NC: SAS Institute Inc.

- Customize data visualizations in SAS Visual Analytics with #D3Thursday: https://communities.sas.com/t5/SAS-Communities-Library/Customize-data-visualizations-in-SAS-Visual-Analytics-with/ta-p/467770

- Custom Visualizations in SAS Visual Analytics- A Strategy for Using the Data-Driven Content Object: https://communities.sas.com/t5/SAS-Communities-Library/Custom-Visualizations-in-SAS-Visual-Analytics-A-Strategy-for/ta-p/504502
- Data-Driven Content: leveraging third-party visualizations in SAS Visual Analytics (part 1 of 2): https://communities.sas.com/t5/SAS-Communities-Library/Data-Driven-Content-leveraging-third-party-visualizations-in-SAS/ta-p/437303
- Data-Driven Content: leveraging third-party visualizations in SAS Visual Analytics (part 2 of 2): https://communities.sas.com/t5/SAS-Communities-Library/Data-Driven-Content-leveraging-third-party-visualizations-in-SAS/ta-p/437352
- Dynamic and interactive bar charts in SAS Visual Analytics with #D3Thursday: https://communities.sas.com/t5/SAS-Communities-Library/Dynamic-and-interactive-bar-charts-in-SAS-Visual-Analytics-with/ta-p/487891
- How to create a basic bar chart in SAS Visual Analytics with #D3Thursday: https://communities.sas.com/t5/SAS-Communities-Library/How-to-create-a-basic-bar-chart-in-SAS-Visual-Analytics-with/ta-p/487852
- VA Report Example: Using D3js in your Report: https://communities.sas.com/t5/SAS-Communities-Library/VA-Report-Example-Using-D3js-in-your-Report/ta-p/509033

My GitHub Repository: https://github.com/idig007/Visual-Analytics-Examples/tree/main/samples
SAS GitHub Repository: https://github.com/sassoftware/sas-visualanalytics-thirdpartyvisualizations
SAS Institute Inc. 2021. *SAS Visual Analytics: Reference*. Cary, NC: SAS Institute Inc. https://documentation.sas.com/doc/en/vacdc/default/varef/titlepage.htm
SAS Institute Inc. 2021. *SAS Visual Analytics: Working with Report Content*. Cary, NC: SAS Institute Inc. https://documentation.sas.com/doc/en/vacdc/default/vaobj/titlepage.htm
www.codecademy.com/learn/learn-d3
www.codecademy.com/learn/introduction-to-javascript

Chapter 8: Additional Examples

SAS Communities Library. Cary, NC: SAS Institute Inc.

- Adding brush and zoom events to a D3.js steamgraph in SAS Visual Analytics with #D3Thursday: https://communities.sas.com/t5/SAS-Communities-Library/Adding-brush-and-zoom-events-to-a-D3-js-streamgraph-in-SAS/ta-p/513331
- Adding Interactivity to a 3D Choropleth in SAS Visual Analytics with #D3Thursday: https://communities.sas.com/t5/SAS-Communities-Library/Adding-Interactivity-to-a-3D-Choropleth-in-SAS-Visual-Analytics/ta-p/571002
- Animating a 3D Choropleth Over Time with #D3Thursday: https://communities.sas.com/t5/SAS-Communities-Library/Animating-a-3D-Choropleth-Over-Time-with-D3Thursday/ta-p/572453
- Animating a D3.js area graph over time in SAS Visual Analytics with #D3Thursday: https://communities.sas.com/t5/SAS-Communities-Library/Animating-a-D3-js-area-graph-over-time-in-SAS-Visual-Analytics/ta-p/517067

- Combining the Power of D3 with Three.js to Create a 3D Choropleth: https://communities.sas.com/t5/SAS-Communities-Library/Combining-the-Power-of-D3-with-Three-js-to-Create-a-3D/ta-p/569501
- Create a radar chart in SAS Visual Analytics with #D3Thursday: https://communities.sas.com/t5/SAS-Communities-Library/Create-a-radar-chart-in-SAS-Visual-Analytics-with-D3Thursday/ta-p/504801
- Creating a 3D Residual Plot with #D3Thursday: https://communities.sas.com/t5/SAS-Communities-Library/Creating-a-3D-Residual-Plot-with-D3Thursday/ta-p/595494
- Creating a split view radar chart in SAS Visual Analytics with #D3Thursday: https://communities.sas.com/t5/SAS-Communities-Library/Creating-a-split-view-radar-chart-in-SAS-Visual-Analytics-with/ta-p/509208
- How to create a donut chart in SAS Visual Analytics with #D3Thursday: https://communities.sas.com/t5/SAS-Communities-Library/How-to-create-a-donut-chart-in-SAS-Visual-Analytics-with/ta-p/487900
- How to create variable view stacked bar charts in SAS Visual Analytics with #D3Thursday: https://communities.sas.com/t5/SAS-Communities-Library/How-to-create-variable-view-stacked-bar-charts-in-SAS-Visual/ta-p/507147
- How to Restyle an Existing #D3Thursday Visualization: https://communities.sas.com/t5/SAS-Communities-Library/How-to-Restyle-an-Existing-D3Thursday-Visualization/ta-p/549628
- Interactive maps in SAS Visual Analytics with #D3Thursday: https://communities.sas.com/t5/SAS-Communities-Library/Interactive-maps-in-SAS-Visual-Analytics-with-D3Thursday/ta-p/487944
- Leverage a Google 3D-PieChart within VA using the Data-Driven Content Object: https://communities.sas.com/t5/SAS-Communities-Library/Leverage-a-Google-3D-PieChart-within-VA-using-the-Data-Driven/ta-p/463917
- Styling a D3 donut chart in SAS Visual Analytics with #D3Thursday: https://communities.sas.com/t5/SAS-Communities-Library/Styling-a-D3-donut-chart-in-SAS-Visual-Analytics-with-D3Thursday/ta-p/487936
- Using a Sunburst to Visualize Pseudo-Hierarchies with #D3Thursday: https://communities.sas.com/t5/SAS-Communities-Library/Using-a-Sunburst-to-Visualize-Pseudo-Hierarchies-with-D3Thursday/ta-p/551876
- Using parameters with Data-Driven Content in SAS Visual Analytics: https://communities.sas.com/t5/SAS-Communities-Library/Using-parameters-with-Data-Driven-Content-in-SAS-Visual/ta-p/609557
- Visualizing nested data with a circle packing graph in SAS Visual Analytics with #D3Thursday: https://communities.sas.com/t5/SAS-Communities-Library/Visualizing-nested-data-with-a-circle-packing-graph-in-SAS/ta-p/553655
- Visualizing nested data with a sunburst chart in SAS Visual Analytics with #D3Thursday: https://communities.sas.com/t5/SAS-Communities-Library/Visualizing-nested-data-with-a-sunburst-chart-in-SAS-Visual/ta-p/511114

SAS Communities: SAS Viya. Cary, NC: SAS Institute Inc.
How to use Google Map in SAS Viya: https://communities.sas.com/t5/SAS-Viya/How-to-use-Google-Map-in-SAS-Viya/m-p/549237

Chapter 9

Kumar, Uttam. 2017. "Concurrent data append and update to a global CAS table." SAS Blogs. https://blogs. sas.com/content/sgf/2017/11/15/concurrent-data-append-and-update-to-a-global-cas-table/

Nelson, Gerry. 2020. Jobs: "Stored processes in Viya." SAS Blogs. https://blogs.sas.com/content/ sgf/2020/02/28/jobs-stored-processes-in-viya/

SAS Communities Library. Cary, NC: SAS Institute Inc.

- Create a SAS Viya Job with a prompt using Task Prompts: https://communities.sas.com/ t5/SAS-Communities-Library/Create-a-SAS-Viya-Job-with-a-prompt-using-Task-Prompts/ ta-p/658639

SAS Institute Inc. 2021. *SAS Studio Developer's Guide: Working with Jobs*. Cary, NC: SAS Institute Inc. https:// documentation.sas.com/doc/en/webeditorcdc/default/webeditorjobsdg/titlepage.htm

SAS Institute Inc. 2021. *SAS Studio with SAS and SAS Viya Programming Documentation: CAS User's Guide*. Cary, NC: SAS Institute Inc. https://documentation.sas.com/doc/en/sasstudiocdc/default/pgmsascdc/ pgmsasacwlcm/home.htm

SAS Institute Inc. 2021. *SAS Visual Analytics: Working with Report Content*. Cary, NC: SAS Institute Inc. https://documentation.sas.com/doc/en/vacdc/default/vaobj/titlepage.htm

SAS Institute Inc. 2021. *SAS Visual Analytics: Working with Report Data*. Cary, NC: SAS Institute Inc. https:// documentation.sas.com/doc/en/vacdc/default/vareportdata/titlepage.htm

SAS Institute Inc. 2021. *SAS Viya Programming Documentation: SAS Job Execution Web Application: User's Guide*. Cary, NC: SAS Institute Inc. https://documentation.sas.com/doc/en/pgmsascdc/default/ jobexecug/titlepage.htm

Chapter 9: Additional Examples

SAS Communities Library. Cary, NC: SAS Institute Inc.

- APIs in action: build an automated profiler with SAS Viya: https://communities.sas.com/ t5/SAS-Communities-Library/APIs-in-action-build-an-automated-profiler-with-SAS-Viya/ ta-p/633060
- Creating JES Prompts and Output Using the Viya Reports API: https://communities.sas. com/t5/SAS-Communities-Library/Creating-JES-Prompts-and-Output-Using-the-Viya- Reports-API/ta-p/664314
- Data Entry in SAS Visual Analytics 8.3: Part 1, The basics: https://communities.sas.com/ t5/SAS-Communities-Library/Data-Entry-in-SAS-Visual-Analytics-8-3-Part-1-The-basics/ ta-p/579076
- Data Entry in SAS Visual Analytics 8.3: Part 2, Write a Viya Job with a form: https:// communities.sas.com/t5/SAS-Communities-Library/Data-Entry-in-SAS-Visual-Analytics- 8-3-Part-2-Write-a-Viya-Job/ta-p/580962
- Data Entry in SAS Visual Analytics 8.3: Part 3, Integrate SAS Viya Jobs with SAS Visual Analytics: https://communities.sas.com/t5/SAS-Communities-Library/Data-Entry-in- SAS-Visual-Analytics-8-3-Part-3-Integrate-SAS-Viya/ta-p/582397

- Embedding an HTML Input Form in a JES Job Definition: https://communities.sas.com/t5/SAS-Communities-Library/Embedding-an-HTML-Input-Form-in-a-JES-Job-Definition/ta-p/571475
- Executing a JES Job Using JavaScript: https://communities.sas.com/t5/SAS-Communities-Library/Executing-a-JES-Job-Using-JavaScript/ta-p/626489
- Getting Details about VA Report's Data Sources Using Viya APIs, CAS Actions and Viya PROCs – Part 1: https://communities.sas.com/t5/SAS-Communities-Library/Getting-Details-About-VA-Report-s-Data-Sources-Using-Viya-APIs/ta-p/676560
- Introduction to Integration of SAS Visual Analytics with SAS Jobs via Data-Driven Content- Part 1: https://communities.sas.com/t5/SAS-Communities-Library/Introduction-to-Integration-of-SAS-Visual-Analytics-with-SAS/ta-p/670823
- Sending Bigger Tables: Integrating SAS Visual Analytics with SAS Jobs via Data-Driven Content- Part 2: https://communities.sas.com/t5/SAS-Communities-Library/Sending-Bigger-Tables-Integrating-SAS-Visual-Analytics-with-SAS/ta-p/672716
- Loading Tables into CAS from SAS Visual Analytics with SAS Jobs via Data-Driven Content- Part 3: https://communities.sas.com/t5/SAS-Communities-Library/Loading-Tables-into-CAS-from-SAS-Visual-Analytics-with-SAS-Jobs/ta-p/674595
- Pareto Example of Integration of SAS Visual Analytics with SAS Jobs via Data-Driven Content- Part 4: https://communities.sas.com/t5/SAS-Communities-Library/Pareto-Example-of-Integration-of-SAS-Visual-Analytics-with-SAS/ta-p/681149
- Outliers Example of Integration of SAS Visual Analytics with SAS Jobs via Data-Driven Content- Part 5: https://communities.sas.com/t5/SAS-Communities-Library/Outliers-Example-of-Integration-of-SAS-Visual-Analytics-with-SAS/ta-p/685469
- Making a Viya Service API Call form a JES Input Form: https://communities.sas.com/t5/SAS-Communities-Library/Making-a-Viya-Service-API-Call-from-a-JES-Input-Form/ta-p/599904
- Running Your SAS Code from the Web Using the SAS Job Execution Web Application: https://communities.sas.com/t5/SAS-Communities-Library/Running-Your-SAS-Code-from-the-Web-Using-the-SAS-Job-Execution/ta-p/666202

SAS Job Execution – a loan application: https://communities.sas.com/t5/SAS-Communities-Library/SAS-Job-Execution-a-loan-application/ta-p/667802

Chapter 10

Morris, Brad, and Robby Powell. 2020. "SAS Visual Analytics SDK: Embed SAS Visual Analytics Insights into your Web Pages and Web Apps." *SAS Global Forum 2020: Proceedings:*

- Paper: https://www.sas.com/content/dam/SAS/support/en/sas-global-forum-proceedings/2020/4309-2020.pdf
- Presentation: https://www.youtube.com/watch?v=zMb3xZxpcK4

Patsilaras, Teri. 2020. "Pick your metric or category with Viewer Customization level set to Data edits!" SAS Blogs. https://communities.sas.com/t5/SAS-Communities-Library/Pick-your-metric-or-category-with-Viewer-Customization-level-set/ta-p/677300

SAS Communities Library. Cary, NC: SAS Institute Inc.

- How to enable guest access in SAS Visual Analytics 8.2: https://communities.sas.com/t5/SAS-Communities-Library/How-to-enable-guest-access-in-SAS-Visual-Analytics-8-2/ta-p/437101

SAS COVID-19 Public Dashboard: https://tbub.sas.com/COVID19/

SAS GitHub Repository for Visual Analytics SDK: https://github.com/sassoftware/visual-analytics-sdk

SAS Institute Inc. 2021. *SAS Visual Analytics Apps*. Cary, NC: SAS Institute Inc. https://support.sas.com/en/software/visual-analytics-apps-support.html

SAS Institute Inc. 2021. *SAS Visual Analytics SDK*. Cary, NC: SAS Institute Inc. https://developer.sas.com/sdk/va/docs/getting-started/

SAS Institute Inc. 2021. *SAS Viya Administration: Authentication*. Cary, NC: SAS Institute Inc. https://documentation.sas.com/doc/en/sasadmincdc/default/calsecwlcm/home.htm

SAS Institute Inc. 2021. *SAS Viya Administration: Identity Management*. Cary, NC: SAS Institute Inc. https://documentation.sas.com/doc/en/sasadmincdc/default/calids/titlepage.htm

Appendix A

Census. 2021. *Cartographic Boundary Files – Shapefile*. United States Census Bureau. https://www.census.gov/geographies/mapping-files/time-series/geo/carto-boundary-file.html

Hicks, Scott. 2019. "Creating custom region maps with SAS Visual Analytics." SAS Blogs. https://blogs.sas.com/content/sgf/2019/03/27/creating-custom-region-maps-with-visual-analytics/

Hicks, Scott. 2019.. "Essentials of Map Coordinate Systems and Projections in Visual Analytics." SAS Blogs. https://blogs.sas.com/content/sgf/2019/05/21/essentials-of-map-coordinate-systems-and-projections-in-visual-analytics/

SAS Institute Inc. 2021. *SAS Visual Analytics: Managing Data*. Cary, NC: SAS Institute Inc. https://documentation.sas.com/doc/en/vacdc/default/datahub/titlepage.htm

SAS Institute Inc. 2021. *SAS Viya Programming Documentation: CAS User's Guide*. Cary, NC: SAS Institute Inc. https://documentation.sas.com/doc/en/pgmsascdc/default/pgmsasacwlcm/home.htm

SAS Institute Inc. 2021. *SAS Viya Programming Documentation: SAS/GRAPH and Base SAS: Mapping Reference*. Cary, NC: SAS Institute Inc. https://documentation.sas.com/doc/en/pgmsascdc/default/grmapref/titlepage.htm

Schulz, Falko. 2018. "Building and visualizing custom polygons in SAS Visual Analytics." SAS Blogs. https://blogs.sas.com/content/sascom/2018/01/30/building-visualizing-custom-polygons-sas-visual-analytics/

Surratt, Marcia. 2016. "MAPS, MAPSGFK and MAPSSAS, Oh my!" SAS Blogs. https://blogs.sas.com/content/sgf/2016/08/19/maps-mapsgfk-and-mapssas-oh-my/

Appendix B

D3 Gallery: https://github.com/d3/d3/wiki/Gallery

Murray, Scott. 2017. *Interactive Data Visualization for the Web, 2nd Edition*. O'Reilly Media.

My GitHub Repository: https://github.com/idig007/Visual-Analytics-Examples/tree/main/samples

Powell, Robby, and Renato Luppi. 2018. "Create Awesomeness: Use Custom Visualizations to Extend SAS Visual Analytics to Get the Results You Need." *SAS Global Forum 2018: Proceedings:* https://www.sas.com/content/dam/SAS/support/en/sas-global-forum-proceedings/2018/1800-2018.pdf

SAS GitHub Repository for Third-Party Visualizations: https://github.com/sassoftware/sas-visualanalytics-thirdpartyvisualizations

www.codecademy.com/learn/learn-d3

www.codecademy.com/learn/introduction-to-javascript

Ready to take your SAS® and JMP®skills up a notch?

Be among the first to know about new books,
special events, and exclusive discounts.
support.sas.com/newbooks

Share your expertise. Write a book with SAS.
support.sas.com/publish

Continue your skills development with free online learning.
www.sas.com/free-training

 sas.com/books
for additional books and resources.